For Roxanne, with acknowledgements for planting the seed.

Home Ecology

Karen Christensen

Illustrated by
Judy Strafford

Arlington Books: London

HOME ECOLOGY
First published 1989 by
Arlington Books (Publishers) Ltd
15–17 King St, St James's
London SW1

Reprinted March 1989

British Library Cataloguing-in-Publication Data
Christensen, Karen
Home ecology
1. Man. ecology
I. Title
304. 2

ISBN 0–8514–725–0

Typeset by J & L Composition Ltd, Filey
Printed and bound in Great Britain by
Billing & Sons Ltd, Worcester

Cover photograph by Graham Goldwater

CONTENTS

ACKNOWLEDGEMENTS

I am grateful to Julian Clokie, Patrick Green, Michel Odent, Walter Patterson and Tony Webb, who read the drafts of certain chapters and patiently answered many questions. Bob Fromer deserves special mention for having written many pages of notes and suggestions for the book, and for looking through a confused first draft, while Andy Cotton provided invaluable technical assistance with the chapters on transport and health. Staff at Friends of the Earth were invariably helpful, as were Debra Lynn Dadd, Peter and Christopher Belt, Emily Halapatz and Cathy Keir. Amrit Row designed the *Home Ecology* logo. Love and thanks to Andy and Tom, who found themselves submerged in my work for far longer than promised, and to Dad for his continuing support and interest.

INTRODUCTION

The twenty-first century will be ecological, or will not be.
Michel Odent, *Primal Health*, 1986

Have you noticed that the evening news often sounds like a half-hour environmental bulletin these days? There is the greenhouse effect, acid rain, chemicals in our drinking water, radioactive waste—a seemingless endless variety of problems facing us. No one can ignore 'the environment', and all the political parties are painting green banners.

The threats are real, and serious. Coincidentally, the crunch seems to have come as we approach both the end of a century and the end of a millennium, an appropriate time for soul-searching. The way we live has caused these problems and figuring out what needs to be done—translating it into personal terms, New Year's resolutions—is what *Home Ecology* is about.

I am not a lifelong environmentalist. In fact, I used to hate the sound of the word ecology! When I was 13 my father started making 'ecology runs' every Saturday afternoon. This meant driving up into the California foothills, with as many kids as he could muster, and gathering rubbish from along the quiet wooded roads. Aluminium and other metal cans went to the recycling center, soda bottles went back to the grocery store, and the bags of other rubbish were put out with our dustbins.

At home we had to wash glass bottles and jars, and tin cans, which were bagged for recycling. Newspapers were tied into bundles in the garage for the Boy Scout collection day. We used non-phosphate washing powder, and Dad made a valiant effort to get us to save energy by turning off lights and lowering the thermostat on the central heating.

I am ashamed to say that I never once went on one of those ecology runs. Although I was interested in health foods and became a vegetarian for a while, I was far too rebellious to go on a public outing with my father. I couldn't see any connection between the state of the roads and the state of my world, or my future.

Only after my son was born in 1985 did it dawn on me that my concern about health, and especially about his well-being and future, was inextricably connected with the environmental problems I kept hearing about. I knew I should be recycling my bottles and that detergents were a bad thing. But where could I take them? What could I use instead?

The word 'ecology' literally means the study of the home. It comes from the Greek *oikos*, and is a branch of biology which studies the interrelationships between organisms and the environment. *Home Ecology* looks at the home as one kind of ecological system which is part of the larger ecosystem outside. Unlike other living creatures, we have created much of the environment we live in, but until recently little care has been taken to ensure that it is safe, or sound.

Environmentalists sometimes dismiss human health and social issues as of minor importance. In contrast, there are people who are deeply concerned about health—diet, exercise, stress management and so on—who fail to realize that these things are closely linked to wider environmental, or ecological, issues. We cannot improve our health until we improve the health of the earth we live on, and of the society we live in.

While I can sympathize with dedicated environmental campaigners who feel that only serious political action has any chance of changing the course we have set ourselves on, I come back to two certainties. First, personal change is essential to changing people's attitudes, and it is public attitudes which will force the necessary changes in industry and technology, in the way we deal with our rubbish, and in safety standards for serious threats to human health like toxic chemicals and nuclear radiation. Second, we simply must change the way we live—to something sustainable, healthy and humane. While *Home Ecology* by no means provides all the answers about how to do this, it gives us a realistic and practical starting point.

Let's face it, not everyone can work for Friends of the Earth or Greenpeace. In an article entitled 'Activism in Daily Life', Marty Teitel writes that:

For political and social action to become broad-based rather than just the territory of 'professional activists,' the price of admission should be low enough to include as many of us as possible. We should each be able to do small things in our daily lives that we know will work toward changing the world. . . . Those people who will dedicate their entire lives to making changes in society deserve our respect and our thanks. But we can also pay attention to those who care, but whose family responsibilities, economic conditions, or other factors make them unable to single-mindedly devote their lives to activism

Utne Reader, March/April 1988

A common complaint is that what one person does can't possibly make any difference. Why bother? True, your choosing a biodegradable washing-up liquid isn't going to stop our lakes filling up with algae growing on an excess of nitrates (from fertilizers) and phosphates (from detergents). The amount of plastic which you throw out each day is only a miniscule fraction of what has to be dealt with around the world. And your can of hairspray will not make a very big hole in the ozone layer.

A more constructive approach is to recognize that although every choice you make may not change the world, at the very least it changes YOU. And a positive choice this time makes it far easier to make the right choice next time (passing up a fast-food hamburger, say, or walking to the shops instead of driving).

The 'battle for the planet' is one which we can all fight. Every small contribution was welcome during the Second World War. Have you seen the old posters extolling the virtues of cabbage salads, homegrown and full of vitamins? 'Victory' gardens, helping to create a more self-sufficient nation, can be just as relevant now. Small things—turning down your thermostat, reusing envelopes, staying well and fit—do matter.

Some changes are much easier than others. Giving up the car entirely would be a difficult change for almost everyone. A reduction in the amount you use it, however, by walking or taking the bus instead, is easy.

The idea of change makes many people nervous. They imagine that an ecologically-sound lifestyle will be dreary and difficult, and expensive too. Some politicians would like us to think that the costs of cleaning up our act are just too high. Environmentalists are accused of being against growth, or progress. Progress means 'to advance or develop towards a better state'. What do we call progress? The ozone layer above the earth has a hole in it the size of the United States. People in Third World countries are getting poorer and hungrier all the time. The world is heating up as the result of our intensive burning of coal, gas and oil. Civilization—or at least our western version of it—has its own crippling plethora of diseases. Just how are we progressing?

I am not suggesting that we turn our backs on technology. Sometimes the past looks infinitely safe and cosy by comparison with the ever-changing, insistent, demanding world we live in. But this *is* the world we live in, and which we have to learn to interact with in a healthy, sustainable way. This isn't just mystical rhetoric, talking to plants and hugging trees. It means practical choices about everyday things—washing the dishes, feeding the dog, choosing a holiday for next year.

It has to be said that these days environmentalists seem to be fighting the government half the time. But we cannot underestimate the clout of voters' concern—one of the most important steps we can take is to become informed, because otherwise we will be buffeted by conflicting claims about which candidate is greenest, without sufficient means of judging for ourselves. In a sense what *Home Ecology* is about is consciousness-raising, because we need to become aware of the way we live and how it affects the earth and other people, especially people in the Third World.

This book is only a beginning. I hope that as you read your curiosity will be piqued and that you will want to know more about the issues touched upon—there are many sources of information for you to follow up. Concentrate on one or two areas which really interest you and learn as much as you can about them. Be creative—find ways to apply what you learn to your own life. If you have further ideas and suggestions for *Home Ecology*, please write to me c/o Arlington Books Limited, 15–17 King Street, London SW1Y 6QU.

1
TIME

If a man does not keep pace with his companions, perhaps it is
because he hears a different drummer. Let him step to the
music which he hears, however measured or far away.

Henry David Thoreau
Walden, 1854

Are you frantically busy, harassed by incessant demands on
your time and energy? When I suggest that you stop using
disposable nappies or make a pot of homemade soup, your
first reaction may well be, 'But I don't have the *time* for things
like that!' So before we look at the important environmental
issues which face us today, we need to deal with the question
of how we find time and energy to make changes in the way we
live. First, let's look at the way time—or our perception of it—
makes *us* tick.

Time and money
Benjamin Franklin, the American statesman and inventor,
must bear part of the blame for our obsessive attitude towards
time.

1

Remember that TIME is Money. He that can earn Ten
Shillings a Day by his Labour, and goes abroad, or sits
idle one half of that Day, tho' he spends but Sixpence
during his Diversion or Idleness, ought not to reckon
That the only Expence; he has really spent or rather
thrown away Five Shillings besides.

Advice to a Young Tradesman, 1748

If every moment spent relaxing, playing with your family or
contemplating the ocean waves is a penny lost, every human
activity can be quantified in terms of its monetary value. How
much is your baby's smile worth, or a game of chess, or helping a
10-year-old with her maths homework? How about a day spent
lying in the sun or an afternoon in bed with your beloved?

Our attitudes toward time affect every thing we do. On one
hand, we may want it to pass quickly—think of the last week
of school holidays or standing in a bank queue, waiting at the
hospital, months on the dole, or every hour spent at a job you
don't like. But many people long for 36-hour days, when
stretched to the limit by the conflicting demands of home and
family and work.

Some people compulsively fill every second of each day with
projects and things to do, while others proceed at a leisurely
pace, always ready to sit down and natter over a cup of tea.
Who's right?

In economic terms it seems that we always have a role to
play. If we aren't earning money we should be spending it. A
good example of this, pointed out by Ivan Illich in his *Limits
to Medicine*, is the way women have been encouraged to
switch from breast to bottlefeeding: the change has 'provided
industry with working mothers who are clients for a factory-
made formula.'

To some extent money can buy time—for example, by
making it possible to hire someone to do a task you don't like—
but the notion is misleading. People end up trapped by the
need to finance a luxurious lifestyle, and may in fact have
far less free time than those who live more simply. E. F.
Schumacher, the economist and philosopher, summed this up
with what he called a first law of economics: 'The amount of
real leisure a society enjoys tends to be in inverse proportions
to the amount of labour-saving machinery it employs'—and,
presumably, to the amount of money it has.

Contrary to our assumption that we have far more leisure time than our ancestors—perhaps fostered by a culture which needs our contribution both as employees and consumers—people in 'primitive' agricultural or hunter-gatherer societies had far *more* leisure than we have. They spent between 15 and 20 hours a week providing for themselves and their children, leaving the remainder of their time for socializing and relaxing ('Why tribal peoples and peasants of the Middle Ages had more free time than we do', Susan Hunt/*Maine Times*, reprinted in the *Utne Reader*, September/October 1987).

(This is not the case, however, in many Third World countries today, where obtaining scarce water and firewood take up an increasingly large proportion of the day for many women.)

Convenience products—from frozen meals and fast-drying paint to no-iron clothes—are heavily promoted, but the cost of this convenience is a loss of quality, along with hidden environmental price-tags (see page 54). Unfortunately, many people seem to be willing to put up with this: '. . . as far as food engineers are concerned, the microwave oven is one lousy cooking device...but consumers are very forgiving when it comes to microwave foods. They readily swap quality for speed.' ('Brave New Foods', Erik Larson, *Harper's Magazine*, New York: May 1988).

The 'time-saving' of convenience products can be misleading, but more importantly we need to consider the quality of life we want. Cooking and sharing a meal, and clearing up afterwards, takes more time than sticking individual frozen pizzas into the microwave, but eating together plays a vital role in any human group, and shared preparation is creative—and fun.

An expenditure of time—the decision to stop for an impromptu picnic in a beautiful spot instead of hurrying home to get a load of washing hung out—can make an addition to what Christian writer Edith Schaeffer calls our 'museum of memories'. She stresses the importance of traditions and of taking opportunities to add to our precious stock of memories in her book *What is a Family?*. Think of the extent to which friendships are built up by years of shared experiences. Taking a child to a museum or building a doll's house together is likely to mean far more in later years than any number of purchased toys.

The way we spend our time is a reflection of our values.

Only you can decide about your own days and years, but taking time to consider how you want to spend the time of your life is the first step of home ecology.

Energy, stress and pollution

Think of someone you know who is really healthy and vibrant, full of energy and enthusiasm. Isn't it surprising that more people don't fit that description, considering our affluence and knowledge about good eating habits and exercise? Many of us just manage to get through each day, and underneath a superficial energy is a weariness which we just can't seem to shake off.

There are a number of explanations for this—psychological, social and economic. Fatigue and depression are common symptoms of environmental stresses, which range from poor diet or working in a modern 'sick' office block to a sensitivity to

household chemicals. In one way or another, the
to blame.

Look at some of the bigger 'home' issues. Why do
and live where you do? How you travel to work? Wh.
your health—how do you feel most of the time? Wha.
stress in your life? How happy are you?

All these things are interrelated, and need to be conside
as you take on the ideas and suggestions of *Home Ecology*. It's
possible that making changes in your home and the way you
live will cure the 'blues' by dealing with an environmental
problem you weren't conscious of, or by providing a new way
to look at the pressures in your life.

Time Wars

In his book *Time Wars: The Primary Conflict in Human
History*, Jeremy Rifkin, American activist and philosopher,
looks at the social, physiological and political dimensions of
the way we perceive time, and at how the computer is making
'a revolutionary change in time orientation, just as clocks did
several hundred years ago when they began the process of
replacing non-automated timepieces as society's key time-
ordering mechanisms.'

Computers measure time in nanoseconds. The nanosecond
is a billionth of a second, which we can conceive of theoretic-
ally but which we cannot experience. 'Never before,' writes
Rifkin, 'has time been organized at a speed beyond the realm
of consciousness.'

As more and more people use computers—increasingly
powerful computers—psychologists and sociologists are expressing concern about the effects this new perception of time
will have on us, and on our relationships with each other and
with the environment.

The desire, especially of the Western world, to produce
and consume at a frantic pace has led to a depletion of our
natural endowment and the pollution of our biosphere.
Nature's own production and recycling rhythms have
been so utterly taxed by the twin dictates of economic
efficiency and speed that the planetary ecosystems are no
longer capable of renewing resources as fast as they are
being depleted, or recycling waste as fast as we discard it.

Time Wars, p 12

Just as E. F. Schumacher pointed out the holes in the notion that 'bigger is better' with his *Small is Beautiful*, Rifkin takes on the current assumption that 'faster is better'. He claims that our obsession with speed has gone too far. If going faster means a loss of quality (artificial ripening of fruit), of human contacts (shopping by computer) and of human values (traditional village life, for example, and a responsible and responsive relationship with the place we live), we ought to think about slowing down, and we ought to slow down while we think.

● *Time Wars: The Primary Conflict in Human History*, Jeremy Rifkin (New York: Henry Holt & Co, 1987).

In step

Some suffer from compulsive busyness—every minute carefully preplanned in the Filofax—while others are apathetic in the face of the many conflicts of modern life—the so-called 'couch potato' retiring each evening with a microwave meal and a stack of video tapes. Here are a few suggestions.

For the compulsively busy

- ☛ Take your watch off for a day or two. Does it really matter whether it is 14.36 or 14.39? Eat when you feel hungry, go to bed when you get tired.
- ☛ Spend a weekend doing nothing much, preferably in good company. Avoid the television, which ties you to its schedules.
- ☛ Get involved in a time-consuming craft—pottery or knitting or bookbinding.
- ☛ Plant some seeds (or grow lentil sprouts in a jar).
- ☛ Spend ½ an hour or so walking, every day for a week (a different route each day)—use the time for quiet reflection, or concentrate on the trees, sky, houses and people you see.
- ☛ Do something special and extraordinary for someone you care about.

For the apathetic

- ☛ Get *involved* in something—anything—learning a language or finding a new flat or voluntary work.
- ☛ Put the TV away for a few days or more.
- ☛ Cook a special meal or refinish that old pine table (make sure what you do is something you actually enjoy but normally can't find the energy for).

And, as above, the following may help you to tune in:

☞ Plant some seeds.
☞ Spend ½ an hour or so walking, every day for a week.
☞ Do something wonderful for someone you care about.

Chronobiology

Plants, animals and human beings have in-built 'clocks'. Seasonal growth cycles, mating patterns and the way we wake up on London time after a flight to Melbourne are all examples of this.

Chronobiologists have found that a drug will have varying effects on a patient depending on the time of day it is given and that long distance lorry drivers are three times as likely to have an accident at 5 o'clock in the morning. The nuclear accident at Three Mile Island, Pennsylvania, occurred at around 4 am, because of errors made by workers who had been 'rotating shifts around the clock every week for a month and a half' (Rifkin, p 38).

Job satisfaction, general health and productivity were dramatically improved at a plant in Montana when re-scheduling allowed workers to stay on the same shift for three weeks instead of one, and when the rotation went forward rather than backward (this makes a difference because most people's biological clock runs on a 25- rather than 24-hour day).

Shift work and jet lag can cause dramatic changes in mood and mental clarity, but trying to live by 'social time' can pose problems for people whose natural biorhythms have unsocial peaks and troughs.

Organising expert Stephanie Winston stresses the importance of finding your own 'prime time' before you try to start a new task—this includes tackling the suggestions in the rest of *Home Ecology*.

If you aren't sure about your own biorhythms, consider the following:

☞ Are you more likely to feel chilled in the morning or the evening? Body temperature tends to peak along with alertness.
☞ Try doing a crossword puzzle at different times of the day—when is it easiest?
☞ Similarly, exercise for 5 minutes in the morning and again in

the late afternoon or evening. Does one session leave you feeling exhausted and the other energized?
● *Getting Organized*, Stephanie Winston (New York: Warner, 1978).
● *Body Time*, Gay Luce (Paladin, 1974).

GETTING ORGANIZED

An ecological life probably requires a little more organization than an non-ecological one. Separating your rubbish for recycling, for instance, is going to take more foresight and planning than putting everything into one big plastic bag.

I am not suggesting that you take on ecology as a hobby instead of tapestry or tennis. The key is establishing a routine, and good storage arrangements. It will become natural to put glass bottles to one side, and you'll find that with familiarity a new method of washing clothes or feeding your pet will take half the time it did first time round.

Time is not the only thing in short supply. You may worry that this is going to cost too much, but while you may spend more on some things, on balance the suggestions in *Home Ecology* should save you money, while improving your quality of life. Space is also at a premium, particularly in a flat. You may have a tiny kitchen like mine, where we have to move the wastepaper bin to get to the oven and half the time I end up putting milk bottle tops into the compost bucket, instead of into the jar where they belong, because both containers are squeezed onto the same narrow shelf.

Planning

Time to sit down with a pad of paper. In fact, why not start a household notebook where you can keep track of ideas which you want to try and questions which come to mind as you read, and where you can do a little problem-solving too (perhaps about how to cut down on car use).

If you are an inexperienced cook, planning your grocery shopping and meals is a great help. This does not have to be complicated—even a sketchy plan will help, and it's reassuring to know that 'pasta with sauce (use mush.), salad' is on the menu for Thursday.

Planning ahead saves both time and money, and you avoid

last minute dashes to the shops (once again cutting car use). A large wall calendar is useful for recording things like the bimonthly newspaper collection in your area.

Finding time

Home Ecology is not like one of those beauty books which tells you that 'in 10-15 minutes a day you can significantly improve the state of your nails', and in the next chapter asks for 10-15 minutes for your eyebrows, a half an hour or so for your face and 20 minutes for meditation—so that when you add it up you would be spending more time on the author's programme than you spend at work.

To make any change takes a special degree of effort, and possibly (although not necessarily) extra time or money. Living more simply can bring dividends of extra leisure, because you decide that you're just not going to bother doing some things any more!

Think about ways you might eliminate clutter from your home, and about the worries or responsibilities which make for mental clutter. What can you get rid of, stop doing, do less often or get someone else to do (partner, children, even hired help)? What can you do more simply: food, makeup, clothes, decorating, holidays?

Try not to become overwhelmed by the prospect of filtering your water, changing cleaning products and spending more time in natural light, all this week. Specialize—decide what matters to you or bothers you most. Concentrate on the things you like—finding good secondhand furniture for your new flat or retuning your car engine for improved efficiency.

Storage

☞ A good spring-cleaning is the place to start. Try to get the whole household involved in this. Unwanted items can go to charity.

☞ Decide where you can store recyclable materials, reuseable items, donations, mending, etc.

☞ You'll need room for any extra cooking equipment you acquire and bulk purchases of staple foods, as well as bicycles, gardening tools (out of the rain!) and walking gear.

Ecological living is undoubtedly easier in a sprawling house in the country. If you live in crowded quarters, think about storage *before* you start saving bottles or paper for recycling.

Shopping

Shopping may a bit take longer at first, as you buy less at the supermarket and more from other shops, but you will probably find yourself spending less time on it in the end. Organization makes an enormous difference and your shopping time should be much more enjoyable.

☞ Stock up as much as your budget and cupboard space allow. Wholegrains and legumes, toilet paper and cleaning products can be bought in bulk and last virtually forever. This not only saves money and the hassle of running out in the middle of a Bank Holiday, but eliminates a considerable amount of packaging.

☞ Keep track of things you are running low on by ensuring

that there is a pad of paper and a pencil in the kitchen and the bathroom. Everyone in the household should learn to add to these lists. There's nothing worse than cutting up mounds of vegetables for a Chinese stir-fry only to discover that you've run out of something basic like rice.

☞ Make out a shopping check list of everything you normally keep on hand, arranged into categories to speed things up when you get to the shops. The list can be photocopied, or you can put it in a plastic folder and use a chinagraph pencil to mark the items you plan to buy, ticking them off as you put them into your basket.

☞ Try to find shops which you like and can visit regularly—knowing the layout and staff speeds shopping considerably.

☞ Don't forget to check local shops. People who commute may not realize that an excellent butcher or greengrocer is just down the road—there's always Saturday morning.

☞ Save the car for long distance and/or bulk shopping.

☞ Make shopping enjoyable by combining it with outings, to city farms and rural potteries, for instance. The personal contact of buying from small producers is a delightful change from impersonal department stores.

☞ Mail order is a good way to save time while helping small producers of specialist food, clothes and household articles.

Cooking

☞ Decide on the supplies you need on hand to put together the meals you like.

☞ Plan meals—and ensure that you have an emergency cupboard with enough in it to save you a trip to the local fast food joint.

☞ Draw up a rota if you plan to divide the cooking with your flatmates or partner. Some people like to share the task, while others can't bear any company in the kitchen.

Recycling

☞ Establish sensible storage arrangements (above). Buy as little packaging as possible, to keep recycling to a minimum.

☞ Find out where nearby bottlebanks, Save-a-Can skip and paper collection points are from your local Friends of the Earth group.

☞ Combine recycling with other visits whenever possible, but try to establish a routine so you do not end up buried in stored newspaper (which is also a fire hazard).

☛ If you have to throw things away, don't feel guilty but do whatever you can to encourage local stores to provide recycling sites.

MONEY

Orange squash without tartrazine is more expensive than the supermarket brand which contains it, and real orange juice costs more again. At the moment organic vegetables can cost up to twice as much as their chemical counterparts.

But another way of looking at the money question is to ask how much *food* your money is buying. What *is* squash, for example? Sugar, water and flavouring (some brands contain a small proportion of real orange juice). What about those packets of whipped dessert? Sugar and hydrogenated fat, with a substantial dose of additives and colouring.

If you are extremely short of money, you may be limited when it comes to a few of the ideas in *Home Ecology*, but creativity is far more important than cash. Saving money is very often ecological—buying secondhand, refinishing an old chest of drawers, cooking with real potatoes instead of buying oven chips. Reusing everything from yoghurt cartons (for freezing leftovers) to wine corks (saw in half lengthwise and fix on a leftover board with wood glue to make a practical and charming notice board) and growing your own fruit and vegetables are excellent ways to keep your expenses down. Basic non-toxic cleaning supplies are very cheap, especially compared with aerosol products.

You may decide that paying more, when your choice means that you are not contributing to pollution or to the exploitation of coffee pickers in the Third World, is a fair social contribution. Paying more for better quality products, which will last longer, is ecologically and financially sound.

Although green consumption may mean higher prices, it can help to avoid some of the potential catastrophes which now face us, including the loss of irreplaceable forests, wildlife and genetic stock. If we continue to pollute the earth, the long-term cleaning bills are impossible to imagine.

Here are some of the costs and savings of *Home Ecology*:

Extra expenses	**Savings**
+ better quality food	− less processed food
+ organically-grown food	− less meat
+ handcrafted items	− less alcohol/cigarettes
+ DIY/craft equipment	− less for packaging and
+ bicycles	transport
+ gardening tools	− petrol savings
+ water filter	− goods last longer
+ fitness/sports gear	− buying secondhand
	− barter
	− simpler holidays
	− less 'entertainment'

USING *HOME ECOLOGY*

Priorities

If you leaf through this book, you will see dozens of ideas for things to do. Mark those which are relevant and which you want to try, and draw a line through those which don't apply to you—make the book yours.

Start with the chapter on the area of most concern to you, where you are most willing to make gradual changes. Some changes are easy while others are more difficult and long-term. Start with things which are particularly easy or particularly important, and perhaps both (boycotting CFCs, for example). A few things cost a substantial amount of money (like building a conservatory). Some depend on the cooperation of the people you live with.

When you get excited about cleaning up your home environment, that enthusiasm may be contagious and your partner or flatmates or children may jump on the bandwagon. But, let's face it, they may cling ever more tightly to the remote control and the microwave instruction booklet, flaunt their drycleaning and throw away the ketchup bottle you were soaking for the bottle bank. Don't try to do too much, too soon. Change can be very threatening, and you cannot force real cooperation (though a little arm-twisting may be appropriate from time to time!). You'll need the support and encouragement of the people you are close to, in any case.

Procrastination

If after reading through a few chapters you are hesitant about actually getting started on your own *Home Ecology*—even

though you see ideas which you could use—don't feel guilty
and give up. There will be definite reasons for your hesitation,
perhaps one or more of the following:

> opposition from loved ones
>
> fear of ridicule
>
> lack of information or experience
>
> not seeing where to start
>
> feeling overwhelmed
>
> depression at the extent of the problems we face

That last reason needs to be taken seriously, and it is one I
have faced continually while writing about *Home Ecology*.
This is where political action is essential—even if you do
nothing more today than contributing to one of the campaigns
run by Friends of the Earth and Greenpeace. Sue Clifford of
Common Ground suggests that the next step is to get involved
in some local issue which has caught your attention—a new
traffic scheme, the conservation of an historical building
or plans to build a shopping centre on a precious wildlife
site.

No matter how small you start, remember that it is always
better to do something than to do nothing, and that if something is worth doing it is worth half doing. Stephanie Winston
has a few tips for dealing with procrastination:

- Don't be trapped by thinking you have to clear-the-boards
  (finish that mountain of ironing or get all the kids in school)
  before starting something new. Just *start*.

- When the big picture is overwhelming, make a list of 5-
  minute tasks and do a couple each day. This might include
  sorting out obsolete medicine from the bathroom cupboard,
  gathering all aerosols and resolving not to buy more when
  they are gone, and sending a cheque to Friends of the Earth
  for their *Good Wood Guide*.

Sources

Whenever possible I have tried to list a source for any product
I recommend, with an emphasis on mail order suppliers. You
may, however, find the same product in local shops—or something even better than the one I have mentioned (if you do, I
would be pleased to hear about it).

Every area is going to have its advantages. Urban and
suburban centres have a wide variety of shops and facilities,
but if you live many miles from the nearest shopping centre

there may be a local farm which sells fresh honey and eggs, or chemical-free meat. You might decide to keep your own hens, and can easily get hold of manure and bales of straw to mulch your garden—you are lucky enough to *have* a garden!

Ask around, make contacts, read the notice boards at whole-food shops. You may be surprised at what is available where you live. I have only just found that I can have organically-grown produce from Kent farms delivered to my home every week!

Gradual change is far more likely to be permanent than a crash programme, as anyone who has struggled to lose weight will know. Remember, too, that new ways of doing things soon become old ways. After a while your partner will be retrieving egg shells from the paper bin because they belong in the *compost* bucket. Wait till the children get into the swing of saving bottles for the bottlebank, exclaiming gleefully, 'Guess how many wine bottles there were last time!' when your mother-in-law comes to tea.

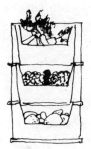

2
FOOD

A change of diet is not an answer . . . [but it is] a way of saying simply: I have a choice. That is the first step. For how can we take responsibility for the future unless we can make choices now that take us, personally, off the destructive path that has been set for us . . .

Frances Moore Lappé
Diet for a Small Planet, 1975

The food we eat affects our health, of course, but our shopping choices have wider consequences too. The store we shop in, the way the food has been processed and packaged, where it comes from, are all important. First, let's just think about what we are buying and eating right now.

16

What does your shopping basket say about you? It's entertaining and educational to look at people's shopping trollies—this makes me look at my own guiltily sometimes—and guess what sort of person they are, or who they are expecting for dinner.

If you do a big weekly shopping trip, you might want to analyse it when you get home one rainy Saturday afternoon—the kids will be fascinated. Just clear a big space on the living-room floor, and sort the shopping into broad categories (make a label for each pile, if you like). Here are some ideas:

fresh fruits and vegetables
grain products (pastas, cereals and so on)
dairy products and eggs
meat/poultry/fish
tinned foods
processed meals and frozen foods
snack foods and sweets
alcohol
sweet drinks

(Ignore the soap powder, toilet paper and shampoo for the moment: these are discussed in other chapters.)

Now look at the piles. Which are the largest? You may be surprised at the amount of tinned and processed food you've bought, compared to fresh things.

If you are concerned about how much much you spend on food, this is a chance to take a look at just why the bill always seems to be higher than you have budgeted for. Advertising on boxes, special displays, bullying from the children and the fact that you skipped breakfast may all contribute to those extra, unplanned purchases.

If you eat out a lot or shop a little every day, getting a clear picture of your grocery buying isn't so easy. You can take a look at what's in your refrigerator and cupboards (pick a time when they are fairly full, not when all you have is a bottle of ketchup and half a lemon). Try to get an idea of the rough proportions. Make an estimate about the food you eat out.

Some people like to keep lists, but most of us know the basics for healthy eating: less fat and sugar, more fresh fruits and vegetables, less meat and more roughage. The most important list to make, if you want to improve your eating habits, is 'Good food I like'. This is a lot more constructive than concentrating on the bad things you eat and feel guilty about.

Processing

The cost of processing and distributing all food in the UK in 1984 was £17,381 million: 53.7% of the total food bill (London Food Commission's *Food Facts*). How much of your weekly shopping was basic, unprocessed food? Processing is not, in itself, a bad thing: when you prepare a meal at home you are processing the food, peeling the onions and blending the pudding.

But commercial food processing has a number of nasty side effects. It removes nutrients and fibre, and adds considerable quantities of salt, sugar and cheap fats, along with a huge range of chemical additives.

It is the high percentage of processed food we eat, going hand in hand with our excessive consumption of fats, sugars and salt, which concerns nutritionists.

Don't think that you avoid waste by buying processed food. The waste just goes somewhere else, and the expense and energy cost of processing and packaging is substantial.

Additives

What are additives for? Manufacturers love to tell us that they are there to improve our food, but the fact is that they are there to make things look and taste nicer than they actually are. Additives can disguise cheap fat and water, and with different flavourings the same range of ingredients can turn into a fluffy dessert or 'creamy' soup.

However, giving something an E number does not make it bad. Ascorbic acid (E300) or Vitamin C, is an antioxidant, and lecithin (E322) is an emulsifier. Both are nutritious and non-toxic. You can use them at home: a little Vitamin C powder will keep cut fruit from turning brown, and lecithin makes sauces smooth and creamy textured.

A healthy awareness of commercial additives is essential. Although *E for Additives* is the best-known of the guides to food additives, several others take a more discriminating and critical approach. You need to have a guide with you when you shop, not when you get home. Keep a copy of the Soil Association or *Foresight* guide in your pocket or bag.

- *Additives: Your Complete Survival Guide*, Geoffrey Cannon and Felicity Lawrence (Century, 1986).
- *Look Again at the Label*, available from the Soil Association for 95p incl. postage.

- *Find Out* additive decoder, £1.35 incl. postage from *Foresight*, The Old Vicarage, Church Lane, Witley, Surrey GU8 5PN.
- Food Additives Campaign Team (FACT), Room W, 25 Horsell Road, London N5 1XL. Send SAE for excellent range of information.
- *The Food Magazine* and other publications from the London Food Commission, 88 Old Street, London EC1V 9AR, telephone 01-253 9513.

Labelling

The Coronary Prevention Group, along with other consumer organizations, is demanding that the government set standards for compulsory labelling of food. They say that we need to know how much fat, sugar, fibre and salt each product contains in order to choose a healthy diet.

The most important thing to remember about food labelling is that the first aim of the manufacturer is to sell his product, not to provide you with accurate information. Advertising adopts a cosy, caring tone, but it is still up to us to demand concrete information, not reassurance.

The vested interest of large corporations takes them into strange arenas. The sugar industry sponsors educational leaflets and videos which blame tooth decay on everything except sweets, while McDonald's puts out a nutrition guide explaining how much they care about quality and nutritional value.

The smart shopper needs to be a cynic. When you read any package, remember that the manufacturer will concentrate on telling anything good about the product (chocolate bars give you a boost, or help you to run marathons). Any negative information will be in small print. 'No artificial preservatives' may be blazened across the label of a product which contains three different coal tar dyes, and a carton will tell you 'Contains no sucrose' when the second ingredient listed is glucose, another sort of sugar.

Reading labels is a discouraging business. You may find yourself buying less at the supermarket and more at a good wholefood shop (they do vary a great deal), simply to avoid the complicated analysis needed these days.

Packaging

It isn't just what's in the food that matters, but what the food is in. Plastics are not biodegradable and should therefore be avoided whenever possible, but they are also undesirable from the point of view of human health. Think of how new plastic smells, or how coffee tastes when you drink it out of a plastic cup. These are both signs that chemicals are being released into the air and into your food.

Plastic film wrapping may not smell but it is recognized that the plasticizers it contains, which are known to be carcinogenic, leak into food wrapped in it, particularly into fatty foods like cheese or bacon. You can now buy wrapping which is 'non-PVC' or 'contains no plasticisers', but it's better to avoid it altogether. Even plastic bags can contaminate food. Natural (and biodegradable) cellophane is preferable if you have a choice.

One of my cookbooks advises against covering a pasta dish containing (acid) tomatoes with aluminium foil because the foil will 'shed' into the sauce. Not a pleasant prospect when you consider recent findings about the relationship between aluminium and Alzheimer's Disease.

Tins, too, should be avoided as much as possible, both because it is seldom possible to recycle them and they require a great deal of energy and raw materials to produce, and because they are soldered with a compound containing lead. (Whole Earth does a range of foods packed in tins with an inert white lining, electronically sealed, but the disposal problem remains.)

A new concern is over dioxin in bleached paper products. Traces of this highly toxic chemical have been found in milk cartons and in the long-life cartons in which fruit juices and other foods are packed (see page 69).

What this adds up to is choosing foods with little or no packaging. You can do this by buying fresh foods and by purchasing in bulk.

ECOLOGICAL FOOD

Organically-grown

For years I didn't bother to look for organic vegetables—I didn't shop anywhere that had them, and the articles I saw in the paper invariably reported that scientists were not convinced that organic food was any more nutritious than 'conventional' produce.

When my son was 6 months old and I started to think about what solid food to start him on, I suddenly realised that I didn't want him to have anything which could possibly be contaminated with dangerous chemicals. His first food was scrapings of organically-grown pears, and our switch to organic food has progressed from there.

Throughout Alan Gear's *New Organic Food Guide*, Safeway stores in the UK are cited as sources because they have taken the lead in offering organic produce, from fresh fruit and vegetables to oatmeal and yoghurt. But the other supermarket chains are now selling organics too.

The International Federation of Organic Agriculture Movements sets out the following points in its document on organic standards: organic agriculture should (1) maintain the long-term fertility of soils, (2) avoid all forms of pollution, (3) reduce the use of fossil energy in agriculture, and (4) treat livestock humanely.

Current agricultural policy and practice are in confusion. Famine in the Third World stands in lamentable contrast to costly over-production in the First World. There is a world-wide problem with soil degradation and the loss of topsoil, and the battle against insect damage to crops is proving far more costly, financially and environmentally, than anyone could have imagined when chemical pesticides first appeared. 'Since the 1940s pesticide use has increased tenfold and crop losses to insects have doubled', according to Lawrie Mott and Karen Snyder, authors of *Pesticide Alert*. Even conventional growers are cutting back on chemical use with a method called Integrated Pest Management (IPM), simply because it is a more effective way of dealing with insect pests. The classic American cookbook *Joy of Cooking* points out that '. . . guarding against losing helpful insects is as important as destroying insect enemies—a fact stressed less often than is the need to solve the equally knotty problem of pesticide poisons in the food chain. We can no longer afford to ignore the interrelationships on which global food supplies depend.'

Another serious problem is nitrate fertilizers. They are used in vast quantities, much of which is washed off into lakes and streams and eventually turns up in our drinking water. Nitrates are also absorbed into plant tissue, in higher concentrations from artificial sources than from natural nitrogen-rich fertilizers like manure, and we ingest them in the food we eat.

In addition, farmers are now threatened with the uncertain effects of the holes in the ozone layer (with a resultant increase in ultraviolet rays) and the 'greenhouse effect' (rising CO_2 levels and global temperature, resulting from the burning of fossil fuels).

Consumer worries about pesticide residues in food have been placated for many years. At last, however, there is some official recognition that we have a serious problem. Baby food manufacturers are refusing to buy produce which has been sprayed with certain chemicals, and even the larger retailers are deciding to get tough with their suppliers in the face of inadequate legal controls.

Government safety levels are seriously flawed; even the

Ministry of Agriculture has admitted that pesticides in common use have been inadequately tested and that new studies are needed. Pesticides, herbicides and fungicides are, by their nature, poisons and it is probably wrong to suggest that there is such a thing as safe levels. Organic agriculture is the obvious alternative.

Fungicides are thought to be particularly dangerous—be cautious of fruit/vegetables from warm, humid climates. Apples, peppers, cucumbers, citrus fruits and aubergines are often coated with a wax, made of petroleum products and animal fat, to improve their appearance and increase shelf life. The wax can also contain fungicides. A detergent will remove some of this, but labelling advice in West Germany warns consumers not to use the peel from sprayed citrus fruits.

The authors of *Pesticide Alert* suggest the following:

- Wash all produce. Plain water or a mild solution of biodegradable washing up liquid and water will remove some, but not all, of the surface pesticide residues.
- Peel produce when appropriate. This means extra work and losing some of the valuable nutrients contained in fresh food, but will completely remove surface residues.
- Grow your own food.
- Whenever you can, buy organic.
- Buy domestically-grown produce and seasonal fruits and vegetables. They are likely to contain less pesticide residues.
- Beware of perfect-looking produce. Many chemical pesticides are used to enhance the appearance of the food. A few superficial flaws do not affect the quality or flavour of what you buy.
- Press for comprehensive labelling of fresh fruits and vegetables.

In her *Fruit Book* Jane Grigson gives details of the processing of dates: 'Commercial dates are customarily dusted with Malathion or a similar toxic insecticide to keep down the date beetle. Commercial dates when picked are customarily washed with detergent. Because they are then wet, commercial dates must customarily be treated with a mould inhibitor. Because of all this, commercial dates must customarily be coated with glycerine or something similar to make them look sticky again.' Since dates are what we would normally consider a 'health' food, this is all the more worrying.

● *The New Organic Food Guide*, Alan Gear (Dent, 1987).

● *Pesticide Alert*, Lawrie Mott and Karen Snyder (San Francisco: Sierra Club Books, 1987).

● The Land and Food Company, Leggatts Park, Potters Bar, Herts EN6 1NZ, telephone (0707) 58561 or (0453) 860844, aim to establish a large scale operation to market organic food and welcome BES investors (minimum £500).

Local food

Food you grow yourself in the back garden is going to be really fresh. While at least a little home-grown food is within everyone's reach (if only sprouted lentils and a few windowbox herbs), most of us depend on whatever shops offer.

If we grew up on packaged and processed food and insipid modern vegetables, we may not know what really fresh food tastes like. Food that has been shipped thousands of miles, and which is bred or formulated for its ability to stand being stored for many weeks, is not going to be really tasty. We are usually satisfied if a banana isn't bruised, without reflecting much on whether it has any flavour.

While we may not be self-sufficient individually, we can aim for considerable regional and national self-sufficiency. The Cornucopia Project began in the United States when a few people at the Rodale Press (famous for its *Organic Gardening* and *Prevention* magazines) realised that New Yorkers were eating broccoli which had been shipped 2700 miles from California, when broccoli would grow *better* in New York's cool climate. After a look at the statistics, it seemed that the only people who were gaining were the trucking and oil companies and the mega-farming firms who control large sections of American agriculture. The consumer was getting food which was less fresh, less nutritious, more expensive, and which did not encourage local employment.

The same situation applies in Europe, and in Britain. At present 70% of the organic food sold in the UK comes from abroad, because there are insufficient domestic supplies to meet demand.

One serious danger with food from the Third World is that agricultural chemicals which are banned in the West are exported to Third World countries, so we can be consuming trace chemicals which have been proved cancer-causing or mutagenic. Recent trials in the United States have found that pesticide residues on imported fruits and vegetables were higher than on domestic produce, and the types of pesticides were often more hazardous.

Try to find local sources for some of your food. A neighbour may be willing to sell excess from a flourishing garden, there may be farms nearby where you can buy eggs or milk or honey, and there are city farms in urban areas.

Most of the wheat used to make British bread comes from the U.S. and Canada, because English wheat is too 'soft' (low in gluten) to be suitable for super-expanded commercial loaves. High gluten Canadian wheat holds more air and water, thus producing a bigger loaf for less money.

Check your local wholefood shop or supermarket for bread made from organic English wheat (Goswell's and Dove Farm are two brands). Better yet, bake your own. Shortly after the Second World War, Doris Grant came up with a method for making bread from English wheat which required no kneading. It's simple, solid and delicious. Here's a recipe:

The Grant Loaf
3 lb stoneground (organic) wholewheat flour
2 teaspoons salt
2 pints water at blood heat
3 level teaspoons dried yeast
3 rounded teaspoons dark brown sugar, honey or molasses

Mix the flour (in cold weather, warm it first in a tepid oven) and salt in a large mixing bowl. Put a few tablespoons of water in a small dish, stir in the sweetener and yeast. Leave for about 15 minutes, until the yeast foams up. Add the rest of the water and pour this mixture into the centre of the flour. Mix well for a minute or two—preferably by hand—until the dough feels elastic and pulls away from the side of the bowl. The dough should be slippery, and you may want to add a little more water, or flour. Divide the dough into three well-greased 2 pint bread tins (sprinkling the greased pans with wheatgerm or sesame seeds makes getting the loaves out very easy—sprinkle some more seeds on top of the loaf). Place tins in a warm place, cover with a clean cloth, and allow them to rise for 20–30 minutes, or until the dough is within ½ inch of the top of the tins. Bake in a 400°F (Gas Mark 6) for 35–40 minutes. When the loaves are done they should sound hollow when tapped.

If you are going to try home baking, be choosy about flour. While you probably won't want to grind your own, packets from the supermarket are frequently stale and dull. Flour should have a wonderful fragrance of freshly ground wheat.

Thinking about using local produce has changed the way I shop. As an expatriate American I frequently bought 'food from home', even though most of it was dreadfully expensive, and frequently stale. Now I try to find suitable British alternatives. While it is exciting to buy French cider, Italian parmesan and Greek olives, this may lead us to ignore and undervalue Devon cider, Welsh butter, Stilton cheese and innumerable other British specialities. Best, of course, is to get local products wherever you live.

Seasonal

When I first came to England I was astounded to find that fruits and vegetables had such definite seasons: there were peas and new potatoes in the spring, and in June the strawberries arrived. Fresh food is, delightfully, best when it is cheapest, so you can save money *and* eat nicer food by concentrating on whatever is in season.

'Fresh' fruits and vegetables are not necessarily fresh. They may have been shipped thousands of miles and kept in a cold / storage for months. These lengthy delays lead to deterioration in food value, especially volatile vitamins like vitamins A and C. One food scientist tested supermarket brussel sprouts and cabbage and found *no* detectable vitamin C! Fruits stored for long periods need extra doses of pesticides and fungicides to preserve them.

Many cookbooks have guides to when fruits and vegetables are in season and therefore cheapest. Eating seasonally should save you money, as well as providing better quality food with somewhat fewer chemical residues.

Real food

After the immensely successful Campaign for Real Ale, there have been many similar campaigns set up. Oddbins is promoting Real Sherry, there is the Real Meat Company, and a growing movement amongst environmentalists, organic farmers, worried consumers and culinary professionals amounts to a Campaign for Real Food.

The *Good Food Guide 1985* listed common 'unreal', or processed, foods found in restaurants, including pâtés, mousses, soups, onion rings, Chicken Kiev and most gateaux. Sauces are frequently boil-in-the-bag. Is this really what we want to eat? The *Guide* now specifies restaurants which do not use processed foods (all vegetables, for example, are fresh) and which support cottage businesses.

The British Culinary Institute was set up in early 1988 and aims to promote quality in British food. The BCI symbol will be awarded to producers and restaurants which meet its high standards, and the BCI is consulting organic growers organizations about improving the supplies of fresh food. One of the problems they want to highlight is a basic one of the varieties which are grown commercially, whether chemically or organically. There are many different varieties of any given fruit or vegetables, as you will know if you've ever looked through a seed catalogue (and seed catalogues by no means have all the possible varieties—see 'The seed scandal', page 295). But the potatoes and cauliflowers and strawberries we buy come from an extremely limited range of varieties, and the 'popular' varieties are the ones which growers like: they look good, have bigger yields and grow larger, travel well and can stand storage.

Eating quality, however, has not been a commercial criterion. The BCI, however, is insisting that we need to go back to old vegetable varieties and breed again—this time concentrating on flavour. The vegetable seed bank at the Henry Doubleday Research Association will be vital in this process.

● British Culinary Institute, 33 Longfield Road, Bristol BS7 9AG, telephone (0272) 424045.

WHAT ABOUT MEAT?

Butchers feel beleaguered these days, what with all the publicity about the evils of animal fats and intensive farming practices. Public awareness about dietary fibre has made many of us shift to eating more pulses and whole grains, and less meat. To make matters worse, my local butcher tells me that people just aren't willing to pay high prices for a good piece of beef.

Responsible meat eating

Traditional farming methods depend on animal manures, and 'mixed farming' creates a neat ecological cycle: animals graze fallow land and eat scraps which would otherwise be wasted (free-ranged chickens do even more: they eat large numbers of pests), and provide manure to fertilize the next crop. In China farmers even provide attractive roadside outhouses (for humans), hoping to entice passersby to add to the farmer's stock of fertilizer.

On the other hand, factory or intensive methods of raising animals for slaughter are appalling, and the emphasis for environmentalists should be on eliminating these practices, via the marketplace and political pressure. We hear a great deal about battery chickens, but other animals are kept under similarly barbaric conditions.

There is now a 'Real Meat' movement, spearheaded by Richard Guy and Gillian Metherell. They have set up the Real Meat Company and will supply meat from animals raised without routine antibiotics, growth promoters and hormones, and without chemical additives or water being added to the meat (the law allows bacon to contain up to 10% added water, which explains why your Sunday bacon fizzles instead of sizzles). Richard Guy explains that supplies of meat reared on organic food are still sporadic, but that the company will be moving in this direction as supplies become available.

A number of butchers around the country sell real meat, and you can order by post (minimum order 60 pounds in weight, so get a couple of friends interested). Or talk to your local butcher about stocking it (promise to buy the meat yourself and to tell all your friends).

There are other suppliers of real meat, some of it from rare old breeds. Heal Farm in Devon provides an overnight delivery service, and although this sort of meat is more expensive than the intensively reared product, it has a robust flavour and you do not need to serve huge portions.

If you are buying from the supermarket, lamb is probably a better bet than other commercially reared meat. Stick to free-range chicken, game and fish as much as possible. While offal is nutritious—and delicious—these organs, especially the liver, tend to store poisons. Avoid them if you do not have a source of 'real', and preferably organic, meat.

● Compassion in World Farming, 20 Lavant Street, Petersfield, Hants GU32 3EW, telephone (0730) 64208.

● Chickens' Lib, P O Box 2, Holmfirth, Huddersfield HD7 1QT.

● The Real Meat Company Ltd, East Hill Farm, Heytesbury, Warminster, Wilts BA12 OHR, telephone Warminster (0985) 40436/40060.

● The Pure Meat Company, 1 The Square, Moretonhampstead, Devon TQ13 8QD, telephone (0647) 40321.

● Anne Petch, Heal Farm, Kings Nympton, Umberleigh, Devon EX37 9TB, telephone South Molton (07695) 2077.

Food and famine

Cutting down on the amount of meat we eat will contribute to a more equitable and balanced agriculture and economy throughout the world. Frances Moore Lappé's *Diet for a Small Planet*, which was first published in 1972, set out a startling discovery. If the grain (corn, wheat, soyabeans, etc.) we in the West use to feed our animals was instead used directly as food for humans, there would be plenty to feed everyone on the planet.

The conversion ratio of pounds of grain and soyabeans fed to get one pound of meat, poultry or eggs ranges from 16:1 for cows and 6:1 for pigs, to 3:1 for eggs and broiler chickens ('*A Protein Factory in Reverse*', *Diet for a Small Planet*, p 70).

The waste involved in commercial meat production is taking food out of the mouths of the starving, especially when the grain comes from the Third World. More than half the world's grain harvest goes to feed livestock, an enormous and incredible waste of food. *Food First* by Frances Moore Lappé and Joseph Collins (Abacus 1982) and the Institute for Food and Development Policy which they founded continue to explain the misconceptions most of us have about the causes of world famine. In light of this, a switch to a mainly vegetarian diet seems in line for all of us.

● *Food First News*, Institute for Food and Development Policy, 1885 Mission Street, San Francisco, CA 94103-3584, USA—publications available in UK from Third World Publications, 151 Stratford Street, Birmingham B11 1AG, telephone (021) 773 6572.

Vegetarians and vegans

A common misconception is that a vegetarian diet is unhealthy, whereas the oppposite is true. Vegetarians and vegans have lower rates of heart disease and tend to be slimmer than meat eaters. Although in the Third World many people don't get enough protein, we get more than enough without meat or soyabean substitutes. Premature ageing and degenerative diseases have even been associated with eating too *much* protein. There are dozens of excellent cookbooks available and a vegetarian diet is relatively easy, interesting and inexpensive.

Meat substitutes, including the mince look-alike TVP (Textured Vegetable Protein), seem the wrong approach to a vegetarian diet. They require specialised commercial processing and encourage us to think, unnecessarily in terms of a 'meat course'.

Veganism means eating no animal products whatsoever, with the possible exception of honey. In our society this is a demanding choice to make, especially because you eliminate those great instant foods, eggs and cheese. Substitutes are often made of soyabeans, and take considerable processing which you are unlikely to undertake at home. Vegans also use synthetic materials to replace leather and wool.

On the other hand, all of us can eat some vegan meals. I've experimented lately and been very pleasantly surprised, and you might want to consult a vegan cookbook for occasional ideas—the *Vegan Health Plan* by Amanda Sweet (Arlington Books, 1987) is one. Most wholefood and vegetarian restaurants now provide vegan dishes.

- The Vegetarian Society, Parkdale, Dunham Road, Altrincham, Cheshire WA14 4Q6, telephone (061) 928 0793.
- The Vegan Society, 33-35 George Street, Oxford OX1 2AY, telephone Oxford (0865) 722166.

HEALTHY FOOD

General principles

Perhaps you feel pulled this way and that by diet advice. Don't eat breakfast. Have nothing but raw fruit. Eat a hearty breakfast to start the day right. Plenty of bran fibre. Wheat bran is bad for you, but oat bran will cure cancer. Who's right? How should we eat, to avoid illness and to achieve good health? Some of my favourite cookbooks are the ones which show blithe disregard for fussy modern fads. 'Plenty of salty farmhouse butter' says a recipe, and I feel inclined to obey.

Nonetheless, our Western diet is an unhealthy one. Here is one summary of basic principles for change:

1 Eat only as much as you need to maintain a healthy weight.
2 Reduce fat from all sources.
3 Eat less sugar (we average 4 oz per day, per person!).
4 Increase dietary fibre.
5 Eat less salt.
6 Moderate alcohol consumption.

Moderation is a useful rule, because however much nutritionists and health writers talk about what our bodies need, food is much more than just fuel.

Raw food

For many years raw food has been used for health cures, and has been promoted recently by Leslie Kenton. If you are concerned about your health, do look at her books.

A simple aid to good digestion is eating something raw—a salad or crudités, a piece of fruit or some fresh fruit juice—before every meal. This prevents a process called 'digestive leucocytosis' in which white blood cells are mobilized when we eat cooked food, and which is thought to adversely affect the immune system.

● *Raw Energy*, Leslie and Susannah Kenton (Century, 1984).
● *Ageless Ageing*, Leslie Kenton (Century, 1985).
● *The Biogenic Diet*, Leslie Kenton (Century, 1986).

Kenton also discusses environmental toxins and how to compensate for them with dietary changes and supplements. Her books are good guides for environmentally-sound weight loss, too.

Supplements

Concentrate on good food before considering nutritional supplements (for details, see page 188). There are a number of nutritious foods which you can emphasize in your diet, and Kenton's books are a good starting point if you want to know more about the benefits of yoghurt, sprouts and garlic.

Britons traditionally ate a variety of seaweeds, or sea vegetables, and the iodine content of these offers some protection against the effects of radiation. You can buy delicious Scottish sea vegetables from Julian Clokie, The Sea Vegetable Co Ltd, Pitkerrie, Balmuchy, Fearn, Ross and Cromarty IV20 1TN, telephone (0862) 87272.

The fat fallacy

There is considerable disagreement amongst scientists about the role of cholesterol in heart disease, although the public has now been thoroughly indoctrinated with the idea that polyunsaturates are desirable and saturated fats are bad.

Recently, many researchers have changed their minds, while we continue to down highly processed, chemically extracted (and cheap) oils, thinking that they will prevent heart attacks. There now appear to be two different types of cholesterol, one good and the other bad. Good cholesterol is called high density lipoprotein (HDL) and actually helps to prevent heart disease. Bad cholesterol is low density lipoprotein (LDL), and this is the sort which blocks arteries.

Too much unsaturated fat seems to have the deleterious effect of suppressing the immune system and promoting tumour growth. According to Michael Weiner, author of *Maximum Immunity* (Gateway Books, 1986), 'Some scientists suspect that the increased use of polyunsaturated fats in our diet is responsible for the high incidence of cancer in Western civilization' and 'The more unsaturated a fat is, the more it can harm your immunity' (p 81).

Unsaturated fats—containing essential fatty acids (EFAs) are indeed needed for good health, but only in small amounts. They should come from a natural, untreated source—such as fresh raw seeds, unrefined oils or fish and fish oils. Biscuits and cakes which give 'vegetable fats' as an ingredient are likely to contain highly saturated palm or coconut oils, or hydrogenated vegetable oils.

Monosaturated olive oil seems particularly desirable although researchers are not entirely clear about the reasons for the relatively low incidence of heart disease in Mediterranean countries, where it is the main source of fat.

Commercial vegetables oils are extracted with a solvent, which may be benzine, ethyl ether, carbon tertrachloride or methylene chloride (known carcinogens which leave minute traces in the final product), and are then bleached and deodorized.

In her *Fruit Book* Jane Grigson quotes a description of the processing of vegetable oils: 'First, the oils have to be degummed and neutralized after, of course, being chemically extracted from the rapeseed or soyabeans. Phosphoric acid is injected into the oil and mixed under pressure to precipitate the gums. Then it is mixed with caustic soda which forms a soap containing gums and colour which can be separated easily from the oil. Next stage is to wash the oil, dry it, bleach it with fuller's earth and filter it. At this point it's a fully refined oil but the original taste and smell still remain, making it unacceptable for consumption. The final stage, therefore, is deodorization to ensure a bland, odourless oil that won't tinge the flavour of what's cooked in it.' Grigson adds that this is why 'in this book, butter, lard, and olive oil are the fats preferred'.

Another point to consider is that pesticides and other chemicals concentrate in fats, both animal and vegetable.

What to do

1 Reduce fats from all sources. The 'good' fats recommended below are more expensive than those you've probably been using, an excellent deterrent to over-consumption.

2 Use unrefined, mechanically-expressed (first pressing; extra virgin) vegetable oils, and heat them as little as possible. Use olive oil for pan frying when the flavour is appropriate (peanut oil will be more suitable for an oriental stir-fry). They should be stored in a cool place.

3 If you must deep fry, use fresh oil and do not reuse it.

4 Use small amounts of butter in preference to highly processed margarines.

5 Choose organic dairy products whenever you can, and buy meat which has been raised without antibiotics, growth promoters and hormones.

6 Cut the fat off your meat and choose lean cuts especially if you are buying meat from an ordinary butcher. Fatty meat will contain higher levels of pesticide residues than lean meat.

7 Lard is a useful cooking fat, but commercial varieties not only contain traces of pesticides and growth promoters but have added antioxidants as preservatives. To get traditional lard you will almost certainly have to make your own (it's not difficult, if you are inclined to leisurely kitchen tasks).

Cold-pressed oils have distinctive flavours, unlike bland commercial oils. You'll need to experiment to find ones you like. I find sunflower and safflower oils far too strong, and prefer to use corn oil. Sesame oil (not the dark 'toasted' kind used as a flavouring) is also bland. On salads, use olive oil or (even more expensive, and delicious) walnut or hazelnut oil. Euvita brand organic olive oil is a good one to try.

EATING AT HOME

Keeping costs down

You may be alarmed that many of the foods I am recommending cost more than similar items from a supermarket. This is largely compensated for by a reduction in meat consumption and cutting out the many convenience and snack foods many of us depend on, but it is still important to think about how to obtain good quality food at reasonable prices. People on a low income have far poorer diets, and spend a larger proportion of their income on food, than do people who have more money. Only by making a truly adequate diet accessible to everyone (this includes food free from dangerous additives and pesticides) can there be real improvements in the national health.

As the organic food market grows, prices will come down— your purchases are a sort of investment in organic agriculture. Neighbourhood food co-ops are an excellent idea but require quite a bit of time and commitment, especially in the beginning. Organizing a cooperative scheme amongst a few friends is much easier. Get together to order 'real' meat, buy from your nearest wholefood warehouse (grains, legumes and dried fruits keep for long periods, so you can stock up) or directly from a farm. I go to New Covent Garden to buy organically-grown produce at wholesale prices. Look in the *New Organic Food Guide* for organic farms and dairies in your area where you can buy direct, or contact the Soil Association or the Henry Doubleday Research Association (HDRA)—addresses, page 306.

Emphasizing seasonal foods, and eating inexpensive grains, legumes, vegetables like potatoes and carrots as the mainstays of your diet will keep basic costs very low. Equipping yourself with several good vegetarian cookbooks is essential, so you aren't trapped with steamed brown rice and jacket potatoes day in and day out. There are endless variations possible using these staple foods, and cookbooks provide the necessary ideas and inspiration.

Where to shop

Frances Moore Lappé, tireless campaigner on world hunger, points out that the question may not be which supermarket to shop at but whether we wouldn't be better off shopping somewhere else. The assumption is that we save masses of time by using supermarkets and shopping centres, but in fact a smaller wholefood store, which you get to know and which doesn't offer an overwhelming range of unhealthy and over-packaged goods, is likely to be faster.

Of course you are not going to give up your weekly supermarket shop immediately, especially when you are not sure what the alternatives are. Such changes have to be gradual. Over the past couple of years I have found my supermarket shopping lists grow shorter and shorter as we've got to know where else to get our food.

A friend who doesn't have a car buys most of her groceries

from local shops, instead of travelling three miles to the nearest supermarket once a week. As she says, this helps keep the local shops going, and she enjoys seeing the shopkeepers. She probably spends less than she would if she went to the supermarket, even though shop prices are generally higher, because she isn't tempted by a huge range of goods. Shopping frequently means that she can buy exactly what she needs. On top of that she gets fresh air and exercise.

Try to buy from small farms and cottage industries. A demand for real ale has put small brewers back in business, and a demand for real British food is encouraging many small producers into the market. T. S. Eliot, who was a great cheese fan, mourned the demise of English cheesemaking some 40 years ago. He would be delighted to see that it's back in the news and on our plates.

Many items are sold by post, and some is available in specialist shops. There is a burgeoning market in guidebooks to local producers. While buying from farms isn't as convenient as piling everything into a trolley at the supermarket, you can combine weekend outings with a little shopping—we keep shopping guides in the car so we don't find ourselves in a new county with no idea of what treasure might lie down one of the little lanes we pass.

(If you don't have a car, you might pick up something when out walking or cycling, or discover that there are firms in your town which make ice cream or smoke fish.)

- *The New Organic Food Guide*, Alan Gear (Dent, 1987). Not entirely up-to-date, but the introductory chapters and reference material are excellent.
- *Shopping for Health*, Janette Marshall (Penguin, 1987).
- *Fine Food*, Simone Sekers (Hodder & Stoughton, 1987).
- *The Good Food Directory*, ed. Drew Smith and David Mabey (Consumers' Association, 1987).
- *British Food Finds 1987*, ed. Henrietta Green (Rich & Green Ltd, 1987). For shops and restaurants, or bulk buying.
- *RAC Food Routes*, ed. Henrietta Green (George Philip & Son, 1988).
- National Federation of City Farms, The Old Vicarage, 66 Fraser Street, Windmill Hill, Bedminster, Bristol BS3 4LY, telephone (0272) 660663. City farms often have goats' milk, eggs, honey and even meat for sale.

Boycotts

Although the *Green Consumer Guide* suggests that boycotts are 'negative', avoiding certain types of food or the products of particular countries or companies is a powerful consumer tool and one which we must use. I cannot give a list of things to boycott, but a few current campaigns ask that shoppers avoid buying tunafish (tuna fishing is causing the death of thousands of dolphins because of the types of nets which are used) and Icelandic fish (Iceland is one of the few countries which allows commercial whaling; Japan is another).

Avoiding South African goods is another ethical choice we can make while doing the grocery shopping.

Susan George, researcher on international food issues, has suggested a boycott of products from 'corporate junk-food mongers'—Coca-Cola and Kellogg for example—because these companies aggravate malnutrition in the Third World by promoting their nutritionally marginal products as alternatives to indigenous staple foods. The same could be said of junk-food promotion in Britain.

COOKING

Equipment

Even a stainless steel pan needs to be looked after with care: there are suggestions that if it is even once scoured with abrasive powder or steelwool, tiny amounts of toxic metals such as chromium and nickel will leach into whatever you cook in the pan.

A far greater concern is aluminium, which has been associated with a number of brain disorders. Have you noticed that you can clean an aluminium pan by cooking something acid (tomato soup or rhubarb, for instance) in it? Guess where the surface of the pan has gone. Try to get rid of your aluminium cookware—and, most importantly, throw out any aluminium teapots.

Enamelled pots and pans (like Le Creuset) are probably safest of all, and uncoated cast-iron pans can add small but beneficial amounts of iron to your diet. Glass is safe, and so is terra cotta (as long as the glaze does not contain lead).

Teflon is a fluorine-based plastic which should be avoided. If teflon-coated pans are put over a high flame they release toxic fumes. Non-stick coatings—even Silverstone—are made from types of plastic and will gradually release their constituents. The surface eventually gets worn and small particles chip off into your food.

The best stainless steel and enamelled iron pans are very expensive. Accumulate them gradually, and in the meantime try to stop using aluminium, particularly for acid foods and long-cooking soups and stews. Woolworths sells a range of mock Le Creuset, and there are a variety of less expensive stainless steel pans and glass baking dishes around.

Women in the kitchen

As we lead more hectic lives, convenience foods become an increasingly, and excessively, important part of our diet. Many women, especially women who work outside the home, feel these foods are the only way to escape the tyranny of hours spent over a hot stove. One of the most important changes needed to help us to eat ecologically is more cooperation from our partners.

A recent survey found that the maximum amount of time American women wanted to spend preparing a meal was 30 minutes, while the average amount of time men wanted to spend was 15 minutes. This is probably comparable to statistics on cleaning, but whereas men (in general, of course) have somewhat more relaxed housekeeping standards than women, they believe in Hot Meals. Many women would be happy to come home and eat a piece of cheese and some cherry tomatoes, or a bowl of muesli, but our partners are miserable if there isn't a plateful of something *serious* in the offing, and they wouldn't mind a snack to tide them over until then.

Of course this phenomenon is partly caused by women's concern about slimming, and by men's childhood mealtimes uncluttered by either preparation or clearing up. It also has something to do with fundamentally different approaches to food: because women are usually responsible for preparing it, there are times we can't bear to be within 10 feet of a saucepan.

Let's establish the fact that men *can* be left to fend for themselves, and so can older children. Make sure they understand that anything they cook *they* clear up—or you'll end up with the remains of a complicated curry to deal with while they are pleased as punched about having cooked dinner.

If you are a man, think hard about your actual, manual

contribution to preparing meals. Many men simply feel awkward in the kitchen, and hate cooking under someone else's supervision. Learning to cook takes time, and practice, and a few mistakes along the way—but you should be able to count on a sympathetic reception if you decide to master the art.

Ensure, jointly, that you always have a supply of things you don't need to cook: fruit, vegetable sticks, yoghurt, cheese and good bread. Even small children can make an adequate supper on these.

Inexperienced cooks

If you are inexperienced in the kitchen, enlist the help of a couple of user-friendly cookbooks or, preferably, a skilled friend. Be prepared to scrub vegetables and whip egg whites while you watch and learn.

Start by making a list of 'Things I want to to be able to make myself', and work up to them gradually. It's fun to specialise a little: Indian food, Japanese, old-fashioned English cooking, soups, salads and vegetables or whatever else you fancy.

My own choice is soups, and I can recommend them as the ideal unprocessed fast food, especially in during cold winter months. A couple of years ago we replaced our aluminium soup kettle with an enormous stainless steel pot. It has a thick bottom which heats evenly and prevents sticking, and in the winter it is kept pretty constantly full of things like corn chowder and spinach-kasha soup.

Quick meals

Frankly, much of what many of us eat falls into this category. When it gets to the table it may not look like it came out of *Fast and Furious* (the cookbook I keep meaning to write), but when it comes to making a meal after a long day at the office or coping with a pair of toddlers, or with teenagers whining that they are hungry, plans for a leisurely cassoulet go out the window.

I once saw a newspaper column called 'The 60 Minute Gourmet'. What I'd like to read is 'The 60 *Second* Gourmet'. Well, up to about 10 minutes would be okay. What I have in mind is meals that take minimal effort and don't dirty more than one pan.

In fact, a good rule for deciding whether a recipe is easy or not is to count the number of bowls and pans it requires. Another clue is the number of ingredients, though this can be misleading because some cookbook writers list ten herbs and spices for a single sauce, and that really doesn't complicate things much (you can always leave some out).

Make out a list of your own Rock Bottom Six easy meals, just to prove that you can get through a week of eating at home. Baked potatoes, omelettes or scrambled eggs, pasta, grilled fish, cheese and salad, stir-fried vegetables, for example. That'll take you through a week, at a pinch. The seventh night you eat at your mother's, cadge a meal from a friend who loves to cook, or go to a restaurant. Or don't eat at all!

Microwave ovens are not the answer. They are good at cooking prepared and heavily processed foods, dishes which have been 'engineered' to suit their peculiar requirements, but they are a flop when it comes to real, fresh food. Have you ever read a microwave cookbook? Prawn curry, an 'easy' dish which takes 20 minutes according to one recipe, has six separate stages of microwave cooking. Minted lamb chops, 'less easy', requires ten separate stages. Although you might be able to produce a dish in slightly less time (and the cookbook times do not take account of chopping and measuring, exactly the same for conventional and microwave cooking), you are almost certain to spend just as much time actually working at it. (For more information on microwaves, see page 255.)

Cooking for one

The main problem here is inspiration. It just isn't as much fun to cook for yourself as for or with other people. Why not eat with other single friends, perhaps on a regular basis by forming a supper club?

A freezer makes it possible to cook in quantity for one person: make a batch of soup or casserole which will serve six, divide it into portions depending on your figure and appetite, keep one out to eat tonight and freeze the rest. (Don't be careless about labelling—you'll end up thawing a tomato sauce when you wanted the blackcurrant mousse.)

Mollie Katzen, author of *The Enchanted Broccoli Forest*, includes a section called Light Meals for Nibblers, and starts with 'A Pep-Talk for Solitary Eaters':

> Do you regularly miss out on the pleasure of Dining, because it doesn't seem worth the trouble to make things Nice if they're only for you (and the 6 o'clock news announcer, who is your steady dinner companion)? Perhaps you can be convinced that you, yes you, are indeed deserving of good food and a little extra attention. Try these suggestions, and dinner with your Self can become something you eagerly anticipate, . . . a Pleasurable Experience.

She suggests setting aside time each week to prepare one soup and one main dish, which you divide into single portions and freeze. With a steady supply of fresh fruits and vegetables, and good bread, you are set. Soup with raw vegetables and a simple dip from her Nibblers chapter one night, and a portion of the main dish with a spectacular salad the following night. Vary with omelettes, which can be made quickly and easily in single servings.

Eating your greens

The trick to eating fresh vegetables, something we all need to do more of, is preparation. If the salad greens are washed and the spring onions trimmed, you can pull out a bowl, spend a minute or two slicing and tearing, and be ready to eat. A little dressing mixed up in advance or some good oil and vinegar make it a cinch.

Katzen writes that 'a major deterrent to the use of fresh (as opposed to frozen or canned) vegetables is an aversion to chopping'. While a food processor makes this much easier, it does not have the skill of a good chef handling a good knife. Learning to prepare fresh vegetables yourself is an essential culinary skill, and *The Enchanted Broccoli Forest* has five pages of tips on cutting, with illustrations.

If you can't stand plain steamed vegetables, switch things round and start making a vegetable dish the main course. Cauliflower cheese is the obvious example, but broccoli (very nutritious) can be prepared in exactly the same way. And so could finely shredded cabbage for that matter. Or all three, coarsely chopped with sliced carrots for colour.

Rather than stick with vegetarian cookbooks, excellent as many of them are, consult Jane Grigson's *Vegetable Book* and any of Elizabeth David's books for hundreds of vegetable-based dishes to try.

Avoiding waste

Even though clearing our plates is not going to save a child in the Sudan from starvation, some changes in the way we use the food we buy can change our attitudes (and where else does any real change in the world start?), as well as saving some money. And that money might actually help the starving child.

Why not skip the occasional meal—or fast a whole day? Make a guess at how much money you have saved and donate it to Oxfam or Save the Children or Intermediate Technology. Some people like to do without meat, or sweets. A concerned slimmer could put 15p in a piggy bank each time s/he passes up a packet of crisps or a chocolate truffle.

An important and rare culinary skill is making full use of every bit of food. Of course most of us don't have farmhouse kitchens or time to make our own sausages, but we could make far better use of the food we buy.

Leftovers are something of a joke, but if you establish one area of the fridge for things to be used up, the family will know to look there for that piece of lasagna to warm for lunch, and you'll notice the juice left from a tin of tomatoes in time to add it to a sauce.

It has been estimated that every year the average family throws away in its potato peelings the amount of Vitamin C in

95 glasses of orange juice, the iron in 500 eggs, and the protein in 60 steaks. I have a simpler reason for not peeling potatoes— lack of time. Scrub them with your vegetable brush and cut out any eyes or bad bits (some organic potatoes have more skin blemishes than chemically grown potatoes, but don't worry about that—just watch for worm holes and follow them).

Unpeeled potatoes roast and mash perfectly well—though if you are accustomed to creamy white mashed potatoes they'll take a little getting used to. If you love jacket potato skins, that's a good start.

Another point of view, vehemently espoused by my partner, is that mashed potatoes *should* be white and that they taste different with the skin left in. I don't mind, as long as *he* does the peeling. Anna Thomas, author of *The Vegetarian Epicure*, makes soup stock from potato peelings and says that she is sometimes hard pressed to use up the peeled potatoes!

Making a proper clear meat stock is not a skill I've mastered, but one can make delicious broth (to eat as it is or use as a soup base) with more casual techniques. Almost all vegetable trim- mings can go into the pot (be cautious with cabbage, however, and its sister vegetables like cauliflower). If you can get decent, meaty bones, they should be browned in a little fat before you add water. A little salt helps draw out the flavours—a good reason for not salting vegetables you are cooking to eat— and I often add dregs of wine or a dash of vinegar. The acid will dissolve bones slightly, adding a bit of calcium to the stock.

Cookbooks, especially budget cookbooks, are full of ideas for making the most of what you buy. Candied citrus peel is easy to make (there are clear instructions in Jane Grigson's *Fruit Book*)—this is a good way to use the peels of organically- grown oranges, and makes a lovely gift.

Organization

A common mistake amongst the health conscious is to make huge bowls of salad each mealtime, because we *ought* to eat more salad, and throw half of it away afterwards. Some dishes need to be eaten while they are fresh. On the other hand, many soups and most stews taste much better after standing overnight, and even better on the third day.

Knowing your audience is crucial, as is having the right equipment and a good stock of basic ingredients and season- ings. Favourite recipes should be somewhere accessible, and it's a good idea to keep cookbooks in or near the kitchen, rather than on the bookshelves above your desk in the bedroom, so they are at hand to provide inspiration and information.

Planning meals and shopping—with anyone who is going to share in them—is another great help, even if you aren't terribly precise about it. Keeping tabs on what you have on hand in the fridge helps to avoid shrivelled carrots and mouldy cheese, and prevents a buildup of unidentifiable containers lingering on the back shelf (eventual clearance because of the nasty odour).

Conserve energy by letting dishes cook in their own heat. Nutritionist Adele Davis recommended bringing a soup or spaghetti sauce to the boil and then turning off the flame and allowing the pan to stand for a couple of hours, instead of simmering.

You can save yourself a great deal of work by doubling or even tripling recipes, assuming you have the right size pans and bowls (but be careful with this if you're an inexperienced cook). It's not much more trouble to make a huge batch of lasagna than a tiny one. Eat half now, and save the other half for another meal. Double cooking is easiest if you have a freezer, because you can have the second dish a week or two later. If possible, freeze food in the dish it will be cooked (a collection of cheap glass baking pans make this possible).

Cookbooks

● *Diet for a Small Planet*, 10th Anniversary Edition, Frances Moore Lappé (New York: Ballantine, 1982) and *Recipes for a Small Planet*, Ellen Ewald (Ballantine, 1973). Both essential reading and recipes for ecological cooks, and available by post from Wholefood, 24 Paddington Street, London W1M 4DR, telephone 01-935 3924.

● *Diet for a Small Island*, Patrick and Shirley Rivers (Turnstone, 1981).

● *The Moosewood Cookbook* (Berkeley: Ten Speed Press, 1977) and *The Enchanted Broccoli Forest* (Ten Speed Press, 1982), both by Mollie Katzen. Order through your bookshop.

● *The Vegetarian Epicure* by Anna Thomas (Penguin, 1973).

● *The Vegetarian Feast* (Thorsons, 1982) and *Fast Vegetarian Feasts* (1983), both by Martha Rose Shulman.

● Jane Grigson's *Vegetable Book* (Michael Joseph, 1978) and *Fruit Book* (Michael Joseph, 1982).

- *The Cranks Recipe Book*, David Canter, Kay Canter and Daphne Swan (J. M. Dent, 1982).
- *Food Combining for Health*, Doris Grant and Jean Joice (Thorsons, 1984).
- *Confessions of a Sneaky Organic Cook . . . Or How to Make Your Family Healthy While They're Not Looking*, Jane Kinderlehrer (Emmaus, Pennsylvania: Rodale, 1971).

EATING OUT

Restaurants

One fellow I spoke to at Friends of the Earth was all in favour of res`aurant eating because, he said, it meant fresh, bulk purchase food (saving packaging), prepared in large quantities (saving energy). Fundamentally, he is right, but there are a few special hazards:

1 Many restaurants, even expensive ones, serve prepackaged and processed foods. Good ethnic restaurants may be the best choice, and you can always ask if the vegetables are fresh or frozen when you order, and whether the soup is homemade.
2 Most restaurants cook in aluminium because it is cheap and light. (There is concern in the catering business about the fact that it pits easily and is therefore not as hygienic as stainless steel or enamel pans, and talk of its being banned.)
3 Restaurant food can contain hefty amounts of monosodium glutamate and salt, as well as cheap fats (why should they care about your heart, or waistline?).
4 Even many wholefood restaurants microwave food these days. Although some waiters look terribly offended, the only thing to do is ask in advance.

What this boils down to is knowing your restaurant. Guidebooks are helpful even if you find that your criteria and budget differs from theirs.

Fast food

Why do people go to McDonald's? They want something NOW, are in a hurry and don't want to spend much. Yet fast food restaurants contribute to the destruction of tropical rainforests (destroyed forever in order to raise beef for a couple of seasons, until the soil is utterly depleted), contribute huge amounts of plastic and paper waste to the 'disposal stream' and our streets, and give us proverbially unhealthy food to boot. International hamburger chains also tend to homogenize cultures (why on earth should we be able to eat the same American hamburger and French fries in Tokyo and Peking and Paris?).

If you frequently find yourself going out for a hamburger because it's 10 at night, you are starving, and there is nothing in your refrigerator except a couple of mouldy tomatoes, get a piece of paper right now and make a list of ways you can avoid that situation in the first place. This is a lot more constructive than feeling guilty and simply resolving to do better.

Laying in a supply of some kind of wholesome, non-perishable and almost instantaneous food at home is probably the most helpful step, and ensuring that you always have, say, a box of eggs will also help.

Bread, wine and cheese make a good alternative meal, especially with the right companions.

Travel alternatives

Not only is the food at motorway stops and on most trains heavily processed and wrapped, for the most part it is pretty awful to eat! You can enjoy better food and save money by ensuring that you always have basic picnic equipment in the glovebox, or your overnight case. During the day you can stop at a market or shop to buy provisions—and if you travel with one of the food guides mentioned on page 36 you can often pick up a regional speciality along the way.

While British shops do not as a rule offer the same variety and quality as continental ones, it is still possible to assemble the ingredients for a pleasant and satisfying meal if you have the following supplies with you: a sharp knife (for cheese, fruit and bread—a Swiss Army knife is good if you are travelling on foot or by train or bicycle); corkscrew; a few pieces of cutlery; small hand towels (to use as napkins and for wiping up); salt, pepper and mustard.

For long journeys it helps to lay in plentiful supplies of drinks and snack foods. A big flask of iced water is good in warm weather, and in the winter there is nothing more welcome than a hot drink (apple juice, spiked with cinnamon, is delicious). Cartons of juice, crackers, fresh fruit, cut-up raw vegetables in a plastic bag, dried fruit and nuts, all travel well and are easy to eat.

You might think about carrying real mugs along to avoid getting takeaway coffee or tea in a plastic cup (saves waste and tastes much better). With an old-fashioned wicker picnic basket you can transport wine glasses, and a tiny camping stove makes it possible to brew fresh tea.

When you travel by air, you can ring ahead and order vegetarian meals, which are generally better than ordinary plane fare. But it is fun to plan a survival pack, with fresh fruit and some special cheese or whatever you fancy. Leslie Kenton suggests that jetlag is far less a problem if one avoids eating anything but fruit during the flight, and says that she simply brings along a bag of apples to munch. Drinking plenty of water and avoiding alcohol is important too.

EATING TOGETHER

Psychologists have begun to point out that sitting down for a meal is an important part of family life—something which should surprise no one. Eating together is fundamental to human groups, in every society. Sadly, mealtime is one of the casualties of our way of life and restoring it sometimes requires quite a lot of effort.

Edith Schaeffer writes, in her *Hidden Art*, about restoring shared meals to their proper place in our lives:

> The art of living together, of being a family, is being lost, just as the wealth of the earth is being lost by man's carelessness in his ignoring the need for conservation of forests, lakes and seas. The 'conservation' of family life does not consist of sticking a rose in the middle of the table, it is a deeper thing than that. However, whether one is sketching a face, building a house, designing a dress or planting a forest, one has to start *somewhere*. And in this need to get back to 'gracious living', to real communication amongst people living together, it seems to me one place to start could be the meal-time moments, and the careful preparation of the background for conversations at that time.

Food is an absorbing, and nearly endless, subject because it's a continual part of our daily lives. The purchase, preparation and consumption of food has important ecological consequences—and even more importantly it is central to the fabric and substance of our families, work groups and society. I hope that an ecological approach to the home and to food will encourage people to see shared meals as essential to good living.

Don't let worries about health or the environment stop food being a source of pleasure. Food is the simplest, most socially acceptable sensual experience we can have. 'Breaking bread together' promotes harmony and it is always good to hear that world leaders have shared a meal. Regular, happy meals with people you love will do more for your health than careful food combining with no joy. As Proverbs 15:17 says 'Better is a dinner of herbs where love is, than a stalled ox and hatred therewith.' *Bon appetit*!

If you want to enjoy organic wines—which are reputedly less likely to cause a hangover—check at your local wholefood shop, or contact the following:

● Henry Doubleday Research Association, Ryton-on-Dunsmore, Coventry CV8 3LG, telephone (0203) 303517.

- Vintage Roots, 25 Manchester Road, Reading, Berks RG1 3QE, telephone (0734) 662569.
- Vinceremos Wines, Beechwood Centre, Elmete Lane, Leeds LS8 2LQ.

3
HOME ECONOMICS

Good workmanship—that is, careful, considerate, and loving
work—requires us to think considerately of the whole process,
natural and cultural, . . . because the good worker does not
share the industrial contempt for 'raw material' . . . .The good
worker understands that a badly made artifact is both an insult
to its user and a danger to its source. We could say, then, that
good forestry begins with the respectful husbanding of the
forest that we call stewardship and ends with well-made tables
and chairs and houses, just as good agriculture begins with
stewardship of the fields and ends with good meals.

Wendell Berry
Preserving Wildness, 1986

Why should an ecology book tell you about buying things?
Surely I ought to be talking about recycling newspaper, not
where to buy your sweaters.

But all the things we throw away—and should try to recycle
—are things we have bought. This includes packaging: the
cost of a sturdy cardboard box and polystyrene casing is included in the price you pay for your new home computer
(packaging accounts for approximately 5% of all consumer
spending). Of course the computer needs to be packaged, to
protect it, but the polystyrene was probably expanded with
CFCs, contributing to the breakdown of the ozone layer, and
will never biodegrade.

When the cheap beach shoes you bought at the end of last
summer go into the wastebasket, there is still a price to be paid
for disposing of them. We jointly generate more than a quarter
of a million tonnes of rubbish each year. A small proportion of
it is burned (which creates air pollution) and the remainder
goes into landfill sites. Estimates reckon that approximately
75% of our rubbish could be reused or recycled (plastics and
toxic products being the main exceptions). Recycling is infinitely better than disposal, but we need to consider how we
create so much waste in the first place.

Do you have a bathroom cabinet full of makeup and different brands of cough syrups or half a dozen different bottles of
shampoo by your bathtub? The packages were tempting, you
were in a hurry, or a friend recommended that new shampoo.
Perhaps the salesgirl insisted that 'Cerulean Blue' was just
heaven on you, and you were in a mood to believe anything. In
the same way, your closet may be groaning with clothes or the
workshop with gadgets. Consumption has become a way of life.

More and more of the goods we buy are 'disposable', specifically designed to be used once and thrown away. British
Telecom's phonecards are an example: a durable, reusable
coin is being replaced by a disposable plastic card packaged
in a plastic envelope. Of course British Telecom has sound
reasons for switching many public phones to phonecards and
customers benefit by having working telephones, but the
ground around them is littered with used and broken cards
now, and with the plastic envelopes they come in. (It's a small
thing, but the concerned consumer can try to use a coinbox
when one is available and save the phonecard for emergencies.)

Consumer society

Economic growth is supposed to be a good thing. Increasing
productivity and efficiency is supposed to be a good thing, no

matter what the human and social cost. The more people buy, the better this is for the country.

Think this through. An ever-rising standard of living, for everyone? Or a rising standard of living for some, with a corresponding deterioration for others? As long as we measure standard of living in terms of cars and washing machines and other things we own, instead of giving some thought to quality of life, we're simply on the wrong track, a course which leads nowhere.

Measuring quality of life is not a task suited to charts and figures, but the notion of limitless growth is a foolish one. All production depends on the input of raw materials which come from the earth, and which are in limited supply or replace themselves relatively slowly. What happens when they run out? It makes no difference whether this happens in 10 years or 1000—is it appropriate to simply use things up, without ensuring that they will be replaced? At present we treat oil reserves and the tropical rainforests as if they were leftovers which are going to get mouldy if we don't use them up fast enough.

There are costs involved in this kind of development which are not taken into account in companies' annual statements. In the process of economic growth we have the capacity to destroy the world we live on. Increasing output depends on *our* willingness to buy ever-increasing quantities of things. More cars, more clothes, more toys (for children *and* adults), more kinds of writing paper, fancier diaries and kitchen equipment.

To keep the wheels of commerce oiled we have to keep buying—and throwing other things away. Goods aren't made to last, because if they did you wouldn't need to buy more next year, or next month.

In contrast, alternative economists promote the idea of sustainability and sustainable growth. If you are interested in this idea, contact one of the following organizations.

● The Other Economic Summit (or TOES) and the New Economics Foundation, both at Thames House, South Bank Business Centre, 140 Battersea Park Road, London SW11 4NB. Developing principles for a new economics, aiming at human well-being, sustainability, good work and economic self-reliance.

● Schumacher Society, Ford House, Hartland, Bideford, Devon EX39 6EE, telephone (02374) 293.

● Intermediate Technology Development Group, Myson House, Railway Terrace, Rugby, Warwickshire CV21 3HT, telephone (0788) 60631.

Advertising

The typical American consumer receives 5000 advertising messages every day according to a recent study, so many that even the marketing people are worried about overloading the public with 'advertising clutter'—perhaps we could call this advertising pollution. In the US it is possible to read blurbs for local restaurants in public toilet cubicles!

Some advertising is informative, and necessary. We put up with a lot more because it pays for our newspapers and magazines and television programmes. Most advertising, however, is designed to make you unhappy with what you've got.

Your hair needs a lift and your bed hasn't got the latest support system. Good grief, if you settle in with that nice tweed jacket and neat little pigskin Filofax you bought in 1987 (both of which will easily last till the end of the century at least), business in Britain will take a nosedive. You need a denim jacket, they tell you, and some new organizer will be essential this autumn. Our insecurities grease the wheels of commerce.

Value judgments

While recent moves towards a 'green consumer' ethic are welcome, we need to think primarily of reducing the volume of consumption and what Jonathan Porritt has called 'the prevailing ethic of consumerism'.

Do we want to be 'consumers'? Consumers consume—that is, use things up—not a particularly satisfying function for most human beings. Most of us would prefer to think that we are acting in the world, affecting other people, creating something of value.

The first step towards ecologically-sound consumption is to think carefully about what you really need and want. This is not as simple as it might appear. Take time right now to jot down a list of your goals and aspirations. Do you think more about what you want to buy than about what you want to do, or be? Are your choices about the future determined by what you own?

Some people have made a conscious decision to simplify the

way they live, putting money aside for causes which matter to them. We could all resolve to live a little more lightly on the earth.

Maybe if you stop buying so much you'll end up with too much money. But you can give some away or invest it (ethically of course—see page 73). Or you could cut back on the hours you spend working, so you have more time for your family, or gardening, or travel—for campaigning on environmental issues or writing the novel you've always talked about.

ENVIRONMENTAL PRICE-TAGS

A friend of mine was bemused as she looked round her crowded flat, 'How can one person buy this much stuff?' If you are a compulsive consumer, perhaps considering some of the following points will help you slow down. Environmental price-tags are not written in pounds and pence—though they do have a long-term financial cost—but they can make even cheap items far too expensive for a concerned shopper.

CFC's and the ozone layer

Aerosol manufacturers are at last responding to scientific and public concern about the deterioration of the ozone layer (or at least to the likelihood of boycotts, should they ignore the warnings), although they have continued to insist that a link between the use of CFCs (chlorinated fluorocarbons) and the hole in the ozone layer has not been scientifically proven. Some manufacturers are adopting a label which says that their product does not contain propellants 'alleged to damage the ozone layer'. Friends of the Earth and the television programme *What on Earth is Going On?* suggested a more succinct label reading simply 'Ozone Friendly' and a number of companies plan to use it.

While companies switch over to different propellant gases for aerosols and adopt the new labelling, it's not easy to decide which product to buy. Friends of the Earth publishes a guide-sheet, listing all the 'Ozone Friendly' products they know about. But aside from the ozone problem, aerosols are a wasteful and expensive form of packaging. Besides this, the propellant gases they contain can be dangerous and the very fine particles into which they disperse their contents are a health threat. They can explode if left near a source of heat or even in sunlight, and are a hazard to disposal workers. Choose an alternative product whenever possible—for example, shaving soap and a brush instead of aerosol foam.

Polystyrene also contains CFC gases, which are used to 'expand' it. As it breaks up the CFCs are released into the atmosphere. Hamburger restaurants have been much criticised, and most of them are now switching to 'Ozone Friendly' foam packaging.

Energy and transport

The price of everything we buy includes a percentage for the energy needed to produce and transport it. Chemical-based agriculture is extremely energy-intensive, both in the fertilizers and pesticides required and in the mechanical equipment used. (Cotton, a difficult crop to grow successfully, requires the equivalent of its own weight in oil to produce it.) Keeping this energy cost to a minimum is an essential part of controlling a number of environmental problems, including the 'greenhouse effect'.

Pernicious plastic

Plastics can be water-resistant, light and almost unbreakable. They are also cheap. The trouble is that they last for ever, and although recycling is possible in theory it is a long way off in practice. Much packaging is made from layers of different plastics, which cannot be reprocessed in combination. There are also toxicity problems associated with many plastics, and dangerous dioxins are given off when they are incinerated.

Litter

Do you have to kick your way through a sea of broken hamburger cartons, crisp wrappers and paper cups on your way to catch the bus each morning?

Very little of this rubbish could be recycled, even if someone wanted to. MPs are talking about the litter question, aware that Britain's image is tarnished by the squalour of her streets, but it seems that little is likely to be done.

Concern about the social impact of litter and the difficulty and expense of disposing of the mountains of non-biodegradable packaging we generate has led to important and innovative leglisation in Suffolk County, Long Island. They are *banning* almost all non-biodegradable packaging at retail establishments throughout the county, and voice particular concern about polystyrene and polyvinyl chloride (common plastic packing materials).

The environmental question includes the aesthetics of walking through drifts of rubbish every time we go outside. The problem isn't restricted to urban areas: walks in the countryside are marred by inescapable and unmistakeable signs of the people who have been there before you and who couldn't be bothered to pick up after themselves. Bright purple chocolate bar wrappers and 'disposable' nappies catch the eye, instead of cowslips and hawthorn blossom. Plastic lemonade bottles have eternal life.

It is all too easy to throw a wrapper down, especially when there's no bin available and your scrap is only a drop in the oceans of plastic. Each of us needs to think about this, and discuss it with our children. There is no excuse, ever, for adding to the mess.

The ecologically-sound alternative snack is an apple, preferably British, best of all from a tree in your garden. Keep one in your handbag or briefcase at all times if you are a snacker.

You'll never be embarrassed by an apple the way you are by a Mars bar, and it isn't messy like a peach or fussy like grapes. Eat the core (more roughage) and toss the stem into the nearest potted plant.

NIMBY: Not In My Backyard

Just as we think of what comes into the ecosystem which is our home, we also need to consider what goes out again. Have you ever thought about what happens to the contents of the one, two or even three bins you leave out on Friday morning? The dustmen heave the bags into the huge metal jaws of their truck. That's it, as far as we're concerned.

But landfill sites throughout the developed world are already filling up. Rubbish has to be transported farther and farther for burial, adding to costs. Landfill tips pose special problems: primarily the dangerous leakage of methane gas (which could, however, be used as fuel) and toxic leachate which enters the ground water supplies (even domestic rubbish contains its share of toxic waste).

Incineration is a potentially useful source of heat and energy, but has special hazards. When some materials are burned they emit dangerous gases unless special filtering systems are used.

None of us wants this rubbish in *our* backyard, but everywhere is someone's backyard. There are some obvious ethical questions raised by the prospect of American rubbish being buried in Cornish tin mines, or West German industrial waste in Northern Cyprus. It should be obvious that our waste is our problem, while the waste of other nations is theirs. Responsible waste management is essential domestic housekeeping for everyone.

Ethical issues

Many of the things offered in our shops come from countries with oppressive regimes or where production is causing ecological degradation or economic hardship. Countries which could easily produce enough food to feed their own population instead grow crops for sale to richer nations in order to pay off high interest bank loans (often taken in order to finance expensive and inappropriate Western technology). This cannot be separated from land issues in the producer countries, or from the economic hold which multinational companies have on Third World economies.

What we can do is try to buy from companies or organisations which promote equitable and conscientious development. Traidcraft, for example, sells a wide range of household goods, clothes, tea and coffee from the Third World and ensures that the producers themselves receive a fair price for their goods.

Another matter for concern is animal welfare. Avoiding meat which has been raised by intensive farming methods and cosmetics and toiletries which are tested on animals are perhaps the most important things to consider. For more information, contact the following:

● Traidcraft plc, Mail Order Department, Kingsway, Gateshead NE11 ONE. Free catalogue.

● *New Internationalist*, Subscription Office, 120-126 Lavender Avenue, Mitcham, Surrey CR4 3HP. This magazine covers many topics, but is a good source of information about the various ethical issues which may affect your choices next time you go shopping.

● *The Real Cost*, Richard North (Chatto & Windus, 1986).

● *Cruelty Free Shopper*, Lis Howlett, available from the Vegan Society, 33-35 George Street, Oxford OX1 2AY, telephone Oxford (0865) 722166.

● Royal Society for the Prevention of Cruelty to Animals (RSPCA), The Causeway, Horsham, West Sussex RH12 1HG.

THE GREEN CONSUMER

Green Consumer Week in September 1988, organized by a 'green development' company called SustainAbility and used to launch their *Green Consumer Guide*, brought the idea of green consumerism into the public eye. There is much to be said for buying 'green'—that is, choosing CFC-free aerosols, energy-efficient cars which run on unleaded petrol, and patronizing a supermarket which stocks a wide range of organic produce—and the *Guide* is full of useful information to help us make practical choices.

However, this approach doesn't tackle some fundamental ecological and economic issues. The main problem is simple— we consume too much. Buying green is not going to affect that (perhaps we will feel so virtuous that we will buy even more). Neither does the *Guide* concern itself with the question of our dependence on a few large firms and the vast multinationals, whose primary interest is and will always be profits, and profits alone.

Frances Moore Lappé, tireless campaigner on world hunger, points out that the question may not be which supermarket to shop at but whether we wouldn't be better off shopping somewhere else. Conscientious consumers, of whatever persuasion, have no valid role as far as many manufacturers and retailers are concerned. Informed consumers are to be discouraged because scepticism about the grand claims of various brands of washing powder is not what keeps the marketplace going round.

As green consumers, we need to be aware that the power of industry and of the multinational corporations is not something to be easily challenged and brought into line with our principles. Exerting pressure at the shop till is important, but to some extent we need to step away from the shops themselves.

Local shopping

No doubt you've read about the demise of the corner shop, and perhaps you've seen old favourites close down or move away. Shopping centres are increasingly taking shopping away from our homes into centralized sites which are geared to car owners. Doing your shopping near home saves time, transportation costs and fuel, and by keeping your neighbours in business you enrich your own locality.

Architects at the Center for Environmental Structure in Berkeley, California, write: 'we believe that people are not only *willing* to walk to their local corner groceries, but that the corner grocery plays an essential role in any healthy neighbourhood: partly because it is just more convenient for individuals; partly because it helps to integrate the neighbourhood as a whole.' (Alexander *et al.*, *A Pattern Language*, p 441). In fact, neighbourhood shops are one of the most important elements in our perception of an area as a neighbourhood.

Everyone needs a local shop for spur-of-the-moment purchases, a pint of milk or packet of butter or the Sunday paper, but many people only use local shops for these few purchases and give their real allegiance to the high street giants. Instead, we should get to know the shops near our homes and use them whenever we can. Of course you won't find the same range of goods at a small shop, but they can often obtain things for you if you ask. The much vaunted 'choice' we are offered in big stores can be misleading (aren't things often much of a muchness?), and dazzling variety is a spur to over-consumption.

Just as our diet should emphasize locally-grown food, we ought to choose goods which have been produced or crafted locally when this is possible.

Craftsmanship

John Seymour wrote in the January/February 1985 issue of *Resurgence*: 'Slowly and steadily, I am ridding my home, as far as I can, of mass-produced rubbish, and either learning to do without certain things or replacing them with articles made out of honest materials by people who enjoyed making them and who, by long diligence and training, have qualified themselves to make them superbly.' This is a constructive approach which we can all adopt to some degree or other.

There are hundreds of small businesses and craftspeople around the country, and abroad, who sell their goods direct to callers as well as by mail order. The only difficulty is finding them. Scottish tweeds, handmade wooden toys, wrought iron kitchenware and smoked salmon from the Outer Hebrides are a few of the many things available. Prices are relatively low because there are no middlemen, and it's satisfying to know that your money is going to the person who has actually made the thing you are going to use. The contact is delightfully personal, too, compared with going to your high street department store, and you won't find yourself wearing the same sweater as ¼ million other people.

Ask around—there may be a potter who lives down the road, or a skilled seamstress a few doors away. This principle means using a local joiner instead of going to a large building contractor, and buying prepared food for a party from a local vegetarian caterer instead of from a big chain store.

Look at your local paper and check the classified columns in national newspapers and magazines (especially around Christmas). The small ads in many 'green' journals and newsletters are full of fascinating offers. Oxfam and Traidcraft sell many household items made by people in the Third World.

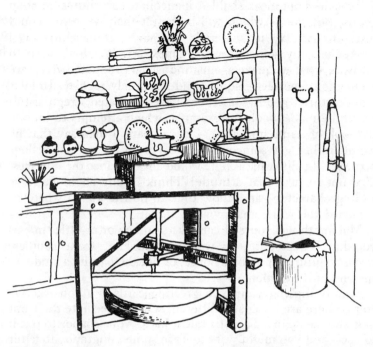

Do It Yourself

When you realize that your toddler's toys have multiplied like hampsters over the summer holiday, even without a birthday or Christmas, do you immediately plan a trip to the shop to buy a new plastic toybox? Or do you look around the flat to see if there is something else which would do, or think about how you could make some new toy shelves out of that old washstand?

When we buy everything ready-made, our creativity and inventiveness is stifled. We become incapable of seeing the potential in the things around us; preparing for Christmas becomes simply a matter of choosing the right gifts, spending days fighting through crowds, utterly depending on what the shops offer.

But think how many people trained at art college or did an O level in pottery, or simply always wanted to write poetry. Everyone has creative ability, and using whatever skills and talents we have (and developing them) will contribute to a richer, more interesting environment in the home, and reduce our dependence on commercially-produced goods.

This does not mean shabby, inadequate substitutes for shop goods, but things which will be better than what you could buy—in quality, in materials and in workmanship—even when made by someone who is inexpert. We don't need to measure what we make against industrial products, which are bound to be perfectly square and absolutely regular. In fact, manufactured goods sometimes have simulated irregularities (machine-made wool, for example, which attempts to imitate the look of hand spinning). I once heard a man say that he would rather get someone else to lay his new kitchen floor because if he did it himself he would always notice the mistakes. Try not to take that attitude! Think of any slight flaws as adding character—and allow time to do the job to whatever standard you will be happy with.

Making things yourself can take as much or as little time as you have, depending on whether you knit, make candles, carve furniture for a doll's house, or decide to build a studio at the end of the garden.

Simply making your own greeting cards is a constructive step. There are dozens of different ways to decorate the front —if you have buried artistic talent here's your chance to put it to use—and you might want to learn some calligraphy to letter the inside. Even if you just use cutouts from other cards and a coloured felt pen to write 'Happy Birthday Daddy', the result will be far more interesting than most of the cards one can buy.

Look around the house for odds and ends which can be put to good use in your artistic endeavours. Good materials are essential, no matter what craft you choose—try to go to professional suppliers instead of to a 'hobby' shop. Get your children involved, or a friend. To share planning and making something—a set of painted wooden blocks or a woven arbour for the garden—adds an immensely satisfying dimension to a relationship.

● Check at the library for books on every conceivable craft. An especially nice general one is *The Pauper's Homemaking Book*, by Jocasta Innes (Penguin, 1976).

● *The Forgotten Arts*, John Seymour (Dorling Kindersley, 1984).

Sympathetic materials

While plastics last virtually forever, cluttering up the planet, natural materials like paper, cloth, wood and fur will disappear into the soil in a year or so, and actually enrich it. To see this, bury a variety of household items in your compost heap or in a deserted patch of ground: a milk bottle top, an old beach shoe, a piece of cellophane wrapping, a cereal box and plastic liner, a worn out polycotton shirt, a glass jar and a tin can. Which will disappear first? Which items will outlive you, and your grandchildren? If you choose natural materials— sisal door mats, a wooden file box, leather shoes—they will not pollute the earth long after you've left it.

Natural materials have another important advantage. Edith Schaeffer writes: 'synthetics seem a step away from the basic simplicity of the production of wool, cotton, linen and silk: a step away in somewhat the same way as a highway, a car or a building separates man from experiencing the "earth" . . . One feels the softness of lamb's wool and thinks of sheep grazing on Scottish hills among the heather and gorse. One irons linen until it is crisp and tries to remember what one has heard of growing flax . . . .' (*Hidden Art*, p 166–7). By choosing materials which come from the earth, we become more conscious of our connections with it, and perhaps more appreciative in our use.

Sympathetic materials come from natural sources, do not create other environmental or social problems, encourage local enterprise and small firms, and do not have an excessively high energy cost.

Durability

It's natural to want pretty things, and to want new and different things. But the cycle of buy and throw away and buy and throw away has reached dizzying proportions. We feel slightly sick when we read about the hundreds of pairs of shoes Imelda Marcos left behind when she fled the Phillipines, but perhaps don't think so much about just how many pairs are cluttering up our closets. Certainly, there's a big difference between 500 and 15. But where does need turn into desire, and desire turn into greed and dependence?

A big part of the problem is that so much of what we can buy is of such poor quality that in a couple of months a new pair of shoes is looking shabby and down at the heel. And they often aren't made of materials which can be touched up and repaired. Who could repair them anyway—and wouldn't you be told that they aren't worth mending?

There's a curious contradiction here: good quality, expensive items (from shoes to umbrellas to shaving brushes) tend to be made of natural materials which, when they do eventually find their way into the rubbish, will gently break down and disappear, while cheap items which will only last, at best, a couple of months are made of synthetic materials which will not.

A really good piece of clothing might last 50 years. This may sound crazy in these days of cheap and cheerful high street fashion and ever-changing fashion silhouettes, but quite a few of us have a 'vintage' tweed jacket or a Victorian nightdress amongst our clothes. Furniture, assuming that it is well-made in the first place, can last for centuries.

Buying more costly items is an incentive to choose carefully and to make things last. A fountain pen will outlast dozens of plastic biros, and is a pleasure to write with. A good one will last a lifetime. (If you could never trust yourself not to lose an expensive pen, just try to be frugal with ordinary plastic pens and biros, and use refills.)

Most ordinary household mugs and glasses are easy to break, and you'll get better wear by buying things designed for restaurant and hotel use. These range from simple and serviceable to elegant. The place to look is in catering shops, which are also a source of heavy cooking pans and utensils.

The fact that a towel is 100% cotton isn't enough: hotel-grade bath towels weigh 1½ pounds each, while a cheap towel might weigh a third of that. If you've stayed in hospital perhaps you noticed their wonderful heavy cotton sheets, which have to survive innumerable boil washes. They are designed to give maximum use, and feel delicious.

Think about durability, and repairability, when you shop. This doesn't necessarily mean spending more. Good quality secondhand furniture is often a far better buy than new store-room items, and a reconditioned vacuum cleaner may give many more years of service than a bright new plastic one.

SHOPPING SPECIFICS

Guidelines
- ☛ Shop locally.
- ☛ Buy from charities, environmental groups and development organizations like Traidcraft.
- ☛ Choose beautiful, durable items made by craftspeople.
- ☛ Look for natural, sympathetic, non-toxic materials.
- ☛ Select goods with least packaging.
- ☛ Buy recycled paper and stationery.
- ☛ Recycle by buying secondhand goods.

Secondhand strategy

1 Quality varies considerably. It's worth getting to know good shops and popping in regularly to look at new stock.

2 Jumble and boot sales have the lowest prices. Good jumble sales tend to be held at churches and schools in reasonably prosperous areas, and there is likely to be a fierce queue ready long before the doors open. Take your own bags and plenty of small change, and be ready for a fight to get to the tables. (Jumble sale helpers are likely to get first chance at the better articles, something to consider when you are asked to lend a hand.)

3 Remember that charity shops do not exist to give you a bargain but to raise money for the organization's projects. Prices, however, vary a great deal. While an Oxfam shop in the country might charge 50p for a not-very-fashionable skirt, you might see a similar garment in central London for £5 or more (due, presumably, to higher rents and rates).

4 Don't be too squeamish. To find treasure—and it's there—you will probably have to wade through piles of stretched-out synthetic jumpers and horrendous polyester trouser suits.

5 'Vintage' clothes which sell at high prices at market stalls can sometimes be turned up for next to nothing at these sales.

6 'Surplus' stores are full of peculiar things, some of which can be very useful. Military and other work gear is

designed for rugged use and will wear well. I've seen heavy ex-army cotton sheets which would make excellent table-cloths, napkins or curtain lining as well as a wide variety of kitchenware.

7 Factory seconds are sometimes available direct, and are everywhere during annual sales. Buying goods with slight flaws is good domestic management and makes ecological sense. (This goes for eggs from a local farm, too.)

8 Check the advertisements in newsagents' windows. Better yet, place your own, asking for the things you want.

9 Some areas have lots of junk-cum-antique and house clearance shops—worth a browse.

10 There are resale shops in many towns which sell good quality clothing, with the shop taking a percentage of the sale price (some sell very expensive designer garments at a considerable reduction).

11 For household items there are auctions and salerooms, ranging from cheap and seedy to very exalted indeed.

12 Remember that antiques, too, are second, if not fifteenth, hand. People often feel conscience-bound to confess if something they are wearing is secondhand, especially if they are complimented on it. If you want to make a point, or crow over the bargain you got, fine. Otherwise, say 'thank you' and leave it at that.

As I was writing this chapter I decided to go to a nearby shop, run by the Spastics Society. Frankly, it was pretty grim, with racks of shabby sweaters, tired shirts and polyester knit dresses. But even on a quick visit, I found (and bought) a navy corduroy Jaeger skirt for £2.50.

● *Style on a Shoestring, a Guide to Conspicuous Thrift*, Carolyn Chapman (Hutchinson, 1984), is an excellent guide to buying and repairing old clothes.

Pooled labour and tools

Anyone who has seen the Amish barnraising in the film *Witness* will have some idea of the way small rural communities traditionally share labour. No money needs to change hands and the work is a social event which binds the community together. Some version of this is possible even in modern urban neighbourhoods. Why not help a friend draughtproof his house in return for a hand with laying a new floor in your children's playroom? Or have a house-warming and painting party—everybody wears old clothes, and you provide plenty of hot food and cold beer.

Sharing equipment and tools is another way to save money. A modern home is full of gadgets, many of which are seldom used. Why not think about what you'd be happy to share and see that friends know about it (which will encourage them to do the same in return).

Creative Acquisition

I once stayed with friends in a tiny New York apartment. They were both designers and wanted their home to demonstrate their talents, but had little money. I was astonished to hear how many of their things had been scavenged from the street—including a pretty chair, several lamps and an area rug. Apparently it was common for people to put anything they didn't want out on the pavement, and a scouting trip early Saturday morning was almost certain to turn up something useful.

There are always people looking furtively into the builders' skips which abound in areas being gentrified. Why not make it easier for them by setting out any potential useful item with a sign offering it to anyone who wants to carry it away?

Skips are good sources of firewood and scrap timber for building a compost bin, but you can also find anything from old bricks to bathtubs in them. We once carpeted a flat with attractive wool carpet from a skip in front of a Belgrave Square embassy (it needed to be cleaned but was virtually unworn).

Keep your eyes open. Our local library replaced its wooden bookcases with adjustable metal shelves a couple of years ago. We talked to the workmen as they were breaking up the old ones, and were able to carry home beautiful hardwood shelves which would have cost several hundred pounds.

Building Materials

The authors of *A Pattern Language* suggest that 'good materials must be ecologically sound: biodegradable, low in energy consumption in production and in use, and not based on depletable resources' (Alexander *et al.*, p 965). Nor should making them pollute the environment.

In West Germany there are 'biological' architects, and firms which supply ecologically sound and non-toxic building and decorating materials. Some of these can be ordered by post (see page 231), and one hopes that similar products will become available in the UK before long. In the meantime, when you start building or decorating, look for natural, unprocessed materials. This means wallpaper made of paper rather than plastic, wood, cork or tile floors, and wool carpets or cotton rugs. Many people choose these things because they are inherently more congenial to live with, and because they usually last longer than synthetics. When they do wear out, they won't be lingering in a landfill site for hundreds of years. See 'The Plastic Free Home' in *Blueprint for a Green Planet* by John Seymour and Herbert Girardet (Dorling Kindersley, 1987).

If you are restoring an older home, what could be more appropriate than to use original materials, which are almost all biodegradable and non-toxic? There are many sources of both secondhand 'salvage' and good reproductions, virtually all of which will be in natural materials and designed to last. *Putting Back the Style*, ed. Alexandra Artley (Evans Brothers, 1982) has detailed lists of sources for everything from water-based distemper paint to Victorian bathroom fittings, for houses built between 1700 and 1930.

Good Wood

Wood is a satisfying material to work and live with, but the choices we make when we buy wood have huge environmental consequences. In 1984, Britain imported 1.5 million doors from tropical countries! These are sold through a variety of retail outlets, and you may have bought one without having the slightest idea that this was contributing to the destruction of the earth's precious rainforests. How will you know what to buy next time?

Friends of the Earth and the National Association of Retail Furnishers have produced a Good Wood Guide to promote the use of sustainably-produced timber, from Europe and North America as well as from a very few well-managed tropical forests. On the whole, tropical hardwoods (such as iroko and mahogany) should be avoided, and the FoE guide will enable you to make informed choices as to what you buy and where you buy it. DIY products are often made from tropical hardwoods, and if you use a builder ask him about the timber he uses.

● *The Good Wood Guide* consists of loose pages which will be periodically updated, and can be obtained by sending £1.50 to the Rainforests Campaign, Friends of the Earth, 26-28 Underwood Street, London N1 7JQ, telephone 01-490 1555.

Paper products

An environmental and practical problem has been presented by recent research into the bleaching process used for virtually all paper products—from kitchen towels to disposable nappies —and is being highlighted in a campaign run by the Women's Environmental Network (WEN), who are especially concerned about the bleached paper used in women's sanitary products.

Chlorine bleaching of wood pulp creates the chemical dioxin (along with another 300 or so chlorine-containing compounds, some of which are similar to polychlorinated biphenyls, the infamous PCBs which are known to cause sterility and cancer, and which have been associated with the death of seals in the North Sea). A Greenpeace statement before the Canadian House of Representatives Committee on Public Works (13 June 1988) stated that 'dioxin was found to be the most potent carcinogen ever discovered' in animal tests. It also appears to enhance the cancer-causing effects of other chemicals.

The US Environmental Protection Agency (EPA) has concluded that the chlorine used in the bleaching process is the source of dioxin contamination of water—which has a serious impact on water life around paper mills—and of the paper products themselves. Dioxins have been found in facial tissues, kitchen towels, paper plates, sanitary napkins and tampons, as well as in milk and long-life juice cartons. Research is being done on the way the dioxin 'migrates' into food or into the body through contact, but tests have already found dioxin in coffee made with paper filters (a prominent US scientist doing research on this has switched to a metal filter!).

It appears that we will have to stop using chlorine and its

derivatives for bleaching, and to start marketing unbleached products as such. In Japan, Sweden and some other European countries consumer consciousness has made unbleached paper products available (sold as 'chlorine-free'). Changes in pulping technology, such as the use of oxygen bleaching and extended cooking of paper pulp, can greatly reduce the use of chlorine. Sweden has already reduced its discharge of organochlorines by 80%, and is talking about zero discharge by 2010.

Unbleached paper ranges from the brown envelopes we are all familiar with to the grey-beige of some recycled loo paper. If other products were to be left unbleached, the colour would take some getting used to because we have learned to associate white with cleanliness and purity. However, many of us have made the switch to brown bread—a similar psychological leap. When it comes to paper, white means danger. In her statement to the Canadian House of Representatives, Renate Kroesa said: 'Greenpeace will not be convinced that consumers, when made to understand the real tradeoffs between breastmilk contamination and the color of their toilet paper, will not make a wise choice when given one.'

Safe choices are few and far between at present, but the Women's Environmental Network hope to see Swedish manufacturers introduce unbleached products in Britain and expect British manufacturers to follow suit shortly. In addition to choosing unbleached paper we can switch to reuseable items, as suggested below.

Alternatives

Many common household articles have been specifically designed to be disposable. These are usually made from paper or plastic, placing unnecessarily heavy demands on natural wood and oil resources. There are times when modern disposables are very handy, but why not try some of the following:

Paper towels

Use terry towels for your hands and a dishcloth for the worktop or spills. Drain fried food on brown paper bags saved from the greengrocers or on opened cardboard egg cartons.

● Domestic Paraphernalia Co, 2a Pleasant Street, Lytham, Lancs FY8 5JA, telephone (0253) 736334, sell a sycamore roller towel holder and cotton towels.

Plastic sponges

Cellulose sponges are a good (biodegradable) choice. Especially nice ones are available in French supermarkets (they are labelled *éponge végétale*). Dishcloths last much longer than sponges and can be knitted with scraps of cotton yarn.

Disposable cleaning cloths

Accumulate a good supply of cotton cleaning rags, cut from old sheets or clothes (if you are short of old clothes, buy some for 50p at a jumble sale). Linen is good for windows. Cleaning expert Don Aslett suggests making super-efficient cleaning cloths by folding an 18x18 inch square of cotton terry in half and sewing up the long side to form a tube. All the edges will need to be hemmed, unless you start with outgrown terry nappies. Refold the cloth and use both sides, then turn inside out for another four fresh surfaces.

Paper napkins

Cloth napkins are efficient, and far nicer to use than paper napkins. For every day, choose a sturdy cotton fabric which does not need to be ironed. Many ready-made napkins are made of synthetics (useless on sticky fingers) or linen (too much trouble for daily use), so you may want to buy a suitable fabric and make your own. Terry works well. A good shortcut is to buy textured cotton teatowels in a suitable pattern, cut them in half and hem the cut edge.

A personalised napkin ring for each family member saves washing – when the napkin is still clean, tuck it back into the ring and put it aside for the next meal. Plain wooden rings (available at Habitat) or curtain rings can be painted, and glueing on seashells is an attractive way to decorate them.

Coffee filters and tea bags

Use a percolator or a cafetière, and loose tea instead of tea-bags. Instant coffee is not the answer because it is hugely expensive in terms of the energy required to make it (see Richard North's fascinating book, *The Real Cost*).

Bin liners

Line bins with sheets of newspaper, or those plastic carrier bags you can't bring yourself to throw away. Most of your rubbish will be dry if you compost food scraps.

Carrier bags

You can buy durable canvas shopping bags, and string bags are great to tuck into a handbag or pocket. Although these seem to have disappeared from British shops they are readily available in France. Buy a half dozen and share with friends.

Nappies

For lots about switching to cloth nappies, flip to page 331.

Baby wipes

Some tissues and a flannel will do the trick most of the time, and you'll avoid the various 'medicated' cleaners these are saturated in.

Facial tissues

There are times when these are almost essential – when the whole family comes down with a cold, for example – but cotton handkerchiefs are a nice alternative.

Loo paper

While there is no satisfactory alternative, unless you don't mind using newspaper, it is possible to buy loo rolls made of unbleached, recycled paper from some wholefood shops and by post from Traidcraft.

Razors

Disposable plastic razors are astonishingly cheap, but an appalling waste of raw materials. While you might consider switching to an old-fashioned open razor, a reasonable compromise is to use a razor for which you only need to buy refill blades.

Sanitary products and miscellaneous

When you buy supplies like cotton wool, cotton buds and tampons, look for those made from biodegradable materials: paper and 100% cotton. (The presence of synthetic fibres in tampons increases the growth rate of the bacteria which cause Toxic Shock Syndrome – another good reason for choosing cotton.) Choose tampax with cardboard, not plastic, tubes. As unbleached products become available, buy them.

Tights

Some 500 million pairs of tights and stockings are sold each year in the UK – 23 pairs for each woman. Since nylon is not biodegradable and this is a 'disposable' article of clothing, you might think about going barelegged, wearing more socks or switching to cotton stockings. (This is a good health move, as nylon tights are associated with persistent thrush problems.)

● Funn Stockings make cotton, silk and wool stockings on traditional equipment. Available from Liberty's of London and other department stores.

Batteries

Batteries contain a wide variety of toxic substances, including zinc, mercuric chloride, lead and cadmium. In Japan they are deposited at petrol stations for separate toxic waste disposal. According to the *Green Consumer Guide*, manufacturing batteries takes 50 times more energy than they produce. Avoid buying battery-powered toys, and choose equipment that can run on mains power. Buy rechargeable batteries (far cheaper in the long run) – you can even get a solar recharger!

ETHICAL INVESTMENT

In the United States, socially-responsible investment funds have shown tremendous growth in the last few years and accounted for some $350-400 billion of investment as at April 1987. Although this idea is new in Britain, it has already found considerable interest amongst investors.

These funds avoid companies which produce tobacco or alcohol, armaments, which are involved in gambling, the fur trade and cosmetic research with animals, or which have links with oppressive regimes, including South Africa. They seek investment in companies with good records in employee welfare, environmental awareness and community participation. The criteria varies from fund to fund, however, and the vast majority of investment in the US is screened only for South African links. South Africa and tobacco are the most common exclusions in the UK.

People who take a highly moral tone about political and social affairs sometimes see their investments in the stock market as something unaffected by normal values and ethical judgments. I knew a woman whose husband had died of emphysema and who was extremely conscious of how deadly smoking is, and was dumbfounded to hear that she was enthusiastically investing in a multinational tobacco firm.

In the US there is an ethical credit card, called Working Assets VISA (and part of the worldwide VISA network). Every time you use it, 5 cents is donated to an organisation like Greenpeace or the Environmental Defence Fund. In the UK, you can apply for a Girobank Oxfam VISA card—0.25% of each transaction value goes to Oxfam. Write Oxfam, 274 Banbury Road, Oxford OX2 7DZ.

● Ethical Investment Research Service (EIRIS), 401 Bondway Business Centre, 71 Bondway, London SW8 1SQ, telephone 01-735 1351. Set up in 1983, the EIRIS provides an independent information service (they are not brokers or investment advisors). For £45 you can have an analysis of your current investments and a list of acceptable companies, based on your personal ethical or social criteria.

● There are quite a number of firms which run 'conscience funds' and the EIRIS can send you a current list (enclose SASE).

● The Ecology Building Society, 8 Main Street, Crosshills, Keighley, West Yorkshire BD20 8TB, telephone (0535) 35933. Does not pay 'gold' rates of interest, but you will get a reasonable return on your money. Lends on small-scale businesses with an ecological bias, organic smallholdings and farms, and properties which will contribute to the regeneration of rural areas and inner cities.

4
RECYCLING

What poverty makes poor countries do—value their resources too much to use them only once—rich countries must learn to do as a matter of ecological good sense.

Richard North
The Real Cost, 1986

When you piled your weekly shopping on the floor (in Chapter 2), did you notice how much packaging there was? Cardboard boxes, plastic and polystyrene trays, plastic film, plastic bags, foil packages, plastic and glass bottles, and tins. Packaging seems to get fancier and fancier: in fact, if you were given an elaborate box of chocolates or glacé fruits last Christmas you probably to fight your way through three, four or even five separate layers of wrapping.

One reason waste packaging has become such a problem is that we don't really notice it, or have to deal with it. Into the bin or down the chute—and the dustmen come on Tuesdays. People who do not have public rubbish collection are far more aware of the quantities they generate, and have an incentive to keep waste to a minimum.

Recycling is an essential adjunct to careful buying habits. To *not* recycle costs a great deal: not only is there the value of the raw materials which are being wasted, but the high cost of collecting, transporting and disposing of them. Then there is the growing problem of finding room for it all: rich countries are trying to send their waste abroad, and poor countries have not only accepted ordinary domestic rubbish but toxic waste, in spite of the long-term risks to their own citizens. (Fortunately this is changing, and Nigeria recently forced Italy to reload a hazardous cargo which had been dumped, nightmarishly, on open ground near a river which provides washing and drinking water for the local population.)

Recycling is the *second* step. First, we need to rethink our buying, and particularly the way we expect goods to be packaged. Become a canny shopper. Try not to buy things you don't need or want. If you're not sure, try a sample or buy a small size. Go away and think about the purchase for a couple days, particularly if it is a major one. Buy in bulk and choose goods with minimal packaging. This approach not only saves money but makes recycling at home much easier because there just isn't so much to deal with.

MAKING THINGS LAST

Repairs

Mending is an art which many women would rather not hear about, and there's no way I can promote the darning of socks because I have no idea how it is done. (It does seem a shame that socks wear out so quickly; people who are hard on socks might want to try all-wool Unwearoutable Socks made by Nicholl Knitwear, Piper Close, Corbridge, Northumberland, telephone (043) 471 2283.) But making things last is important and only needs a little bit of advance planning.

1 Buy things which can be repaired and for which you can buy replacement parts. Ask about servicing when you buy.
2 Learn to do basic repairs yourself. Everyone should be able to replace buttons and to sew a straight seam, for example. Something as simple as replacing the inner filters in a vacuum cleaner can add years to its life.
3 Patch early. You know where certain things are going to wear out, so protect them from the beginning. My mother

used to sew patches on the boys' jeans *before* they started wearing them. A rug in the right place will save wear on the carpet.

4 Build in sections. Think how easy it is to repair damage to a brick patio, whereas cracked concrete would have to be removed and relaid. Work can be done gradually, making DIY projects easier.

Love Your Tools

A cook's spoon, a carpenter's hammer and a gardener's trowel are the tools we use to perform the tasks each day confronts us with. The pen, the potter's wheel and the computer keyboard are tools which make it possible for us to accomplish and create.

But most of us are pretty feeble when it comes to looking after them. Think how you envy people who are 'good with their hands', and how much in demand a handy man or woman is. I know the breed well, having grown up with a father who could do everything from electrical wiring to building a house and now living with a man who thinks the best way to fix anything is to take it completely to pieces and then put it back together (and who does this successfully).

Think of the amounts of money we pay to have our machines serviced. And of how often we call out the repairman only to find that one of the kids has unplugged the machine. This mechanical ineptitude—which I suffer from too—leads to a great deal of waste. I once retrieved an Anglepoise lamp from a friend's rubbish. 'It doesn't work', she warned, but I took it home thinking Andy might be able to fix it. He simply changed the fuse.

1 Learn the obvious: how to wire a plug, change a fuse and check the oil.
2 Find out where the fuse box is, how to turn the water off at the mains and so on.
3 Read the instructions. These are sometimes rather freely translated from the Japanese or German, and not very inspiring pieces of literature, but it's well worth coming to grips with their terminology and structure.
4 Buy sturdy, well-made tools, from a specialist shop rather than the nearest superstore, and keep them in good condition.
5 Read *Zen and the Art of Motorcycle Maintenance*, by Robert Pirsig (Bodley Head, 1974).

GOOD DISPOSAL

First, a summary of the principles which we will look at in more detail in this chapter:

1 Cut waste to a minimum by buying only what you need and by avoiding excess packaging.

2 Avoid non-biodegradable plastics, plastic-wrapped products, and synthetic fabrics.

3 Buy recycled products (stationery, for example) and returnable packaging (milk in glass bottles) whenever you can.

4 Compost kitchen scraps—for details see Chapter 13. This is extremely satisfying, and you won't need to buy commercial fertilizers or manure for a small garden once you get a compost bin going.

5 Reuse envelopes, paper, jars and other containers. Fabric scraps can be turned into a quilt, rugs or dolls clothes.

6 Have worn articles repaired or restored whenever possible, either doing the work yourself or having it done professionally. Buying goods when can be repaired is essential.

7 Give things you no longer want to friends or a local charity.

8 Paper, wood and cardboard scraps can be used as tinder, if you have a fireplace or suitable stove.

9 Take bottles to the bottle bank and tins to a Save-a-Can scheme (but don't make a special trip in the car for this!).

10 At present you have no choice but to put plastics out for the dustmen (they should eventually be biodegradable or recyclable).

11 Toxic wastes, including used batteries, old paint and paint thinners, need particularly thoughtful disposal. Used motor oil should be taken to a garage which collects it.

DONATIONS

Many charitable organisations and voluntary groups will welcome donations of clothes, books and miscellaneous articles, which they resell to raise money. If you have things to get rid of, please don't put them in the dustbin! Here are some guidelines:

1 Pin sets of clothing, and bag articles which should stay together.

2 Do not remove buttons or other useful parts!

3 Ensure that anything you pass on is clean and still useful (really worn clothing is better turned into dust cloths, or sold to a rag merchant: Oxfam's Wastesaver scheme does this on a large scale).

4 If you give away an appliance or an old record player, attach a note to say whether or not it works.

5 Some groups will collect jumble from your home. Telephone shops to find out when they accept donations (do not leave bags outside the shop).

6 Playgroups and scrapstores welcome a wide variety of household items, such as yoghurt tubs and egg cartons.

7 Our local doctors' surgery was delighted with a large bundle of magazines (fairly current issues).

8 Save cancelled stamps—charity shops often accept these or you can send them to Save the Children Fund, 17 Grove Lane, London SE5 8RD.

9 Disaster appeals do not take used clothing, because it would need to be fumigated and is often inappropriate for the countries in need. Do enquire before donating any large items.

10 Charitable appeals can sometimes use the following: old television licences, road tax discs, Co-op books, Green Shield stamps, foreign coins and notes, old or new postcards, stamp albums and collections, UK and foreign stamps (keep these separate if possible), and old Christmas cards.

PACKAGING

We hardly notice that it's there. A pair of chocolate Easter bunnies, each wrapped in coloured foil and packed in a box (cardboard with cellophane windows), goes into a small plastic bag at the till and then, with other shopping, into a plastic carrier.

That's 4 layers of packaging. Start counting when you are next out shopping—you can probably get up to 5 or 6 without too much trouble. Some stores box and bag and wrap their goods so thoroughly that you have to empty the dustbin before you can start cooking. Safeway now offer a line of organic lunchpacks, an excellent idea, but they are sold on plastic trays with plastic wrapping. The food is wholesome and environmentally desirable, but the packaging is a disaster. Organic food at the supermarket seems to be packaged *more* than the 'conventional' produce—organic swedes, for example, are wrapped in clingfilm to differentiate them from chemically-grown produce.

The UK packaging industry uses 39 million tonnes of materials each year, for which we pay £5,000 million. This is no paltry sum we're talking about—remember, you bought the package too!

Packaging performs certain functions. It protects the product during transport and storage; keeps it dry; enables it to be boxed or stacked neatly; displays it to advantage; makes it easy to carry or easy to use; and carries information. But the packaging of an item can vary a great deal, and you can make constructive choices.

What makes for 'sympathetic' packaging? It should be the minimum necessary to protect the goods inside, and should be reuseable, recyclable or biodegradable. Plastics are the least desirable, and Suffolk County, Long Island—who sent the infamous 'garbage barge' on its abortive trip south—has banned all non-biodegradable packaging because they cannot cope with the waste disposal problem it represents.

An alternative is the natural, biodegradable cellophane film which Infinity Foods of Brighton use to package dried goods. The Body Shop offers to refill its plastic shampoo and lotion bottles (at a savings of 20p per bottle), but the take-up on this is only 4%. Placing a deposit on bottles would increase the percentage—a number of American states are now making this mandatory for a variety of bottles and cans.

How to avoid packaging
- ☛ Buy in bulk.
- ☛ Buy in returnable/refillable containers.
- ☛ Buy loose items.
- ☛ Choose paper wrapping over plastic.
- ☛ Carry your own shopping bags, and use boxes.
- ☛ Ask stores to take their own-label bottles and jars back.
- ☛ Cut down on tinned and bottled food.

A wholefood store in Santa Barbara, California, displays this sign: 'To help keep our deli prices down as well as to encourage individual environmental awareness, please feel free to bring your own containers when purchasing our food. Thanks.'

PAPER

Newspaper nexus

Friends of the Earth in London gets more phone calls about what to do with old newspapers than any other subject. And Vera Elliott, who runs the Centre for Environmental Information in Sutton, says that no matter what subject she talks about at a meeting she is always asked what to do with newspapers.

Recycling is the obvious choice, but this isn't always easy. The price of low quality paper (to see the differences in quality, compare newsprint to the paper a book is printed on and to a piece of company letterhead) makes it difficult even for voluntary organisations to justify the time and money required to collect, sort and bundle old newspapers.

Some bottle banks have paper bins next to them, and if this is the case where you live your problem is solved. Otherwise, you might consider cutting down on the number of papers you buy. Time management expert Alan Lakein considers reading newspapers something of a waste of time, and getting the news from a daily paper has been compared to telling time by the second hand. Katherine Whitehorn suggested in the *Observer* that one could take things by the week, relying, say, on the *Spectator* and New Statesman/Society, 'with a possible top up from *Time*, *Newsweek* or a good Sunday' (16 October 1988).

Of course newspapers are inexpensive, 'light', and a form of entertainment too, but you could consider some modification of your reading habits. How many of us claim never to have time to read a book, but spend many hours each month reading the paper, perhaps one each morning and evening? (Books are also a lot easier to handle on the train or bus than a full spread of newspaper.)

There are lots of good things to do with newspapers. They can be used as firelighters, for making paper hats and boats, paper patterns, homemade 'peat' pots, underlay for carpeting, or as a disposable doormat. You can turn them into papier mâché. They can be spread on a newly washed floor to protect it, or on the table while you prepare vegetables for soup (the whole bundle goes into the compost bucket), or under the table where a toddler is eating.

Substantial amounts of newspaper can be turned into efficient 'logs' for your fireplace with a hand-operated machine available by mail order (one source is Axford Marketing Ltd, Bell Lane, Ellisfield, Basingstoke RG25 OQD—their Double Brikker costs approximately £35). This is an ideal way to make use of old papers—yours and the neighbours' too, and provides a pleasant occupation for the children, as long as they don't get so keen that they get to the Sunday paper before you do!

At the moment I use most of my newspapers as a weed-smothering mulch on my allotment. Perennial weeds like dock, couch grass and ground elder will eventually die if deprived of light, so one simply covers the ground with opened newspapers (at least 6 sheets thick, but the more the better), making sure there are no gaps between them. Hold them down with earth or small stones, or with a layer of another mulch material like straw. Tabloids and quality papers seem to be equally efficient, but avoid coloured pages. Ordinary black newsprint is quite safe. (For more on gardens, and mulching, see Chapter 13.)

Paper waste

You shouldn't have to make many trips to the stationers if you reuse as much paper as possible. Much of what we write, from shopping lists to interoffice notes could easily be done on some sort of scrap paper.

An easy source of jotting paper is envelopes. Open incoming

letters with a paper knife and stack the envelopes, face side down, next to the phone or in a small basket on your desk. This soon becomes second nature, and is particularly handy for shopping lists because you can put coupons or a swatch of fabric to be matched inside the envelope.

There are many reuse labels available, sold by everyone from Friends of the Earth to the Bodleian Library in Oxford. These can be used to cover over the old address on the front or to reseal an envelope you have opened with a paper knife.

Make use of the paper which comes through the door or passes through your hands at work. Cut attractive cards in half and use the front as a postcard next time you need to drop a note to a friend. Save sheets of paper which have been used on one side for drafting notes or for the children to draw on. I was once given some out-of-date letterhead bearing the title 'Histopathology', and a friend's children spent days writing out lists of words they could make out of it.

If you get lots of postal solicitations, you can use the outside envelope for notes, the reply-paid envelope inside for paying bills (with a reuse label), and the back of the letter asking you to subscribe or invest for more scrap paper!

Eliminate at least part of the problem at source—and save yourself constant aggravation, especially if you are one of the many people who loathe junk mail—by having your name removed from solicitation lists. When you join an organisation or subscribe to a magazine, they sometimes give you the option of *not* having your name sold to or shared with any other organization. Take advantage of this. Or write to Mailing Preference Service, FREEPOST 22, London W1E 7EZ for their brochure and application form to have your name taken off participating companies' mailing lists. (There is no charge.)

Recycled paper

Have you noticed that those brown On Her Majesty's Service envelopes are made from recycled paper? And a few shops have bags made from recycled paper.

Why should we use recycled paper? Over 2 billion trees are chopped down every year to make paper. Although paper production is only one of the causes of the world's increasing shortage of trees, the potential savings from recycling paper are very important. Trees play an essential and irreplaceable role in the earth's ecological systems, and their destruction is a contributory factor in the 'greenhouse effect' (see page 92).

Paper production consumes large quantities of energy and water, and the bleaches, dyes and other chemicals used contribute to air and water pollution (as well as posing a danger to human health when we use bleached paper—see page 69). The plantations of fast-growing conifers which provide most of our paper pulp lead to the degradation of precious countryside and the loss of important wildlife habitats.

In Britain, 2 million tonnes of paper currently thrown away every year could be recycled, requiring no new raw material, cutting energy consumption, and reducing air and water pollution by up to 50%. Paperback Ltd points out that 'Recycling 2 million tonnes of paper would also save £500 million on the balance of payments, create more than 10,000 jobs and save money on waste collection and disposal.'

Until recently, recycled paper was rather coarse and rough. The quality has, however, improved by leaps and bounds, and you can now get fine laid stationery, photocopying and art papers, and glossy board made from recycled paper. Choose recycled whenever you can, but watch out. McDonald's has some of its fast food packaging printed 'Recyclable Paper' next to the international recycling symbol. That is, it is not made from recycled paper but *could* be recycled, just like any other paper! This is the equivalent of labelling food 'edible'.

A few retail shops sell recycled paper products, but for the most part one has to depend on mail order sources.

- Traidcraft plc, Mail Order Department, Kingsway, Gateshead NE11 ONE. Free paper catalogue.
- Conservation Papers, FREEPOST, Reading RG6 1BR, telephone (0734) 668611. A wide range of personal stationery and greeting cards.
- Paperback Limited, 8/16 Coronet Street, Hoxton, London N1 6HD, telephone 01-729 1382. Wholesalers—retail sales within London and the Southeast.
- Friends of the Earth, 26-28 Underwood Street, London N1 7JQ. Directory of Recycled Paper £1 from the Recycling Unit.

RECYCLING

Getting organized

Separation of different types of waste is crucial to any recycling programme, whether in your home or nationwide. The problem is being tackled in some areas of the North America with legislation forcing businesses to separate bio- and non-biodegradable waste. In some schemes residents are provided with different coloured bags or stackable containers, while in others there are collections on different days, for different sorts of household rubbish. At home, you'll need to develop a system too.

My mother had a laundry basket which was divided into three sections, labelled Whites, Coloured, and Delicate. A similar principle is involved here. Once you get used to sorting rather than putting it all into the rubbish bin and get a system going which works for you, the battle is won.

Recycling at home:
- Bucket for compost, lined with newspaper.
- If you have pets, some scraps can go to them (see Chapter 14).
- Cardboard box for glass—if you have a lot, use three boxes (Clear, Green and Brown).
- Box or bag for aluminium cans and milk bottle tops.
- Box for metal cans, if you have a way to recycle them.
- Your regular bin, for plastics (and metal cans), lined with a bit of newspaper rather than a plastic liner.
- Basket by the fireplace for paper and cardboard.
- Shelf for jars and plastic containers.
- Somewhere to stack newspapers and other recyclable paper.
- Box or shelf for 'jumble' and other donations.

This will probably seem daunting, although in practice it is easier than it sounds. You'll find that you think twice before you buy, once you start taking responsibility for disposing of the rubbish. Don't let recycling take over your life, or your home. If the boxes destined for the bottle bank threaten domestic harmony, do some rethinking and maybe some negotiating.

Label the boxes to make it easy for your family. If you have a small kitchen—and most of this recycling will go on there—use small boxes and move them out frequently.

If your council insists that all rubbish be bagged, empty it into one large bag rather than many small liners.

Step by step around the house

1 Vegetable and fruit trimmings and leftover food scraps go into the compost bucket. Line this with newspaper for easy emptying (the newspaper will not add nutrients to the soil but is a fine source of garden fibre). For neat vegetable preparation, spread a sheet of newspaper on the worktop, setting the trimmed vegetables aside for rinsing. When you are finished put the whole thing in the compost bucket.

2 Meat scraps can be offered to pets. Birds like fat (mix it with stale cereal or leftover rice). Some garden books advise against putting any meat scraps on the compost because it could attract rats, and a whole carcass would probably be a bad idea, but the tiny amounts which we have left over have never been a problem. Bury them well, of course. Make bones into soup, then add them too.

3 Some people have large amounts of frying fat to dispose of.
  The easiest and healthiest solution is to cut down on frying. Dripping and chicken fat from free-range animals is
  perfectly good for cooking and adds flavour. Otherwise
  you'll have to put it in a carton or bottle and throw it in the
  dustbin.
4 Small amounts of paper can go into the compost heap, and
  newspapers can be used as a mulch. I always throw match-
  sticks into the compost bucket too.
5 Some paper and cardboard wrapping can be reused. Breakfast cereal with a waxed paper lining is useful for wrapping
  sandwiches. Great for your iron, too: run a warm iron over
  the paper, then over a cotton cloth. Cereal boxes can be
  used, at home or a local playgroup, for children's cutouts
  and drawing. Paper bags from the greengrocers are good
  for draining fried food, instead of paper towels. If you have
  a fireplace, no doubt you already save paper scraps for
  tinder.
6 Plastic bags can be used many times. Try to keep them
  clean, because it's a hassle drying them and they clutter up
  a small kitchen. Stick them over an empty wine bottle or a
  whisk in your drainer—or buy a swinging towel rack to dry
  them on. For safety as well as convenience (because I
  prefer not to let fatty food come into direct contact with
  plastic) I often wrap cheese or leftover meat in a piece of
  greaseproof paper and then put it into a plastic bag.
7 Plastic yoghurt pots and other containers can be used for
  storage and freezing, although you may find it frustrating
  to see 3 identical pots when you know that one is leftover
  curry, another parsley and the third macaroni salad. (Glass
  jars are better for identification purposes.) Labelling them
  is probably unrealistic so try to stick to casual divisions of
  the fridge—leftovers go on the top righthand shelf, for
  instance. (This system breaks down when you have guests
  staying, or if you share with a number of people.)
8 Glass jars and bottles can be reused—if not by you,
  ask around for an enthusiastic jam maker. They are terrific
  for kitchen storage: seeds and chunks of Parmesan and
  chopped parsley in the fridge. Large jars make permanent containers for flours and grains and beans (they
  look nice and are easier to cope with than plastic
  bags). Wine bottles can sometimes be sold or given to

home-winemaking suppliers, and charitable groups may want jam jars.

9 A painless way to clean bottles for the bottle bank (only necessary if they contained something messy, which could smell—wine bottle are fine as they are) is to fill with warm soapy water (the dregs from your washbowl, say) and leave overnight. Pour out half the water, put the lid back on and give a good shake, then rinse. Throw lids away, and remove any metal or plastic (paper labels are okay).

10 Aluminium is a valuable metal. Although we use over 2 billion aluminium drinks cans in the UK each year, only 1% of them are recycled. Recycling not only saves 95% of the energy needed to produce aluminium but reduces the amount of tropical rainforest being destroyed to mine the bauxite ore it comes from. Use as little aluminium as possible, and do not let it come into contact with food (particularly acidic dishes)—aluminium has been associated with Alzheimer's disease. Drinks cans, milk bottle tops, pull-tabs, aluminium foil and trays can all be washed and taken to your nearest Oxfam shop.

11 Other cans are harder to recycle because they contain several metals which have to be separated in processing, and because they are not so valuable in the first place. Try to cut your use of these, and find out whether there is a can recycling scheme in your area.

12 There is some interest in recycling PET (polyester terephthalate) plastic bottles—this is the hard plastic which soft drinks and other beverages are sold in—but it is likely to be some time before this is done. At present there is nothing you can do with plastic packaging except throw it in the bin. Not into the fire, as the smoke given off by plastics is often toxic.

13 Keep one or two plastic carrier bags folded in your handbag or briefcase or rucksack. A supply in the car boot is a good idea, to ensure that they are on hand when you get to the market, and they are useful for clearing away after a picnic, for muddy boots or sandy wet clothes at the beach. But try not to accumulate them in the first place. (Bags made of biodegradable plastic are now available and a few shops are using them.) Some small shops welcome clean plastic carrier bags and egg boxes.

14 Another thing to think of when throwing rubbish away is the potential danger to wildlife. Animals can be caught in plastic netting, and deer have been known to die as the result of swallowing plastic bags. The plastic rings which hold packs of beer and soft drinks cans together can be lethal too. Used condoms are an increasing litter problem in the countryside, and they pose a hazard to wildlife. Take your rubbish home with you!

15 Tie newspapers into bundles with natural fibre string, or pack in paper bags or cardboard boxes.

16 You may want to keep a small container in the bathroom for compostable material. (Personally, I end up trailing out to the kitchen with damp bits of cotton wool.) Once you become enthusiastic about composting—after seeing the good results in your garden—everything goes in the compost bucket: hair trimmings, (100%) cotton wool, even nail clippings!

17 Body Shop bottles can and should be washed and taken back to be refilled (with another product if you like). The small sizes are also good for travelling (decant a little shampoo into one you've saved)—they are sturdier than the empties you can buy at the chemist.

18 Pump-top and spray bottles are useful for homemade cleaners or for repackaging products bought in large containers. Save any you have, or beg them off unecological friends—label them carefully and prominently! (The Body Shop sells pump and spray tops to fit their bottles.)

For details about local recycling sites and groups which want scrap materials, contact Friends of the Earth and ask to be put in touch with your local group. Many groups put together a recycling register for Recycling Week in October 1987, and can tell you about Scout groups who want newspapers or shops which want carrier bags, where the nearest bottlebank is and whether there is a Save-a-Can scheme in your area.

● Friends of the Earth, 26/28 Underwood Street, London N1 7JQ, telephone 01-490 1555.

● *Recycling for Change, A handbook for fundraising by recycling*, Jon Vogler (Christian Aid, 1985). 80p (incl p&p) from Christian Aid, Publications Department, P O Box 1, London SW9 8BH.

FUTURE

We should look for a return to returnable bottles. Glass is far better reused than recycled, and this would become easier for both consumers and manufacturers if there were standard sizes for all bottles and jars. In the United States, the Environmental Protection Agency estimates that returnable bottle legislation would save an annual 500,000 tons of aluminium, 1.5 million tons of steel, and 5.2 million tons of glass—and in turn 46 million barrels of oil.

The present use of plastic packaging is unsatisfactory, but work is being done on developing practical, biodegradable plastic materials. Development of sympathetic packaging is slow, but as the demand for landfill sites and disposal problems grow more intense, there will be increasing public and legislative pressure for alternatives.

Rethinking our notions of convenience and disposability is the first step towards changing the 'throwaway' society we live in. We can all adopt a more appreciative, frugal attitude towards the things which pass through our hands—to start seeing them as resources, not rubbish.

5

ENERGY

The return to designing buildings in response to climate, and employing passive or natural methods of heating and cooling, may be as healthy for us as it is for our planet. It not only conserves fossil fuel and reduces pollution but also reintegrates us with climatic cycles, both physiologically and mentally.

Carol Venolia
Healing Environments, 1988

My father used to stomp round the house turning off the lights and shouting about saving energy. He would call all five of us kids together and demonstrate that light switches were designed to be two-way, and could be turned off as well as on.

Saving energy seemed so boring and mundane. Now that our energy habits are threatening us with catastrophe, the decisions and changes we need to make look a lot more interesting, if undeniably daunting. It is encouraging to know that there are many things we can do to cut our personal use of energy, and that new technologies are being developed which have astonishing potential for reducing overall energy use.

Perhaps you want to know if it really matters—after all, oil prices have fallen in the late '80s. Rather like a horror movie—you know, 'just when you begin to feel safe'—the worst is yet to come. The supply of cheap power available at the moment involves heavy costs which we will eventually have to pay. *Home Ecology* is about how this affects you and what you can do about it, but before looking at the practicalities of home conservation, insulation and even simple solar energy, we need to consider the basic problems of present energy use.

Climate change

Fossil fuels—coal, oil and natural gas—provide most of the world's commercial energy. Supplies of these are limited (estimates range from 20 to 300 years for different fuels). When they are burned carbon dioxide (CO_2) is released—and this CO_2 is the primary cause of the 'greenhouse effect'. The amount of CO_2 in atmosphere is now more than 15% higher than in pre-industrial times and could easily double within the next 50–100 years. The Meteorological Office predicts a 5.2°C rise in global temperatures, which will lead to extensive flooding around the world.

CO_2 is transparent to incoming radiation but impedes the escape of heat (infrared radiation) from the earth. This heating effect is amplified by a roughly comparable amount of heating owing to a build-up of other trace gases (methane, chlorofluorocarbons—CFCs, and nitrous oxide). The precise effects of the expected rise in temperature are uncertain, but according to the Washington DC Worldwatch Institute, 'Climate change looms as the ultimate environmental threat. Its impact would be global and, for all practical purposes, irreversible.' Weather patterns and global water levels will be seriously affected.

No technical solution to this problem is known except reduced combustion of fossil fuels, which account for 4/5 of global energy use. Worldwide energy efficiency is the main way to limit the temperature rise to no more than 1°C, which would still mean serious consequences around the globe but probably enable us to avoid the worst climatic effects.

The cutting down of tropical rainforests is also making a substantial contribution to the greenhouse effect, both because there are fewer trees to use available carbon dioxide and because unused plant material, burned or left to decay when forests are cleared, releases CO_2. Another suspected factor is a reduction in the oceans' photoplankton caused by marine pollution.

Everything we can do to prevent the release of more carbon dioxide into the atmosphere—from energy conservation and planting more trees to using recycled paper—is a step in the right direction.

Acid rain

We've all *heard* about acid rain. What is it? When fossil fuels are burned—to generate electricity, power our car engines or run the factories which produce steel—a number of gases are released, in addition to the carbon dioxide which is causing the greenhouse effect, and these cause acid rain.

Approximately 100 million tons of sulphur dioxide are released into the atmosphere each year. This sulphur forms a dilute sulphuric acid solution in rain water, and the resultant acid rain is killing plant and animal life in lakes across Europe and North America, has already damaged or destroyed more than ⅕ of Europe's forests, and dissolves the surfaces of buildings and historic monuments. Many lakes in Scandanavia and in the US are dead, completely empty of any aquatic life.

It is possible to filter the sulphur in a properly designed power station, but the current British government's policy has been to resist these changes—an attitude not appreciated by Norwegians, whose forests are being killed by the sulphur emissions from *our* power stations.

Nuclear power

The nuclear industry is making an effort to portray nuclear power as as good clean fun, with family outings to Sellafield advertised on TV. While only about 7% of our electricity is nuclear-generated at present (half of that in old Magnox stations which are already being closed down), we are still encouraged to think of nuclear power as the Great White Hope for clean energy in the 21st century. More than that, we are told that *without* it we will shortly find ourselves living in mud huts, chewing on bark for supper.

The government supports the nuclear power industry to the tune of some £400 million each year—government research spending on renewable energy sources is about £12 million per annum—a price which private investors may well be unwilling to pay in the event of privatization. In fact, privatization plans seem to be forcing a fresh appraisal of the nuclear industry. Its record is unimpressive, and the £200 million fall in Central Electricity Generating Board (CEGB) profits in 1987 is attributed to difficulties with Advanced Gas-cooled Reactors.

Nuclear power is being phased out in some countries, and is at a standstill in the United States, where no nuclear power stations have been ordered within the past decade, and all orders since 1974 have been cancelled. Its 'technical, economic, and political problems now appear severe enough to rule out substantial expansion' (*State of the World 1988*, p 25).

One of main problems with our present energy path is the threat of nuclear weapons proliferation that goes along with spread of nuclear power. Nuclear reactors produce substantial quantities of plutonium, a material which is needed to make nuclear weapons. A report from the World Resources Institute of Washington DC, *Energy for a Sustainable World* (September 1987), states baldly, 'If a nation without nuclear weapons acquires plutonium recycling technology, it thereby acquires nearly all the technology and materials needed to make nuclear weapons quickly.' This risk is much less if plutonium-recycling is not readily available, but without recycling only about 1% of energy in uranium can be utilised in present reactors.

The only way to reduce this risk is by limiting the overall level of nuclear power—by regarding it as the energy source of last resort. (Most environmentalists would say that nuclear power should be reduced and eventually eliminated altogether, and replaced with economic renewable energy supplies.)

The day-to-day health threat from nuclear power stations is discussed in Chapter 11, but it is interesting to note that even the Nuclear Installations Inspectorate is not happy with safety standards at a number of power stations. These problems are forcing the early closure of some stations. The cost of decommissioning is uncertain, and there is still no solution to the problem of radioactive waste.

The disposal versus storage debate is a misnomer, as this waste (in Britain, an estimated 2 million cubic metres by 2030) is not 'disposable'. The question is simply one of where it is to be stored, whether at processing stations, buried in land or in deep sea storage.

I hadn't given nuclear power a second thought (frankly, it was the last thing I wanted to think about) until a couple of years ago when I came across *Race to the Finish? The Nuclear Stakes* by a favourite travel writer, Dervla Murphy. This coincided with my new baby, making the nuclear issue of special poignancy. Murphy writes for non-scientists, and points out that the staggering potential danger of this industry, and its dependence on and inextricable connection with the weapons industry, make the fact that it is in some senses 'cleaner' than coal or oil irrelevant. As Dervla Murphy says, 'This unique danger presents a unique challenge to human wisdom. A new technology has never before been abandoned and it goes against man's exploratory nature to seem to retreat from the Fissile Society just because unprecedented difficulties have arisen. But the nature of those difficulties makes retreat essential.'

● *Nuclear Power* (Penguin, 1976) and *Going Critical* (Paladin, 1985), both by Walter C. Patterson.
● *Race to the Finish? The Nuclear Stakes*, Dervla Murphy (John Murray, 1981).

Western waste

It is good news that we in the West are using no more energy now than we were 15 years ago, contrary to even the most optimistic forecasts made at the time. There is still considerable potential for cutting down the amount of energy we use, personally and nationally.

As long as we use more than we generate or can renew, conventional sources of power won't last for more than a few generations; in financial terms, we are living on capital, instead of interest—and, as *State of the World 1988* explains, as long as 'consumers have neither the means nor the information to make cost-effective investments in energy efficiency, we will continue to squander our remaining fossil fuels.'

Part of the cost of each item we buy is the energy which has been used to make it. Potato crisps have to be fried and iron ore has to be smelted to make steel for bicycle chains. Chemical farming techniques are energy-intensive because of the equipment used and because man-made fertilizers and pesticides are made from petroleum derivatives. Added to these is the energy needed for packaging and transport.

Perhaps worst of all, we waste a prodigious amount of heat. Strange as it sounds, this heat is a form of pollution. Water is used in industrial cooling (just as you might cool a boiled egg by filling the saucepan with cold tap water), and the resultant hot water is generally pumped into neighbouring rivers and streams, where it is extremely harmful to water plants and animals.

Cheap energy supply has enabled us to be wasteful; *State of the World 1988* points out that 'energy prices in most countries reflect neither the true replacement cost of non-renewable resources nor the environmental damage that their use can cause.' Attitude changes, including a willingness to pay more for our energy supplies, are essential (with the proviso, of course, that any price rises or a 'climate protection tax' do not hurt the poor).

The other energy crisis

In the Third World, the most serious energy crisis is the shortage of firewood. This has led to overcutting and deforestation, and causes soil erosion, flooding and food shortages. People in need of fuel burn animal dung and agricultural waste which would otherwise be used to enrich the soil.

Effective aid must take this into account. If you are wondering about where to give money to help with a current disaster in the Third World, consider sending some to an organization like Intermediate Technology which is helping to develop equipment like efficient cooking stoves which can be made by the people who will use them from locally available materials.

Health

No one who lives or travels near busy roads can be unaware of air pollution caused by our vehicles, and the problem is compounded by emissions from power stations and industry. There are short-term effects on human health like emphysema, bronchitis, asthma and upper respiratory disease. Deaths from these causes have been reduced considerably over the past twenty years, but there remains a second major health concern, human cancers caused by air pollutants. In a 1980 report, Wilson *et al.* estimated that 'general air pollution in the

United States alone is responsible for 53,000 deaths annually.'
(*Health Effects of Fossil Fuel Burning*, quoted in *Well Body, Well Earth*, p 173).

Another useful point to consider is that 'Energy conservation could lead to more exercise, better diets, less pollution, and other indirect benefits to human health.' (Worldwatch Paper 4, *Energy: the Case for Conservation*, 1976).

ENERGY FUTURE

Efficiency first

Four international energy experts claim in a 1987 report (*Energy for a Sustainable World*, World Resources Institute) that by making full use of presently available energy-saving technologies, global energy use can be stabilized—allowing us time to switch to alternative fuel sources and enabling us to substantially avert the crises which threaten us—while providing sufficient energy for everyone throughout the world to enjoy the sort of standard of living we now have in Western Europe.

Super-efficient fridges, long-life lightbulbs and cars which can run at nearly 100 mpg are some of the technologies they have in mind. Buildings are 'the most wasteful energy users in industrial countries', but architects are increasingly conscious of energy-efficient design and there are a number of model building projects around the country where energy use is as little as ¼ of that in similar but conventionally-built houses. With good insulation, the right materials and careful orientation, remarkable savings are possible. Imagine cutting your fuel bill from £60 per quarter to £15! And cutting down on your contribution to carbon and sulphur in the atmosphere at the same time.

Individually, we can choose energy-efficient appliances and products (in the US many are labelled with energy consumption figures). We can also start to adopt, in practice, the idea that ways of saving energy—'negawatts'—are a better buy than energy generation. Energy efficiency has other things going for it: 'Very efficient cars should be regarded not just as attractive consumer products but also as indirect deterrents of war, even nuclear war', because of a reduction in the global insecurity which results from the West's over-dependence on Middle Eastern oil.

They conclude their report by saying, 'The energy future we have outlined here is not the ultimate answer to the world's energy problems. Eventually, the world will need economical and environmentally benign renewable energy sources—the development of which will take time and ingenuity. But this future would give our children and grandchildren a world free of draconian energy-production regimes and, we hope, a world sufficiently prosperous and peaceful to allow them to work out long-term solutions to energy problems. It should give them a little breathing space and some room to manoeuvre.'

● *Energy for a Sustainable World*, José Goldemberg *et al.*, World Resources Institute, Washington DC (Wiley, 1987).

Renewability

The coal and oil supplies we are so rapidly using up were laid down millions of years ago, and once they are gone there won't be any more. Renewable energy sources, on the other hand, can be indefinitely sustained. There are a wide variety of potential energy sources: sunlight, wind, flowing water, wood and plants. These, too, have to be managed with care so as not to be used up more quickly than they replace themselves (that is, one would use only as much wood from a tree as grows each year).

The tapping of renewable sources of energy has made remarkable strides over the past decade, even without anything like the measure of support enjoyed by conventional and nuclear power supplies. They are particularly suitable for small-scale, local projects—another change suggested by many energy researchers. Small does not mean inefficient. In fact, huge electricity generating plants have turned out to be far less efficient than their creators envisaged back in the '40s and '50s, and in the United States small cogeneration and renewable energy projects are now able to sell power to the public utility companies.

Even urban homes can generate some of their own energy— see 'Simple Solar' on page 112.

WHAT WE CAN DO

The rest of this chapter is a summary of energy-saving ideas and techniques. As you read, tick the ones you want to try. There are many books and publications available which give detailed advice on materials and methods. Your local library will have some, *Which?* magazine has frequent articles about cutting fuel bills, and the gas and electricity boards can offer advice. These suggestions do not depend on any of the new technology we can look forward to over the coming years. Instead, they are ways of making the best of whatever system you have now.

Energy conservation may be the easiest step to take in *Home Ecology*, because you can judge your success so directly. The lower your fuel bills get, the better you're doing.

Transport

This is discussed at length in the next chapter, but it is worth reminding ourselves that using less petrol is an essential part of overall energy savings, since one-third of Britain's fuel consumption goes on transportation.

- Walk or cycle when you can.
- Buy locally-made goods and patronize local shops.
- Improve your car's fuel efficiency by keeping it tuned.
- Consider switching to a more efficient, perhaps smaller, vehicle.

Choice of fuels

Using electricity for 'low-grade' energy such as domestic heating and hot water is exceedingly wasteful because it is produced in power stations which burn large quantities of coal or oil to produce it and which are, at best, only 35% efficient. An open coal fire, by contrast, is 20% efficient (ie, 80% of the heat goes up the chimney), and a gas furnace is about 70% efficient. According to Ecoropa's *The Green Alternative*, 'when we heat by electricity we lose over 90 per cent of the fuel's primary energy because of the inefficiency of the transmission systems and electrical appliances'—on those figures, electricity is even less efficient than an open fire. (In other countries, notably Sweden, the waste heat from power stations is used to heat whole districts.)

Gas and coal are the best fuels for space heating and hot water, which make up 80% of home energy use. A better long-term 'fuel' for this purpose is the sun, and very simple systems are available which will provide hot tap water throughout much of the year, even in Britain. Check with the Centre for Alternative Technology for details.

A well-designed wood or coal-fired stove is a good space heating option, and pleasant to live with.

Electricity is suitable only for 'high-grade' energy needs: lights, powering electronic equipment and motorized appliances. The Central Electricity Generating Board (CEGB) has been extensively advertising the use of electricity for heating and hot water in order to even out expensive power station plant load, and John Bennet, a former engineer for the Yorkshire Electricity Board, writes that 'The current promotion drive will obviously contribute to a higher demand during the winter peaks, thus helping to fulfil the CEBG's prophecy of elecricity shortages—shortages which they blame on the planning delays caused by public resistance to their nuclear power programme.' (*The Ecologist*, January/February 1988, p 14).

According to Debra Lynn Dadd, who specialises in alternatives to toxic household chemicals, it was better home insulation which led to awareness of the dangers of combustion by-products, which include formaldehyde, nitrogen dioxide, sulphur dioxide and a host of other vapours and gases. For people sensitive to petrochemicals and those with health problems (including emphysema, asthma and angina), this can be a matter for concern. Robert Matthews wrote in the *New Scientist* that 'Epidemiological studies, such as that of over 8000 children in the US in 1980, hint that gas cookers in the home can increase susceptibility to serious respiratory illness.' (5 December 1985).

Be especially careful to ensure that gas appliances have plenty of ventilation while in operation. They must be correctly adjusted in order to burn efficiently; if they burn inefficiently there will be unnecessary fumes given off. (Your gas board can provide advice and service.)

Efficiency

Draught-proofing

1 Close all doors and windows, light a stick of incense and walk around your home. The smoke trail is a good guide to where particular trouble spots are.
2 Stuffed draught-excluders—those dachshund- or snake-shaped bolsters—are an easy and cheap way to prevent draughts under doors.

3 Fold newspaper into long thick strips and use them to fill gaps between sash windows and frames (windows which you don't plan to open through the winter). Hold the strips in place while you shut the window.

4 Commercial draught strips are useful, but choose the more expensive, durable kind instead of adhesive foam, which disintegrates after a year or two and is a pain to remove. DIY stores have a wide range and you may want to consult a reference book before you buy. Brass 'atomic strip' is durable and quite attractive, though not so easy to find as the cheaper types.

5 Curtains can be nearly as effective as double-glazing at cutting draughts. The longer they are, the better (floor-to-ceiling are particularly good for draught-proofing).

6 Open doors as infrequently as possible in cold weather (put out the milk bottles when you let the cat in, for instance).

7 On doors that are used a lot, try to arrange some sort of airlock. The idea is to prevent gusts of wind blowing straight through the house when the door is opened. You do this by having *two* doors; the outside one is closed before the inside one is opened (or vice versa). This can be done fairly easily in a house or flat with a narrow front hall, by putting in an interior door (solid or glazed). A porch or small conservatory will serve the same function.

(If your front door opens into a living room, you can at least increase comfort, although probably not save a great deal of heat, by creating an entry area with a large screen or room divider arranged to prevent direct draughts on people sitting in the room.)

8 Chimneys have to be well-ventilated in order to draw properly (you can tell that you've over-insulated if your chimney stops drawing—you'll get a house full of smoke). But an unused fireplace can be very draughty. Either (a) install an efficient stove, (b) brick it up—incorporating air bricks as required, or (c) block it up with a fitted frame covered with board, with holes to allow some air through. Then you'll need half a dozen potted plants or a large vase of dried flowers on the hearth.

Insulation

1 Fitted double-glazing is expensive, inflexible and resource-intensive. *Which?* magazine says 'doubleglazing does not

save enough to be worth installing on cost criteria alone (thick curtains and insulating blinds are almost as effective)'. Secondary double-glazing (detachable in case of fire), however, can be installed for a fairly small amount of money, and even cheaper is plastic film fitted with a hairdryer. A more attractive and permanent solution is using double-pane glass in existing window frames.

2 Heavy curtains are cheaper than double-glazing, easier to manoeuvre, and look elegant. I've seen nice 'stately home' curtains in auction rooms, and you can make them yourself (see Jocasta Innes's *The Pauper's Homemaking Book*). The bigger and thicker, the better. Curtains can be used over doors and at the top of draughty stairs. You can buy special lining fabric (aluminium or plastic-coated) for extra insulation. Curtains should be shut as soon as it gets dark outside for maximum heat retention.

3 Shutters are even more effective than curtains, and provide a good measure of security too. They are often boarded over in older houses, and it's worth taking a look in case you have some. If they have been removed, you can replace them with appropriate ones from a salvage firm or with new ones made up by a joiner. There's no reason you can't add shutters to modern windows—*The Self-Sufficient Home*, by Brenda and Robert Vale, gives instructions for making them.

4 Loft insulation has been well-publicised as a means of cutting fuel bills, and for some years there were grants available for this (they are now limited to people on low incomes). Use mineral fibre, vermiculite chips or cellulose fibre (made from recycled newsprint) rather than synthetic materials, and make sure that insulation goes *over* your cold water tank, to prevent its freezing.

5 Cavity wall insulation is suitable for some homes. Do *not* use urea-formaldehyde foam, which has been banned in the US because of health effects (more about this on page 229). Mineral fibre is a better ecological choice than polystyrene beads.

6 Hot water tanks need a warm jacket (like loft insulation, the pay-back period on this is only a couple of months). Get a large size and fit it over the old, thin one. You can also pad it with the same mineral fibre used in the loft, before putting the jacket on, and a layer of old blankets or clothes salvaged

from the jumble sale bag would be a cheap additional layer of insulation. Water pipes should be wrapped too.

7 Floors are insulated by carpeting and sheet flooring, but you can improve on this with thick fibre underlay, a layer of newspapers under the underlay or directly under linoleum (choose old-fashioned natural resin linoleum). Exposed suspended timber floors are best insulated with an under-floor layer of fibre or possibly polystyrene, but this is a big job to tackle. Eliminate draughts by filling cracks with an appropriately tinted filler (papier mâché works well).

8 Reflect heat with aluminium foil under non-vinyl wallpaper and behind radiators and appliances, shiny side facing you (use a heavy duty wallpaper paste).

A note about materials

Many of the products designed for home DIY use are of poor quality, cheap and temporary. They are also ridiculously over-packaged, as you will know by looking at the contents of your wastebasket after even a small DIY project. Look for sturdy, durable products, and choose natural, biodegradable materials when you have the choice. Robert and Brenda Vale believe that the manufacture of plastic insulating materials is 'the best possible way to use the remaining oil reserves'. Using fossil fuels to *conserve* energy is certainly a good idea, as long as the materials produced have a long life.

Ventilation

It's no good insulating so well that bad smells, solvent fumes and moisture in the air have nowhere to go. A high tech, super-insulated building will need mechanical ventilation, and indoor air pollution control will be essential. Avoiding toxic chemical products is going to be all the more important as we continue to improve building standards.

Extractor fans in the bathroom and kitchen can be auto-matically controlled by a 'dew stat' (bathroom fans generally have a timer). Opening a window a little bit is an alternative, as long as you remember to close it as soon as the moisture or smell you want to get rid of has cleared.

In the summer a small ceiling fan helps to keep the place cool, and in winter it circulates the warm air which would otherwise rise to the top of the room and stay there. More elaborate devices for circulating warmed air around the

house are available too, such as David Stephens' VertiVent
(see addresses, page 108).

Condensation

Internal damp is usually combatted by turning up the heat
or by opening a door or window, both wasteful solutions!
In centrally-heated homes the air is often too *dry*, but
some people fight a continual battle with damp. Condensation
occurs when warm, moist air comes into contact with cold
surfaces—when you turn the heating on in a cold house, for
example. To avoid this:

1 Use natural materials and fabrics (they absorb moisture and
   slowly release it back into the air).
2 Cut the amount of water which gets into the air: cover
   cooking pots and don't dry clothes inside.
3 Constant low heating can cost no more than occasional
   (morning and evening) heating, and has the advantage of
   eliminating the main cause of condensation by keeping
   surfaces and air at a fairly constant temperature. See '9' in
   the following section.

Using less

Heating and hot water

1 Use a timer. New ones with electronic programming allow
   you different settings for different days, and to separately time heating and water.
2 Heat only the rooms which you use, when you use them.
   This is standard advice, but in fact you may be better off
   with a different approach—see below.
3 Fit thermostatic valves to radiators, and use room thermo-
   stats. The hot water cylinder needs a thermostat too. Get
   family agreement as to acceptable temperatures!
4 Look for systems with spark ignition rather than a pilot
   light. These are safer (because the flame cannot blow out)
   and do not burn gas 24 hours a day.
5 Radiators should be placed on *interior* walls, contrary to
   the usual pattern—which is intended to warm draughts
   before they enter the room. Draught-proof your windows
   and this becomes unnecessary. If you have radiators on
   external walls, at least paste sheets of aluminium foil
   (shiny side facing you) onto the wall behind them.

6 Shelves above radiators direct warm air into the room rather than allowing it to rise to the ceiling: a layer of aluminium foil on the underside of the shelf makes this more efficient (you can purchase ready-made deflective shelves).

7 If your ceilings are very high, consider building a platform area to take advantage of the warm air near the ceiling, and increase your living space at the same time. A ceiling fan or heat recycling pump will circulate the warm air.

8 David Stephens of *Practical Alternatives* suggests moving your living rooms upstairs, at least in winter, to take advantage of rising heat.

9 As an alternative to timers and electronic programming, he also believes that continuous low heating is more effective, comfortable, and cheaper, than the intermittent heating that most of us use, taking advantage of the thermal inertia of the building. Experiment for a week with a constant, 24-hour a day heating at 62°F/17°C, keeping track of the readings on your gas or electricity meter. (This may be a particularly good idea if you have fine wood furniture—see page 113.)

10 When installing in a new central heating and hot water system, look at versions which run directly off the mains. They can be cheaper to run, give better water pressure (good in a flat if you want a shower), and mean that you do not need water tanks (thus gaining storage space). But first consider whether you really need central heating (see 'Radiant Heat', page 113).

11 If you have a hot water tank, lag it properly, and use the heat it still gives off for an airing cupboard.

12 Avoid letting hot water go down the drain, when possible. Allow bath or washing-up water to get cold before pulling the plug—its heat is given off into the room.

Kitchen

1 Use an automatic switch-off electric kettle and heat only as much water as you need. Upright kettles make it possible to boil a single cup of water, but there is some concern over the fact that they are made of plastic, minute traces of which will inevitably dissolve into the water. Scale deposits will make your kettle less efficient, so clean with a strong vinegar solution from time to time. Filtering water —page 166—can remove the minerals which cause scale.

2 Put extra boiling water from the kettle into a thermos for later, or use it to start soaking a pan of beans. This is a good budget move if you use filtered water for drinks and cooking. An even easier way to keep a constant supply of hot water is to boil a full kettle and put a heavy towel over it after you have used what you need (same principle as a tea cosy).

3 Improve your health and save energy by eating more raw food, salads and fresh fruit.

4 Cover cooking pots to cut cooking time and save energy (you know, a watched pot never boils—put the lid on).

5 Let the fire fit the pan: flame licking up the side of a small saucepan is wasted. Try not to turn the grill on for a single piece of toast.

6 Use a pressure cooker (stainless steel rather than aluminium) to drastically cut cooking time. Useful for beans which you haven't remembered to soak.

7 Fill the oven. For example, bake a pan of apples on the lower shelf while a nutloaf—or joint of beef—is cooking, then put in a tray of meringues before turning the oven off and leave them overnight.

8 Cut vegetables, including potatoes, into small pieces: they cook much more quickly.

9 When preparing foods which take a long time, cook more than you need and save the rest for another meal. Cooked beans and grains keep for about a week in the fridge, and are excellent in salads.

10 A tiered steamer will do several vegetables at once, and you can use the bottom pan of a double boiler to simmer eggs or steam rice while you stir a curry sauce in the top.

11 Chest freezers are more efficient than upright models, though less convenient to use. If you have a freezer, defrost regularly and try to keep it full. Keeping it outside, in a garage or cellar, cuts energy costs, or you can put foil on the wall behind it to reflect waste heat into the room.

Laundry

1 Wash full loads, and keep the cycles as short and cool as possible. Clothes can be rinsed in cold water, but a hot wash is probably preferable to using large amounts of detergent. Let the machine fill with hot water heated by your gas system, rather than allowing it to heat electrically in the machine.

2 In dry weather, even in winter, hang clothes outside (they'll smell wonderful), or on racks indoors; if necessary finish in the airing cupboard, or tumble dry for a few minutes.

3 According to *Which?*, a spin dryer can halve the time and energy needed to tumble dry a load of clothes, even after they have been spun in a washing machine. It makes drying clothes on racks much faster too.

4 It's all to the good if you can manage without your own washing machine at home. Communal laundry rooms are common in American apartment buildings.

5 Iron in bulk rather than one piece at a time, and use a heat reflective cover (or cut a piece of aluminium foil to fit under your cloth cover).

Lights

1 This may be too obvious to state, but I know my father would want me to point out that lights should be turned off when they are not needed!

2 Use low-energy, long-life bulbs when you can find them (the *Green Consumer Guide*, by John Elkington and Julia Hailes, is good on these).

3 Switch to low-wattage bulbs where only a small amount of light is needed (hallways, for example). Friends of mine with a new baby switched to 25-and 40-watt bulbs upstairs because it was pleasanter for night feedings, and found that the soft lighting also made getting up in the morning less of a shock to the system. Just be careful about matching socks! And always make sure you have enough light for safety, and to avoid eye strain.

4 Light provides a certain measure of security, both on the street and at home. Use sufficient lighting to deter burglars —put your lights on a timer when you are away. (Installing security lights which come on only if someone approaches the house would no doubt save a little energy, but I suspect the neighbourhood cats would set it off. And surely it would seem like living in Stalag 13.)

● Centre for Alternative Technology, Llwyngwern Quarry, Machynlleth, Powys SY20 9AZ, telephone Machynlleth (0654) 2400. Send 40p and large SAE for their extensive mail order booklist. Exhibitions and displays open to visitors; weekend courses.

● Bristol Energy Centre/Urban Centre for Appropriate Technology, 101 Philip Street, Bedminster, Bristol BS3 4DR, telephone (0272) 662008. Concentrate on energy saving and fuel poverty, with draught-proofing team and demonstration house.

● Neighbourhood Energy Action (NEA), FREEPOST, Newcastle-upon-Tyne NE1 1BR. Send SAE for details about local projects. NEA was started by Friends of the Earth members, but is now funded by the Department of Energy and offers advice on draughtproofing and loft insulation, especially to low income households.

● *Practical Alternatives* is a business run by David Huw Stephens, Victoria House, Bridge Street, Rhayader, Powys LD6 5AG, telephone (0597) 810929, which 'publishes a magazine and markets practical and durable goods to help people conserve the Earth's resources'. Send SASE for details.

● The Building Bookshop, 26 Store Street, London WC1E 7BT, telephone 01-637 3151. Reference material and manufacturers' literature.

● *How to Cut Your Fuel Bills*, Lali Makkar and Mary Ince (Kogan Page, 1982).

● *The Self-Sufficient House*, Brenda and Robert Vale (Macmillan, 1980). Try the library as this is out of print.

Appliances

Suggesting that we should be conscious of the energy we use doesn't mean giving up all our modcons, but do think about just what you need to be able to live without too much hardship before you acquire more. If you already have masses of electrical appliances, consider how you use them.

Over the past ten years appliance efficiency standards have been developing in the United States, and by the year 2000 these are likely to 'have saved $28 billion worth of electricity and gas and will keep 342 million tons of carbon out of the atmosphere' (Worldwatch Institute).

Of the major domestic appliances, only refrigerators, washing machines and vacuum cleaners seem essential to me, but everyone will have different feelings about this. Tumble dryers are energy-intensive and quite easy to live without. With a decent-sized freezer compartment in your fridge, a separate freezer is only necessary if you have a garden, or parents-in-law with one, or do a *lot* of cooking ahead. Otherwise it may just encourage you to buy frozen chips and boxes of beefburgers.

A dishwasher probably saves time for a large family and certainly keeps the kitchen a lot tidier, but there are sound arguments against having one. You need more crockery, have the hassle of rinsing and loading and unloading, and miss out on companionable chats over the washing-up. They require particularly strong detergents and use large amounts of hot water, as well as considerable amounts of energy for drying. (If you have one, look out for biodegradable washing powder —one is under development—and in the meantime cut the amount you use to a minimum. Choose the economy setting, and turn the machine off when it gets to the dry cycle—open the door and pull the racks out to air dry. The dishes are already hot so this takes very little time.)

Christina Hardyment argues in *From Mangle to Microwave* (Polity Press, 1987) that supposedly time-saving appliances, and their manufacturers' substantial advertising budgets, have created impossibly high housekeeping standards—that they have, in fact, made women's lot harder, not easier (the same might be said of modern miracle cleaning products). She writes that 'properly paid professionals can take over the drudgery of domesticity, and leave men and women enough time to make their home a satisfying place'. That's one approach— and if you have the money for a fancy new cooker with a self-cleaning oven, think about using it to hire some help instead.

New equipment shouldn't be a substitute for adequate assistance from the rest of the family. In her *Living More with Less*, Doris Longacre points out that 'while labor-saving devices are not all bad, neither is labor' and that 'we in the West have to step out of our comfortable cars and run to stay alive'. Like Christina Hardyment, she observes that people with lots of machines are not less harried. In fact, American women spend *more* time on housework now than they did in the 1920s.

1 Think of any appliance as a long-term investment. Buy good quality models (check *Which?*), and keep them in working order by following manufacturers' instructions (except that you can reduce the suggested amount of washing powder) and having them serviced regularly.

2 Do you really need a dishwasher/video machine/second television (or even first television)? Don't get one just because

your friends have one. If possible, borrow or hire one for a month or so, to see if you really make use of it.

3 Doing without a TV can free a surprising amount of time, and maybe your mind too. Watch important programmes at a friend's house.

4 Look for equipment made of metal rather than plastic—which can release fumes, especially when heated. Try buying secondhand, through the adverts in the local paper or newsagents' window, or reconditioned models. Debra Lynn Dadd says that 'older models provide high-quality non-toxic materials at significant savings', and it also keeps useful equipment in circulation, instead of on the scrap-heap. There is no way at present of recycling the CFCs which refrigerators and freezers contain, so avoid buying new ones.

5 While you want to make good use of your appliances, don't let having a food processor tempt you into blending/processing everything. Chefs complain that food processors spoil the texture of food. I find mine invaluable for many things, but Henry Fairlie of the *Washington Post* once wrote that chopping is a 'concentrated physical effort, it is a skill, it is always thoroughly enjoyable, and I can probably chop a leaf vegetable very fine as quickly as any. If I left this to an electrical gadget, I would have to take my fingers jogging.

6 Look for hand-operated models. Carpet sweepers are great, especially if you like to give the main areas of wear a quick going-over every day (carpets last longer if they are swept or vacuumed frequently).

7 A larder can expand your cold storage considerably (unrefined oils, wholegrain flours, seeds and nuts should be kept cool).

8 For hot food, there's the option of slow cooking with a haybox; a pot of stew or soup, or even porridge, is put into a box packed with hay which works like a vacuum flask to maintain the heat. You can build an urban version with some leftover polystyrene packing, as long as you ensure that there is a good layer of newspaper or towelling between it and the hot pan. Even easier, wrap the pot in a thick bathtowel or newspapers.

Staying warm

1 How warm you feel depends on your metabolism, your body fat, your biological rhythms and on how much

exercise you get. Do a little running on the spot to warm
yourself up on cold mornings.

2 Hot food and drinks are a great help. And you can use a
mugful of coffee or vegetable broth to warm your hands.

3 Dress with lots of layers. Tights or long underwear are
good under trousers. Wool and cotton are warmer than
synthetics, but it can be useful to wear a thin synthetic layer
next to your skin when it's very cold, with a cotton shirt
outside (and whatever collection of jumpers seems necessary). Any sweat 'wicks' through the synthetic fabric and
into the natural material, where it slowly evaporates, while
the layer next to your skin stays dry. Remember to keep
your feet warm.

4 Use and enjoy good, old-fashioned warming methods like
soft car blankets to wrap up in when you are sitting at home
in the evening.

5 In bed, a hot water bottle is very comforting. We used to
have an electric underblanket, but got rid of it after reading
recent studies of the effects of electromagnetic radiation
(one newspaper report was titled 'Electric blankets in cancer
enquiry'). Miscarriages are more common in couples who
sleep with electric blankets.

6 Thick cotton flannel sheets make the bed feel warmer—by
comparison, poly-cotton sheets feel like sliding into a plastic
bag. A flannel duvet cover can be made from a pair of
sheets. Flannel—or 100% cotton—is soft and pleasantly
absorbent in hot weather too. A wool blanket *under* the
sheet seems to help the bed warm up too.

7 Warm clothing at night certainly helps—socks, a sweater
over your pyjamas, even a nightcap (most heat loss is from
your head).

Keeping Cool

This may be an infrequent problem for people in Britain,
but in many places in the developed world airconditioning
throughout the summer is as much a fact of life as heating in
winter. The 1988 heat wave in the United States led to a series
of power cuts because of high energy demand. Not only is
airconditioning highly energy-intensive, but dangerous bacteria can grow in the units and some people are sensitive to
sterilizing chemicals used in them.

It also cuts us off from natural light and air, and does not allow or encourage our bodies to adapt to heat. Changes in temperature are a form of natural stimulus which we need to stay tuned to the environment around us—to stay healthy, in fact.

These ideas may be useful when you are on holiday, or when the temperature rises at home:

1 Dress for the heat in loose, light clothing. A sheer dress is more comfortable than tight shorts—think of a sari. Avoid synthetic fabrics like the plague. Cotton and linen may wrinkle, but are infinitely more comfortable.

2 Spray yourself with spring water, sprinkle water on your head, wet your clothes, or go swimming.

3 Drink cool drinks. (Or hot ones, if you are one of those who believe that a cup of tea is cooling.)

4 Open windows at night and close them during the day. Keep the curtains closed too while sun is shining directly on the windows. Outdoor planting can provide welcome shade during warm summer months.

5 Ensure that there is plenty of air movement, either with ventilation or a fan.

6 Use a hand fan—a collection of exotic fans is beautiful arranged on a wall, and you can offer them round at a party.

Simple solar

If you are itching for a new DIY project you could tackle something like solar panels or a wind-generator, but the simplest, cheapest form of renewable energy available to all of us is 'passive' solar heating. This means making maximum use of the sunlight which falls on your home, and works on a few simple principles.

1 Orientation is the the most important factor, and the chapter on light gives many ideas on this which are equally relevant to energy use.

2 Have large south-facing windows and smaller ones in north-facing rooms to avoid excessive heat loss there.

3 Leave curtains open throughout the daylight hours, but close them promptly when it gets dark.

4 Don't use net curtains, especially on south-facing windows.

5 Remember that dark colours absorb sunlight (and heat), while light colours reflect it.

6 Take advantage of the thermal inertia of building materials. A brick floor will absorb heat from the sun during the day

and give it off through the evening, just as a brick garden wall is perfect for espaliered fruit because of the way it retains warmth.

7 Conservatories are an ideal source of passive solar heat, and can make a substantial contribution towards warming your home, as well as providing an extra room (estate agents also consider them one of the best ways to add value to your property). If you are a gardener, consider a conservatory as a greenhouse built against the house—much easier to nurture seedlings in February if you don't have to tramp down a muddy path to get to them.

Choose a south- or west-facing site if possible, out of the wind (you can plant windbreak trees or shrubs). Double glass will help to eliminate any need for heating—you'll need blinds and ventilation for hot weather. This is a major investment and you will probably want an architect's advice about what is suitable for your home.

Radiant heat

We are moving more and more towards central heating in Britain, but before you put in a centralized system you may want to consider the following points. What we really want is not a particular heating system, but a comfortable place to live, and central heating has a number of disadvantages.

Many people complain of the stuffy, dry atmosphere in centrally-heated rooms, and compensate for this stuffiness with humidifiers (or, in my flat, with wet towels hung over the radiators). Winter colds and flu seem to increase when central heating is on because the dry air affects the protective membranes of the respiratory system.

According to the *National Trust Manual of Housekeeping*, 'In this country central heating has become perhaps the largest single factor in causing damage to the contents and even the structure of our houses.' (p 24). A relative humidity (RH) of 50-60% is ideal—for people as well as bookcases—but it sometimes drops as low as 20% in centrally heated houses. The ideal situation is an even low temperature of not more than 60°F/15°C, just what David Stephens suggests as an energy-saving measure (page 105).

The National Trust's *Manual* also mentions that we should avoid Calor gas and paraffin heaters because they produce minute quantities of sulphur dioxide, forming an acid vapour which will harm furniture—indoor acid rain.

In her book *Healing Environments*, architect Carol Venolia discusses the way we have become engrossed in creating 'thermally stress-free environments'—central heating in winter and airconditioning in summer—assuming that constant temperature is desirable, whereas this lessens sensory input and is actually bad for us, mentally and physically.

Everyone has a different comfort zone, depending on time of day, season, and state of health, but in general the most comfortable heating for human beings is a combination of convected and radiant heat. Christopher Alexander suggests that this is biologically built into us by our evolution in the open air, with plenty of sunlight. Examples of this combination are sitting in warm sunshine on a mild spring day, or in front of a glowing fire in a fairly cool room—think of your own experiences.

The proper balance is a radiant temperature about 2° higher than the air temperature. This sounds terribly technical, but it simply means keeping room temperature quite low (as the National Trust suggests) and having a heat source like a stove or an open fire in rooms where people gather in cold weather. A fire provides a delightful focus to a room, far preferable to the television.

Consumer power

Changing government and international energy policy is a task which we can contribute in various ways: by donating money to research and campaigning organizations, writing letters to MPs, choosing our fuels with care and showing willingness to pay higher prices when appropriate.

A delightfully direct method is to join the Consumers Against Nuclear Energy (CANE), whose slogan is 'We have the power to say NO'. The Campaign is organized on a regional basis, along the boundaries of the Area Electricity Boards. Consumers who join the Campaign withhold a proportion of their electricity bill equivalent to the amount being spent on nuclear power (about 17% at present) and pay the withheld money into a CANE Trust account. The withholdings have to be paid to the Electricity Board eventually, but interest on the money is invested in research into renewable energy.

- Consumers Against Nuclear Energy, P O Box 697, London NW1 8YQ. Send SAE for Campaign details, or £1.50 for Briefing Pack.
- Write to Friends of the Earth for their *Energy Resource List*, 26/28 Underwood Street, London N1 7JQ.

6
TRANSPORT

. . . excessive reliance on cars can actually stifle rather than advance societies. The very success of mass motorization has created conditions that cannot be ameliorated simply by making cars more efficient and less polluting.

Michael Renner, *Rethinking the Role of the Automobile*
Worldwatch Paper 84, June 1988

The car dominates our way of life so profoundly that it is difficult to get a clear look at how it affects our lives, our health and the health of our society.

Car ownership is one of the statistical measures of a society's affluence and increases in mobility are generally considered a desirable thing; mobility is equated with independence. But social health requires a certain degree of dependence—or rather interdependence. Complete independence leads to social alienation.

A LOOK AT THE CAR

Roughly 60% of British households have a car, but *everyone* is affected by the social problems cars create. Let's take a look at them.

Air pollution

As we saw in the last chapter, the burning of fossil fuels, including petrol, has a range of serious environmental consequences, including acid rain and global climate change (the greenhouse effect). Car engines emit a number of pollutant gases, including nitrogen oxide, carbon monoxide, hydrocarbons and sulphur dioxide. Worst of all, because it is completely avoidable and because it has well-documented consequences for children, is lead.

Most of us have felt the effects of these pollutants, while waiting for a bus by a busy road or while stuck in a traffic jam. Headaches and smarting eyes and throat are common complaints, but long-term damage is far more serious and ranges from respiratory problems like bronchitis and asthma to lung cancer.

Noise

Traffic noise is an insidious pollutant, perhaps most striking in its absence—when, for example, snow blocks the roads. Many people hesitate to open windows because of the roar of traffic outside their homes, while others have trouble getting to sleep at night because of cars and motorcycles zooming past. Goods lorries with diesel engines are largely responsible for unacceptable noise levels, and emit 8 times more smoke particulant than the equivalent vehicle run on petrol.

Danger

This is a problem inherent in the nature of cars: they are large, heavy objects which travel at high speeds in close proximity to pedestrians and cyclists. Only careful road and town planning, with restrictions on cars in residential and shopping areas, and an overall reduction in traffic volume, can alleviate this.

Space

Cars and their infrastructure (roads and carparks) take up a
great deal of space, approximately one-third of all land in an
average city. Congestion on the roads makes crossing more
difficult for pedestrians and parked cars frequently block the
pavement. Motorways cut swathes through large stretches of the
countryside, obliterating everything in their path (many valuable and beautiful wildlife sites have been destroyed already).

Ill health

You may think first of the effects of pollution as a cause of ill
health, but more important is the simple fact that driving
requires no physical effort. Some of us make up for this with
regular exercise, but many people do not. Cutting down on car
use—switching to cycle or foot for short journeys—could
substantially improve health.

Human consequences

Architects at the Center for Environmental Structure in
Berkeley, California, suggest that cars may 'cause the breakdown of society, simply because of their geometry' (*A Pattern
Language*, Alexander *et al.*). This is an important, and neglected, aspect of car use and requires some explanation.

A person in an automobile takes up approximately 100 times
the amount of space required by a person on foot, and cars
have 'the overall effect of spreading people out, and keeping
them apart.' Rather than meeting people as we go about our
business, to and from shops and school and work, contacts are
mostly in well-defined indoor places. Shopping in a supermarket miles from your home is a different social experience
from walking to a nearby greengrocer, and increased dependence on the car is likely to prevent what these architects
call 'the collective cohesion people need to form a viable
society'.

An interesting aspect of this can be seen by observing the
way people behave in cars. Behaviour which is the social
equivalent of slamming a door in your face is not at all uncommon on the road, although that driver would probably
never consider doing such a thing if you were not separated by
a number of yards and a mass of steel and glass.

In addition, neighbourhood identity is seriously affected by
heavy traffic. The more traffic there is in a particular area, the

less likely are residents to know their neighbours and to think of it as home territory. According to a study by Donald Appleyard and Mark Lintell: 'All aspects of perceived livability—absence of noise, stress, and pollution; levels of social interaction, territorial extent, and environmental awareness; and safety—were found to correlate inversely with traffic intensity.' (*The Environmental Quality of City Streets: The Residents' Viewpoint*, University of California, 1971). The inner city regeneration we hear so much about needs to take this factor into account.

Another social factor is the way motor vehicles have taken over 'common land'—the space between houses and workplaces which used to act as a meeting ground. Streets with motorized traffic are noisy and unsafe, and Alexander speculates that this may be a reason for the new emotional disorder called 'agoraphobia' (literally, fear of the 'agora', or marketplace) which appears in modern cities. Sufferers are afraid to go outside for any reason at all, and it may be that this disorder is reinforced 'by an environment in which people feel they have no "right" to be outside their own front doors.'

The only way to solve these problems is to give higher priority to social criteria in traffic planning, and to cut down

on the total amount of traffic while at the same time moving more and more of it out of residential neighbourhoods and onto major roads.

● *A Pattern Language*, Christopher Alexander *et al.* (New York: Oxford University Press, 1977).

Attitude towards the environment

The less contact we have with a place, the less we care about it. If you drive everywhere, you may rarely go anywhere on foot in your own neighbourhood; driving through the countryside doesn't provide any real contact with the blooming cherry trees or bramble patches or frolicking squirrels. When you read that the countryside is under threat or about urban decay, it won't mean much to you if you are always protected from these realities. (The inside of your car turns into a little home away from home, with stereo, telephone and other technological comforts.)

Urban children may spend little time on foot or bicycle— and this is bound to affect their attitudes towards the world they live in.

CITIES FOR PEOPLE

Friends of the Earth has a campaign called Cities for People, and propose that what we should be after is *accessibility* rather than *mobility*. Instead of clinging to the 'independence' cars give us—worryingly reminiscent of the way many Americans insist that carrying firearms is essential to their freedom—we should be thinking about what we need access to. Most people need to do the shopping, to get to school and work, to see friends and to go to the cinema, theatre, football matches and so on, but we do not need limitless mobility.

If we could do the things we need and want to do, and at the same time cut car use, everyone would benefit.

Car ownership

When I read that the UK automobile industry was celebrating the sale of more than 2 million cars in 1987, my heart sank. At a time when the automobile is having a calamitous effect on our environment, we seem to be turning more than ever towards car ownership. As a result, UK traffic increased by 5% in 1987 and is expected to increase by between 18% and 39% by the year 2000.

The result has been aptly termed urban thrombosis ('vessel blockage'), and is inevitable as long as driving is officially encouraged by building new roads and by tax concessions to companies which provide their employers with cars, and while public transport is unreliable and uncomfortable. In spite of the fact that most people do *not* drive regularly, over 99% of the national transport budget is devoted to the automobile.

Have you ever known anyone who turned down a company car? Probably not. The tax concessions which encourage companies to pay their employees with a car cost the taxpayer some £2,000,000,000 each year in lost revenue, as well as *stimulating* commuter traffic! If owning a car is an incentive to use it, imagine having one which is paid for by someone else. You drive to work even though the bus journey might be faster. The insurance is no worry so you become a little careless about how you drive. If petrol is paid for by the firm, driving by car becomes the cheapest way to travel. Some firms even pay parking fines.

Traffic

All of us suffer the effects of traffic to some extent, but it is often people who do not own cars who suffer most from heavy traffic and badly planned traffic schemes: children, the elderly and disabled, and mothers pushing prams.

Traffic congestion is a source of irritation and stress to drivers (in the United States there have been a number of cases of angry motorists drawing guns on each other). Many people will go to almost any length to avoid traffic jams, even when this means using residential streets, threading through the 'back doubles' favoured by professional commuters.

My own London street has been fighting for a road closure because of heavy traffic—during rush hours some 1100 cars an hour use it in order to avoid the main roads. Unfortunately, even this degree of community coordination can miss the real point, which is the way we all use our cars. At a recent meeting, one speaker was honest enough to admit that if he lived a little further out he too would be driving down our street every morning.

Putting the car in its place

Individually, we need to rethink the way we use our cars, recognising that overemphasis on this particular form of transport is lowering the quality of life for everyone.

Rather than plan for more cars, why not look at ways of making us less dependent on them? Local shops, post offices, hospitals and schools increase a sense of neighbourhood identity, lessen our need to travel long distances for basic facilities, and make life easier for the many people who do not drive.

When it comes to controlling the car, Friends of the Earth suggest four principles in their Kids Alive campaign:

1 *Reduce the amount of traffic*
   Residential streets can be made unattractively awkward for rat-running motorists by adjusting traffic priorities at junctions, and with road closures and chicanes. These schemes help to limit traffic to local residents, and careful planning (including plenty of trees and shrubs, which help muffle noise and improve the air) can make residential streets far more attractive.

2 *Reduce vehicle speed*
   Traffic humps, width restrictions and street 'furniture' all slow cars down and make roads safer for everyone.

3 *Special cycling facilities*
   Cyclists can be exempted from one-way restrictions and road closures, as well as provided with special cycle paths and turning lanes. This extra convenience will encourage more people onto bicycles, as will increased safety resulting from reduced and slower traffic.

4 *Special pedestrian facilities*
   Wider and higher pavements increase pedestrians' security, and a pavement extended straight across the road at a junction forms a clear pedestrian crossing and a traffic hump for motorists. Special footpaths and pedestrian shopping areas are other examples of this idea.

If all this leaves you anxiously clutching your car keys, please stop for a minute and imagine *your* neighbourhood without so many cars. Would you be more likely to stroll over to the park or to a friend's house—or stretch your legs with a bike ride? Play football in the street? Do some digging in your front garden? Or just sit outside, enjoying the peace and quiet with the Sunday papers?

Few would suggest that we stop using cars. It is virtually impossible to imagine a future without some form of high-speed, private vehicle. Nonetheless, with a combination of the following changes, a dramatic, healthy shift in their use is possible:

● Local facilities encouraged rather than being broken up and centralized.

● Better public transportation and provision for pedestrians and cyclists. Friends of the Earth would like to see £200,000,000 a year (6½% of the national transport budget) spent on cycle facilities.

● Increased public consciousness of the real costs of our dependence on the car.

● Social pressure is a potent force. Using a car for short journeys or travelling to work should become as unacceptable as smoking in public.

Women and transport

Transportation is a particularly acute problem for women, who make shorter and more varied journeys than men, and generally have more to carry. Only ⅓ of British women drive, compared to ⅔ of British men, and far fewer have access to a car during the day.

A switch to bicycles, walking and public transportation can be difficult for women, especially when they are coping with children and/or shopping. Safety is a worry, particularly at night. I remember going to an evening meeting in the next street, two minutes' walk away, and being offered a lift home by one of my neighbours, who apologised for her cowardice but admitted that she had brought her car (which meant driving half a mile) rather than walk down a poorly-lit footpath.

Transport planning tends to ignore the special problems faced by women. Staff cuts and poor design of public transport facilities—bad lighting, isolated staircases and subways—make women feel vulnerable and therefore less likely to use public transport, especially at night (many women without access to a car are stuck at home).

Cycle routes and special provision for pedestrians are all the more important to women, particularly if they are escorting small children. Cycling is a lovely way to get around with a child (much faster than walking, and ideal for local journeys, but unsafe road conditions deter most urban mothers.

● Women's Environmental Network, 287 City Road, London EC1V 1LA, telephone 01-490 2511, is running a transport campaign, and Friends of the Earth is researching women's transport problems as part of their general Transport Campaign.

PUBLIC TRANSPORT

Both city and country dwellers need a good public transport network. The closure of rural bus routes and train lines has left people in many villages and country areas isolated, or increasingly (and unnecessarily) dependent on cars.

We should support public transport, with our votes and by using it whenever we can. Join public pressure groups like Transport 2000 and FoE as well as any local association which campaigns on traffic issues. Our present transportation network needs considerable improvement, but government expenditure on public transport is called a 'subsidy', while money spent on more and bigger roads is not. The social and ecological costs of car travel are not yet taken into account, and the many advantages of better public transport are dismissed as uneconomic.

An intriguing point for drivers to consider is that the best way to speed up car travel is to improve public transport.

In spite of this official attitude, access to good public transport has a great deal to do with property prices—which means that it is valued rather more than most of us realise. There was jubilation in my neighbourhood when the evening news announced that there were plans to bring the Underground to our part of London. 'That'll put house prices up 5%, just on the promise', I heard someone say.

Using public transport requires somewhat different planning than travel by car, and the following ideas may make you more likely to choose to take the bus or train.

1 Set aside a shoebox for timetables and maps, and go out of your way to assemble a complete collection (these ought to be much more readily available). Libraries, town halls and police stations often have some, and bus garages and tube stations should be able to provide the full range. Put information numbers in a prominent place by the telephone, and write them on the top of your shoebox. There may also be a number you can dial to get up-to-the-minute information on cancellations and delays.

2 Get whatever reduced price fares or cards you are entitled

to. British Rail has a wide range of travelcards and there are various concessionary tickets available for buses and the Underground. They are great incentives to use the public transport, for weekend outings as well as shopping.

3 Get details of last buses, trains and night buses for your area. The number of a reliable minicab service won't go amiss either.

4 Think about the personal benefits of *not* driving: time to read, doze or meditate, with no worries about parking or about having a drink.

5 Allow yourself enough time, so you can catch the right train without killing yourself with a last minute dash to the station. This is a hard habit to get into if you are used to stepping out the door into a car. A book is invaluable when waiting for a delayed train.

6 A shopping trolley or a rucksack and an easily collapsible pushchair will make all the difference if you have to manage large parcels or a small child.

7 Working on flexitime makes it possible to travel off-peak, avoiding packed buses and trains and sometimes saving money too.

● Transport 2000, 10 Melton Street, London NW1 2EJ, telephone 01-388 8386.

BICYCLES

Some years ago I mentioned that I was thinking of getting a bicycle to two male friends, both regular cyclists. They were horrified. A passing bus would blow me over—IT WAS NOT SAFE. There's no doubt that the main problem for a cyclist is the sheer mass of metal which threatens you every time you venture out, and in a collision the cyclist is always the one at risk. Many drivers behave appallingly to cyclists, while most are simply oblivious of us (the few who are courteous are probably cyclists themselves).

Nonetheless, cycling is a convenient, efficient and enjoyable way to get around—much faster than walking or rush hour driving, and eminently suited to short journeys. While weather is sometimes a problem, safety is the most important deterrent for most people.

Friends of the Earth have drawn up a transport strategy which gives high priority to bicycles, and reading it makes one sigh. How wonderful it would be to have separate bicycle paths, plenty of marked cycle routes and counter-flow lanes on one-way streets. In the long-term, measures like these are essential to getting lots of people onto bicycles.

The more people who cycle, the safer all cyclists are, because this gives us a higher profile in drivers' eyes: they get used to looking for us. As it is, if you want to start cycling but feel nervous, stick to local journeys and streets you know are quiet until you develop the skills and confidence to cope with traffic. Going out with a friend can be a great help, and some areas offer training courses for young cyclists (ring your local council to ask about this).

The fact that you cycled all the time when you were a child—perhaps 20 or 30 years ago—doesn't mean you have the necessary skills to deal with today's traffic the first time you get on a bike again.

Many people wonder whether the exercise and transport benefits of cycling are not outweighed by the stress of travelling in traffic and the damage that exhaust fumes does to your lungs (not to mention your face—blooming but filthy). Cyclists are especially vulnerable to smoke particulant because they are breathing deeply, and some choose to wear masks. But the exercise makes you fit, and therefore less likely to suffer from other health complaints. Nonetheless, the only way to really get away from these problems is to get away from cars.

Children

Cycling is an ideal way for older children and teenagers to get around. Walking is, by comparison, very slow, while public transport can be inconvenient, especially for very short journeys. Safe cycle routes are even more important for children than for adults.

This is well worth considering, because 16% of the car journeys made by families with children under the age of 15 are escort journeys—to and from school, sports activities and music lessons or to friends' houses—and this applies nearly as much to able-bodied 13 year olds as to small children.

If you are nervous about your child cycling because of traffic, sit down and work out routes to frequent destinations. Cycle them together once or twice to assess your daughter/son's skill and concentration.

If you use a bicycle for local shopping, get a childseat for small children (up to 40 pounds)—you can even buy a child-size helmet. Some mothers use a tricycle or a trailer seat, very practical for shopping too.

Your bicycle

Buy a secondhand bike if you can, through a shop or the small ads, or by word of mouth. A relative may have an old bike in the garage which you can resuscitate. You may want to move up to a fancier model when you get hooked and start planning trips over the Alps, but any bicycle which is the right size and in decent condition will manage journeys around town.

If you decide to buy a new bicycle, go to several shops. They can be intimidating to the uninitiated, full of athletic young staff wandering around in cycling jerseys and those funny black shorts, and you may feel self-conscious about flabby legs or asking for a new tyre for the battered Hercules a friend has given you.

Explain that you want a bicycle and intend to use it for commuting/shopping/touring or whatever, have about so many pounds to spend and what can they recommend. You're looking for friendly, intelligent assistance. Make some notes, and compare not only price but the quality of information you get. Do they talk about 'the cotterless cranks' without explaining that this means the bits the pedals go on? What about a guarantee, accessories and service?

Do not think that you have to get a smart touring/racing bike. An old-fashioned upright bike can be more practical for short journeys.

An alternative is the mountain bike. These look like adult versions of a BMX and are designed to cope with any terrain.

City versions are slightly less rugged but their thick, heavy-tread tyres can handle roadways strewn with fragments of broken glass and death-defying potholes better than a touring bike's narrow wheels. They are also good for going up and down kerbs.

Try to get some help and advice from an experienced cyclist, especially if you are spending a lot of money. And resolve that you will get to grips with the nuts and bolts of your bicycle, so you in turn become an experienced and knowledgeable cyclist.

A lightweight bike is easier to manoeuvre up and down stairs, but quality matters a lot more than lightness. Usually, but not always, the two things go together. At low speeds (up to about 14 mph) weight matters more than air resistance, but the difference between a heavy and a light bike is only a small proportion of your combined weight. You're probably not worried about trimming 10 seconds off your home-to-work speed.

Make sure the bike fits you, and adjust the seat to the correct height. A rule of thumb is that with the saddle half extended out of the frame on its 'pin' you should be able to touch the ground with both feet, without being on complete tiptoe. This is important for back and knees, as well as for speed.

Cycling

1 A copy of *Richard's Bicycle Book*, by Richard Ballantine, is the best investment you can make before you start.

2 Low-profile, high-pressure tyres will help you get around with least effort. Keep them topped up weekly.

3 Get a repair kit and a spare inner tube. You may want to carry the repair kit and a small tyre pump with you.

4 Good lights and reflective gear are essential if you will be cycling in the dark. A helmet can save your life. Friends of the Earth point out, however, that there are strict practical limits to how much a cyclist can protect herself, and that the most important thing is to make our roads safer.

5 Decide what you are going to do about rain, in advance. The right gear makes it easy to cope with light showers. Remember that really bad weather not only makes roads slippery and visibility poor, but makes you far less visible to drivers. If in doubt, switch to public transport.

6 Good locks are essential—check at your friendly local bike

shop. Cyclists rarely have special parking places provided, and finding a secure place to lock your bike can be a problem. Parking meters and stout metal railings are ideal. Use U-shaped solid locks—Kryptonite or Citadel, for example—if you want the bike to be there when you get back (these locks even come with insurance against theft).

7 Check tyres for glass and all nuts and bolts for tightness every week. *Richard's Bicycle Book* will take you through most maintenance procedures, but besides this you should try to tune in to your bike so you hear when something isn't quite right. On a regular basis it really is up to the rider to keep everything greased and tight or loose as the case may be. If you use the bike to get to work, plan on a regular monthly check—just 10 minutes on a Sunday afternoon will make a big difference in reliability. (I have to confess to some hypocrisy here, because I live with a bicycle expert and let him do almost everything for me.)

8 If you feel unable to cope with even the simplest maintenance you'll want to develop a good relationship with a handy friend or one of the lads at your bicycle shop. A bicycle which isn't looked after can be dangerous as well as inconvenient, so be willing to spend a little money keeping it in good repair.

9 If you commute to work, sweat is almost certain to be a problem, at least during warm weather (cycling in town also gets clothes dirty). If you can change when you get to work, get a neat cycling ensemble together (t-shirt, shorts and a pair of training shoes would be basic) and carry your work clothes. Getting in early makes this much easier. Think how fresh you'll look when everyone else turns up.

If you can't, wear as light a shirt as possible and open a few buttons while you are cycling. You may have to wipe down with damp paper towels in the ladies' or gents' room. A fresh shirt, rolled or folded inside your saddlebag or left in a desk drawer, is good insurance.

(A few lucky people work for firms which provide changing and shower facilities for those who run or go to dance classes at lunchtime, equally handy for you.)

10 Cycling can be rough on shoes (even without toeclips), and a pair of pretty Italian high heels will not give you sufficient grip on the pedals for safety or speed. A pair of

training shoes works well—carry office shoes or stick them into a desk drawer at night.

11 Buy reflective bands or clips for your trouser legs, or make do with rubber bands. Tucking trouser legs into your socks doesn't look very elegant, but it does the trick. A bicycle chain can chew through expensive fabric in seconds —use a chain guard for commuting. Skirts are hard to manage on a bicycle and can be dangerous.

12 Fit a plastic mudflap at the bottom of your front mudguard to keep feet drier and cleaner.

Finding routes

Car drivers who turn to bicycles may find themselves on the same traffic-clogged routes they used to drive. Once you establish a 'normal' route it can be quite difficult to try something new, although you think about it every time a lorry cuts you off at the traffic lights and drenches you in its foul black exhaust.

Cyclists can be far more flexible than drivers and alternative routes, using quieter residential roads, make travelling less stressful, safer and often faster.

To work out a new route, spread a large-scale map on the table and mark your home and workplace or other destination. It may be worth planning a route which takes you past a good food shop or market, so you can pick up something fresh for lunch or do some of your shopping on the way home. This is an under-valued benefit of travelling by bicycle—try it! Go via parks and take advantage of any cycle lanes. A new route will take longer for a few days, depending on your memory and map-reading skills, so allow extra time.

If you want to go touring and live in the centre of a town, why not take a short train ride out to save yourself the hassle of a long fight through traffic? Long distance rail travel with a bicycle is a great way to get around because you have private transport at the end of your journey, but taking a bicycle on the train has become more difficult, and expensive, over the past few years.

Friends gave me two examples of the difficulties faced by railway cyclists. Although reservations are required on some Intercity trains, you cannot reserve space for your bicycle. They arrived at the station with bicycles and laden panniers and seat reservations, only to be told that there was no room in the baggage compartment! Another time, they had to change trains enroute home, and the guard attempted to charge them another £3 for each bicycle, saying that the fee was for each train, rather than for the journey.

● *Richard's Bicycle Book*, Richard Ballantine (Pan, 1975).

● Friends of the Earth's Cycle Campaign Network will put you in touch with a local group, which can advise on equipment and routes.

● *The RoSPA Bicycle Owner's Handbook*, available from the Royal Society for the Protection of Accidents, Cannon House, The Priory Queensway, Birmingham B4 6BS (90p incl. postage) is a useful guide.

WALKING

Most people in the world travel on foot because that is the only means of transport available to them, but many car owners never walk anywhere. Walking can be a great pleasure. You notice changes in the trees, watch the restoration being done on a dilapidated but beautiful old house, enjoy the tangy scent of newly turned earth or the luxurious smell of a bank of honeysuckle. The fresh air and light are good for your body, and walking gives one time to think, a precious commodity in our hectic lives.

Are we really so short of time that we cannot walk? Travelling by car frequently means fighting through heavy traffic and trying to find somewhere to park, but because we are inside the car we may not 'count' the time spent there.

Country dwellers have the advantage when it comes to pleasant places to walk, but even in urban and suburban areas it is possible to find interesting routes which keep you clear of the travel and noise of the main roads, and offer a look at another Britain. Wildlife groups have helped to turn abandoned railway lines into attractive pedestrian and cycle paths, as well as being preserves for many wild creatures.

In the city, a walker can explore back streets and parks. You may find that it is worth a longer walk to avoid main roads, or to go to a shop which sells homemade Greek specialities or where you enjoy a chat with the owner.

I used to love taking long walks in historic parts of central London, but of late cars seem intrusive almost everywhere. This is a great loss. Piccadilly Circus was once an exciting spot where cars and people met, but the volume of traffic makes it very uncongenial these days.

Have you ever taken a stroll under a cavernous underpass, where there used to be a pleasant wood with riding trails? As you drive down a motorway—delighted by how quickly you can get to Aunt Margaret's—give a thought to the effect heavy motor transportation has on rural communities and the countryside. We city-dwellers can be extraordinarily insensitive to the consequences of our demands on even nearby stretches of countryside, and let our convenience overshadow the destructive impact of more roads on the villages and towns en route to our destinations.

Brisk walking is nearly as good as jogging for your heart and for losing weight, so many people now walk for fitness. Not just a 5 minute stroll down to the sweet shop, but a vigorous 30 or 40 minutes—you might even be able to walk to work!

A small rucksack is more practical than carrying a bag. And comfortable shoes are essential (put your high heels in the rucksack and change when you get to your destination).

Personal security is a thorny question, and one which women face continually. If in doubt, do not walk (get a bus or minicab or ask a friend for a lift—and a few areas have special late-night women's lift services).

Recreational walking ranges from an afternoon jaunt in the country (take a train to one station and travel home from another) to walking holidays. Britain has an incredible range of footpaths, though to find all of them you'll want to become good at navigating by Ordnance Survey maps. The Ramblers' Association is campaigning to preserve and protect the public's right of access to Britain's footpaths, because in some places it is being eroded by resistance and neglect on the part of property owners and local councils.

Even small children can cover a reasonable distance in a day, with plenty of pauses to examine beetles and discuss the life and death of birds. For inspiration, read Dervla Murphy's *Where the Indus is Young*—this Irish travel writer took her 5 year old daughter walking in the Himalayas one winter. Babies and toddlers can travel in a sturdy back carrier.

A compass is a good idea, in addition to maps, appropriate clothing, proper boots, and a bag of snacks and something to

drink (dried fruit and nuts, or a few squares of chocolate, can be tucked into a pocket).
● Ramblers' Association, 1/5 Wandsworth Road, London SW8 2XX.

USING A CAR

Self-appraisal

Grab a piece of paper and make a list of the reasons for choosing to drive, on a local journey to the shops or to a friend's place, instead of using some other form of transport. There are all kinds of factors, from not wanting to put on a coat to avoiding crowds, the fact that it's raining or you're late, or you don't feel safe outside after dark.

If you didn't have a car, how much extra time would you have to spend walking to the bus stop or the station? Perhaps 20 minutes a day, enough to keep you in reasonable shape.

Think of ways you could avoid part of the driving you do and resolve to take at least a couple of steps this week.

Maintaining a car is time-consuming and expensive. If you don't have a car, is this a conscious choice or are you simply waiting until you pass a driving test or can afford the monthly payments? Taking taxis occasionally and hiring a car a couple of times a year works out considerably cheaper than keeping your own vehicle, and may be a happy choice for you.

Another possibility is using a moped or motorbike, which use little fuel, do not add much to traffic congestion and are easy to park. Motorcycles can also be noisy and dangerous, and leave you exposed to the elements just like a cyclist, but without the advantage of getting some exercise.

Lead-free

Lead makes human beings, especially children, stupid. What could be more stupid than continuing to use it? Please don't!

The lead in petrol has two functions: (1) It allows the fuel to burn properly when the engine compresses it—raising the 'octane'—and thereby prevents 'knocking' which would damage the engine. When lead is removed, other octane improvers have to do this job. (2) It forms a thin, tan-coloured coating on the valves which let the exhaust out of the engine. This stops them from getting worn—so called 'valve seat recession'. If lead is reduced this protection becomes less effective in susceptible older engines. Most cars built since 1980 can run without lead since they have harder valve seats which wear less anyway (consult your manufacturer for specific details).

Older cars can be protected by using leaded petrol for one tank in three, as the lead remains on the valves for quite a time. The faster and hotter the engine runs, the more quickly the protective lead coating disappears, so drive sedately.

Far better, have your car converted to run on lead-free petrol. This involves replacing the valves and valve seats with the modern, hard variety, and is likely to cost about £200 for the average family saloon. Every manufacturer has an advisory service—call your local dealer for more information.

The Campaign for Lead-Free Air (CLEAR) runs an information line and can provide a map showing petrol stations which sell unleaded petrol, especially important if you have a car with a catalytic converter because it can only run on lead-free petrol. Carry a spare can of lead-free in the boot.

If your car is modified to run on lead-free petrol but does not have a catalytic converter, using lead-free is completely safe, just more expensive!

● CLEAR, 3 Endsleigh Street, London WC1H ODD, information line 01-387 4970.

Driving as if people mattered

I was talking to a friend about traffic schemes when her son piped in, 'If it was the future and cars were alive, everyone would think they were much more important than people.'

He was right, unfortunately. Those of us who drive can do some soul searching about just what matters: getting to the supermarket as quickly as possible or letting those pedestrians cross the street without fear.

If you have a car and never go anywhere without it, the first step towards increasing your awareness of pedestrian problems is to spend an hour or two walking around your own neighbourhood. There are always a few places where it is virtually impossible for pedestrians to cross, and other places where people hover in the middle of a busy road, waiting for a gap in the traffic.

Apart from supporting local and national pressure groups to improve traffic conditions for everyone, there are a number of things drivers can do immediately to make the roads safer and pleasanter.

1 Do not drink and drive. How many times does this need to be said? (By the way, be careful about drinking and cycling too, especially if you have to cycle home through heavy traffic, where you need fast reflexes and all your faculties.)

2 Slow down. Simply put, speed kills. At 15 m.p.h. (25 km/hour), there is only 3% chance of death for a pedestrian hit by a car, while at 40 m.p.h. (65 km/hour) the chance rises to 90%. Men who get a buzz from driving fast should find another way of exhibiting their virility.

3 Don't let the common courtesies disappear when you get behind the wheel. Let people cross the street, slow down when there are children about, and do not rev your engine to hurry pedestrians at a crossing. Stop when the lights turn yellow instead of streaking through, especially when there is someone waiting to cross. A calmer driving style will be good for your blood pressure—and bank balance!

4 Learn to drive well. This means handling the vehicle, paying attention to what's going on and staying alert. Passing the driving test does not make you a good driver. (FoE wants the driving test made more stringent, and suggests regular testing of drivers rather than a lifetime licence.) Learn to judge how wide your car is, and be responsive to other drivers' signals.

5 Don't get angry at pedestrians or cyclists just for being there. Watch out when you open your car door, or reverse across the pavement, instead of assuming that they will always look out for you. (Young pedestrians who deliberately tease motorists are foolish and annoying, but this is no reason to get involved in a game of chicken.)

6 Friends of the Earth publishes a *Guide to Cycle Friendly Motoring*. This is essential reading if you don't cycle, and might prevent your injuring (or even killing) a cyclist one day. Remember, it is not simply up to cyclists to look after themselves—drivers must learn to look out for them.

7 Don't be bullied by other drivers into driving too fast or dangerously.

8 Slow down to 20 m.p.h. in residential districts (including your own). This is the speed limit recommended by FoE's Kids Alive campaign—even lower maximum speed limits

are in force in some continental cities—and some of us can adopt it now as a personal traffic calming measure.

9 Encourage local residents' groups to tackle traffic problems. FoE's booklet on Traffic Calming has many ideas taken from European cities.

Green driving

1 Think before you drive—don't drive if you can avoid it. A bike is a great way to get around. Think of walking down to the shop as a pleasant outing (if it isn't—because you have to cross busy roads or the pavements are filthy—perhaps a longer walk in a different direction would be better). A walk or a bicycle ride is a good way to get some exercise, fresh air, and your daily dose of sunlight (see Chapter 12).

2 Shop, work and play locally whenever possible.

3 Plan ahead. Make one trip instead of three (and swing by the bottle bank on your way to the shops).

4 Don't drive alone. Try car-pooling to work if you cannot use public transport, share driving the children to school, and why not do your weekly shopping with a friend?

5 Switch to lead-free petrol, and talk to your garage or a clued-up friend about having a catalytic converter attached.

6 Slow down to save petrol. Consumption is highest in start-and-stop town traffic and over 55 miles on the motorway.

7 Driving technique affects car mileage. Avoid slamming on the brakes, use gears to slow down and don't rev the engine. Aggressive driving uses 20% more petrol.

8 Keep your car in good repair, regularly tuned and tyres fully inflated. Rust prevention is vital to keeping cars alive as long as possible.

9 Other ideas for saving fuel include fitting an electronic ignition and using radial tyres.

10 Remove roof racks when not in use (wind resistance means increased petrol consumption). Lighter loads make for better mileage, so empty out the boot.

11 Support public transport. The greater the demand is, the better the service which can be provided.

12 Use asbestos-free brake pads—ring accessory shops or ask your garage.

When you buy a car

I have to admit that we are a two-vehicle family. We've restored a '67 Volkswagen Karmann Ghia and are now working on a '66 VW split screen van. There are advantages and disadvantages to maintaining vehicles this old. We've probably saved both from the breaker's yard, but older vehicles weren't designed to be as fuel efficient as many modern cars or to run on lead-free petrol. At present, we have to make every fifth tank leaded to keep the engines from an early grave.

The lifespan of any car can be greatly extended by good maintenance and, most of all, by rust prevention. Although 2 million cars were sold in the UK in 1987, some 1 million were discarded. Since the manufacture of a car requires a large input of both energy and raw materials, keeping them alive is ecologically sound—buying a new one every time you have the old one paid for is not.

A cheap and effective method for the keen car person is to seal the underneath with used engine oil. Here's how: when you change the oil, save the old oil in the new oil can. In the autumn, while it is still fairly dry, use a powerful hose jet or forecourt jet wash to clean the underside of the car. Put it on stands, take the wheels off and brush the old oil all over, paying special attention to vulnerable spots like the wheel arches. (Keep drain holes in the frame free, and do not get oil on the brakes!)

This is messy, so spread plenty of newspaper and wear suitable clothing and rubber gloves. Done once a year, this should keep your car on the road virtually forever.

An easier method, which a garage will do for you if you don't want to do it yourself, is to spray on a thick coating of 'Waxoyl' underseal (available from car accessory shops), after the same thorough cleaning with a jet wash. This dries to form an impermeable layer, and only needs to be touched up every 3-4 years.

When you do buy, think about these points:

1 Look at secondhand cars, and get impartial advice if you feel you cannot judge yourself (the best help you can have is a really knowledgeable friend on the spot).

2 Get a car you like and will be happy to drive for many years. Buy the right size, not only for your family but for your frame. Minis are no good if you are tall. *Which?* gives useful advice, and *The Green Consumer Guide* has a lengthy section about choosing a new car.

3 Look for low-pollution features, and check on whether the car will need to be converted in order to use unleaded petrol. A car which gets good mileage means reduced running costs and fewer pollutants being pumped into the atmosphere.

4 Do not choose a diesel engine—these are often sold as ecologically sound, but the fact is that they produce far more particulate pollution than standard engines. Technical improvements are needed before they become a good buy (stricter regulation of diesel buses and lorries is essential too).

HOLIDAYS

The importance people attach to holiday plans might be seen as a sign that many of us are not too happy with life at home. How many people come back from a holiday feeling more exhausted than when they left home, with only a pile of photos, credit card bills and a few amusing stories for the office to serve as reminders of that year's trip?

Next time you sit down with a pile of glossy holiday brochures it's worth taking stock of what you really want to get out of those precious weeks, especially when you consider just how much they cost. Perhaps you simply want to enjoy some sunshine and get away from the commitments of home life. Nothing wrong with that. You may want to travel in a new part of the world and see famous sites for yourself.

Tourism can be seen as a sort of pollution, something which destroys the thing it loves. You've probably heard friends talking about Mauritius or Alcapulco 'before it was spoiled'. Hotel complexes line the seafront in popular mass market resorts, catering standards degenerate to ubiquitous hamburgers and fish 'n' chips, and the real life of the region disappears. Added to this is the extremely serious effect tourism has on the ecology of many precious wilderness areas.

The summer of 1988 brought unprecedented, and unexpected, problems with air traffic. In a leader column *The Independent* commented that 'If tourism pollutes, the polluter—innocent as an individual but guilty *en masse*—is now paying the price.' The article goes on to suggest that while technical solutions may help, 'best of all would be a more thinking approach by travellers and the tourist industry alike.' (18 July 1988).

Tourism in the Third World has heavy social and cultural costs, borne by local people. Unfortunately, the notion that we can bring jobs and prosperity to poor regions by travelling there is not confirmed by recent studies, which have found that as much as 80% of the money spent on holidays in the Third World comes back to home countries, in foreign staff salaries, foreign-owned hotel profits, travel agency commissions, payment for imported food and other items, insurance and interest on loans. Most of the remaining revenue goes to a few wealthy locals and government officials.

Dervla Murphy, who has travelled in a number of Third World countries by bicycle and on foot, writes:

> The distortion of human relationships, rather than the building of Holiday Inns or the sprouting of souvenir stalls is the single most damaging consequence of Third World tourism. And let no one believe that those children's families would be better off if Antsirabe were 'developed'. They would not. But a lot of already rich Malagasy would be even richer. *Muddling through in Madagascar* (John Murray, 1985), p 117.

In the main, the tourist industry generates unskilled jobs—responsible positions tend to go to foreign employees—while causing a disruption of local life. Customs and religious rituals are transformed into spectacles, and traditional crafts become souvenirs.

One of the main reasons we go on holiday is to have a break from routine, to recharge our batteries. A camping trip or walking holiday may sound strenuous and tiring, but can do more to energize you than two weeks at a crowded resort. Edith Schaeffer writes that 'Man does not have the same healthy refreshment for his nervous or his physical system if he never gets his feet on the earth, and his eyes, nostrils, and taste buds free from the sights, sounds, flavours and smells of machine, concrete, exhaust and other non-natural things' (*Hidden Art*), and emphasizes the refreshment one gets from walking, cycling, skiing and swimming away from man-made things. Doris Longacre comments that we need wilderness as a checkpoint, so we can see where development is taking us, and, essentially, 'to give us the humbling experience of leaving something alone.' (*Living More With Less*, p 44).

Here are some things to think about while you plan next summer's trip:

☛ How will you travel? Walking and cycling are good for you and put you in contact with the places you visit. When Dervla Murphy cycled around Belfast, researching her book *A Place Apart*, her bicycle chain used to come off opportunely when she wanted an excuse to stop and have a chat.

☛ You may be able to travel by train instead of car. Cars can go on the train—getting you to the south of France quickly and pleasantly, though not especially cheaply—or you can hire one at the other end. In many places a bicycle, whether hired or brought from home, will do as well.

☛ Where will you go? Instead of 'doing' sights, or towns, or countries, choose a spot which holds some genuine interest for you or your family and read up about it in advance. This will not only make your visit more rewarding but will help you to fit in while you are there.

☛ Try to avoid package tours, which have been described as 'mobile ghettos' because they give the tourist no contact with anyone who is not servicing tourists.

☛ Instead of looking for a home-away-from-home, think of holidays as a chance to experience something different from your regular way of life. Interesting options include cycling holidays (even 'Cycling for Softies'), Outward Bound and Working Weekends (or longer) on Organic Farms (WWOOF).

☛ If you are concerned about the impact of tourists on other countries, you may want to contact one of the groups listed below. Respect for other people's feelings and customs is the most important thing you can take with you, whether you stay in Britain or travel abroad. Tourists can be extraordinarily insensitive about taking photographs, for instance.

● Centre for the Advancement of Responsive Travel, 70 Dry Hill Park Road, Tonbridge, Kent TN10 3BX.

● Tourism Concern, 8 St Mary's Terrace, Ryton, Tyne & Wear NE40 3AL.

● North-South Travel Limited, Moulsham Mill Centre, Parkway, Chelmsford, Essex CM2 7PX, telephone (0245) 492882.

● John Button's *Green Pages* lists many intriguing alternative holidays, and he has written the *Green Guide to England*.

● *The Green Consumer Guide* lists tour operators who donate

a share (a very small share, it must be said) of their takings
to wildlife organizations.

FUTURE MOVES

Technological advances are making cars more efficient users of
petrol, but this fuel efficiency will eventually reach some practical limit. We need to find alternative fuels for motor vehicles
and develop public transportation networks, as well as give far
more thought to the way our towns are designed. Some changes
to look for are:

● Increased emphasis on local facilities, local food supplies,
  local businesses and industry to serve residents and provide
  jobs.
● Neighbourhood boundaries restored and protected.
● Improved pavements.
● More and better cycle routes.
● Bicycle parking/locking facilities.
● Car traffic discouraged and routed away from residential
  areas.
● Freight moved by water and rail.

We also need:

● Much better bus and train services.
● Reduced prices for services like Motorail.
● Long distance cycling and walking routes.
● Efficient, non-polluting cars.
● Social discouragement of driving.

While it is unlikely that we will ever give up the private
motor car, perhaps they will become unnecessary and inconvenient for many people when there are sufficient alternatives available.

7
AIR

Move to an open window or go outside if you can. Close your
eyes and take several long, deep breaths. Fill your lungs all the
way down to your tummy. As you breathe, see if you can
remember times when breathing has been a conscious pleasure.
The sharp, ice-clean smell of mountain air, or the exhilarating
scent of fallen leaves in the autumn. Smell plays a vital role in
our consciousness and memory—everyone knows the way certain smells bring back places, events and even people we've
known and perhaps almost forgotten. The oldest, primal part
of the brain controls our sense of smell, and is closely related
to the parts of the brain which control emotion, mood and
personality.

A baby's nose is its first source of information about
the world, but few adults have a finely attuned olfactory

sense. We are not encouraged to use our noses as we are our other senses, but a few humans can sniff out truffles as pigs traditionally do, and wine specialists develop a very acute sense of smell.

Part of the reason many of us have a dull nose may be sensory overload, which starts from a very early age. Scented baby lotions, powders and even disposable nappies will interfere with perception of people and objects. Modern life bombards us with smells, some extremely unpleasant, and we tune these out in self-defence.

Shallow, inadequate breathing is characteristic of sedentary people, and perhaps our heedless pollution of the air around us has something to do with the fact that we don't use it with appreciation, and pleasure.

Air pollution

Ordinary air pollution, the acrid, brown haze which lies over most large cities, results from the burning of fossil fuels and comes from automobile exhaust and industrial emissions. Our outdoor air has been cleaned up a great deal in the past 35 years, especially after a temperature inversion trapped the air over London for several days in 1952 and an estimated 4,000 people died. It is said that theatres had to close their doors because audiences could not see the stage.

Nonetheless, air pollution remains a serious problem throughout the world, causing illness and death, the crumbling of historic buildings and monuments, and damage to trees and wildlife.

Air pollution harms us in a number of ways. It damages the delicate linings of the nose, throat and lungs, causing a variety of respiratory complaints. While in the lungs it can enter the bloodstream and reach other parts of the body. Some of the chemicals in typical urban smog have been found to alter DNA in cells, causing cancer and birth defects. More subtly, it also suppresses the immune system by reducing lymphocyte and antibody production, making us more susceptible to illness.

The ozone layer

We've heard a great deal about the CFCs used as propellants in aerosol cans, and manufacturers have responded to considerable public pressure by agreeing to start switching to alternative gases. This is a great success, but it is disappointing to think that environmentalists have been warning about the danger to the ozone layer since the mid-1970s!

The Montreal Protocol, agreed in September 1987, states that CFC production must be cut to 65% of the 1986 level by 1999, and manufacturers are scrabbling to find suitable and safe substitutes. This is a step, but Friends of the Earth has concluded that an immediate 85% reduction in CFCs is necessary to stabilize the ozone damage at its current level, and a complete ban on CFCs should be made as soon as possible.

This switch poses a formidable problem for the foam industry, and they are looking for viable and safe alternatives to CFCs. Manufacturers of airconditioning equipment are looking for ways to conserve or recycle the CFCs they contain— this has not been done before because it was uneconomic, but is likely to be highly economic in future.

You can help by not buying CFC-propelled aerosols (Friends of the Earth can provide a current list of CFC-free, 'Ozone Friendly' products), foam packaging or new refrigerators and freezers. If possible, do not allow an old fridge to be broken up—sell or donate it.

Aerosols, whether CFC-based or not, are a source of indoor air pollution. Because they disperse their contents as an extremely fine mist, products which contain toxic ingredients (such as hairspray and insecticide) can be inhaled and easily enter the bloodstream. The American Lung Association advises against their use. You can always find a non-aerosol equivalent: pump action, liquid or cream products work very well. Certain propellant gases are themselves lung irritants and depress the central nervous system.

Toxic clouds

Michael Brown is the reporter who helped bring the Love Canal toxic dump story to the attention of the world. In his latest book, *The Toxic Cloud* (New York: Harper & Row, 1987), he argues that the dangers of airborn chemicals present a far greater threat than has been realised.

In 1982 the US Environmental Protection Agency found high levels of toxaphene (a highly carcinogenic insecticide), PCBs, dioxins and DDT byproducts (more nasties) in an isolated part of Lake Superior in the northern United States. Toxaphene was never used in significant quantities by farmers in that part of the country, and researchers concluded that the poisons must have travelled by air from the cotton fields of the southern United States, some 1000 miles away.

Brown claims that this 'toxic fallout', made up of solid particles, invisible gases and aerosol mists, may be responsible for thousands of cancers and genetic mutations. Aside from the known hazards related to individual chemicals, there is the unpredictable danger of what those chemicals may do in combination, or of what the cumulative effect will be as they build up in the atmosphere. Our experience so far with CFCs doesn't give a good prognosis.

Modern agriculture is a source of some of the most dangerous chemicals in use, because they are specifically designed to kill living organisms. Many do not break down in the environment.

You may think that severe air pollution is confined to large urban areas, but the fact is that some people have to move into the city in order to get away from agricultural chemicals! Looking at Britain's pastoral, patchwork landscape, this is a chilling thought. Country folk, from farm workers to weekending stockbrokers, face problems with nitrate fertilizers and agricultural chemicals in drinking water, and dangerous and debilitating contamination from aerial crop spraying.

Friends of the Earth has compiled a dossier of dozens of incidents of people being sprayed with poisonous chemicals (the most horrific was a case in 1985, when a group of school-children were directly and repeatedly sprayed by an aircraft while they stood waving at it). Organophosphate pesticides have severe and long-term neurological effects, and it seems that there is insufficient enforcement of current government regulations. FoE wants to see aerial spraying banned. (FoE's Second Incident Report, *Chemical Trespass—Whose turn next?*, 1987.)

What you can do
For the environment
- ☛ Drive less and choose unleaded petrol (Chapter 6).
- ☛ Conserve energy (Chapter 5).
- ☛ Do not buy CFC aerosols (and, preferably, no aerosols at all).
- ☛ Use non-toxic household products (Chapter 10).
- ☛ Buy organically-grown food (Chapter 2).
- ☛ Plant trees.
- ☛ Write to your MP.
- ☛ Support FoE's Pesticide Campaign.

For yourself
- ☞ Spend as much time as possible outdoors, preferably in 'clean air' spots (these become increasingly difficult to find, but include mountains, beaches and some parts of the countryside).
- ☞ Increase ventilation at home.
- ☞ Avoid synthetic materials.
- ☞ Stay away from smokers.
- ☞ Carry or wear a silk scarf which you can use to cover your mouth and nose when necessary—cyclists may want to try this.

INDOOR AIR POLLUTION

People are exposed to more potentially harmful pollutants indoors—at home, in the office, and in the car—than outdoors . . . Researchers found average indoor levels for 11 chemicals were 2–5 times higher than the average outdoor concentrations . . . The greatest effect on toxic chemical concentration did not come from living close to a chemical plant but rather the building materials, consumer products, and personal activities of the people living inside the house . . . The worst household dangers identified so far include smoking, living with a smoker, using air fresheners, moth crystals, aerosol sprays and storing paints and solvents.

From a 5-year study by the US Environmental Protection Agency, reported in the *Los Angeles Times*,
9 November 1986

Our increasingly energy-efficient houses are leading to more air pollution because concentrations of gases from building materials and domestic products are allowed to build up to dangerous levels. We also spend an increasing amount of time indoors, some 90–95% on average.

US Army doctors at the Walter Reed Army Institute found that colds and flu are less likely in draughty buildings. They attributed this to a build-up of viruses in well-sealed buildings, but it may be that fresh air is needed to keep our immune systems functioning effectively. Many people find themselves

suffering from regular colds as soon as the central heating is
turned on (and the windows are closed) in the autumn. The
dry, stuffy atmosphere of centrally-heated buildings affects
our respiratory systems and makes us more vulnerable to
whatever viruses are about.

Sick Office Syndrome

Minor health problems are common in modern office buildings, affecting up to 70% of staff. This will come as no
surprise if you work in one of these buildings. A friend told me
that in her office, 'someone is always sick and we all get
headaches—a couple of people are being treated for migraines.'

Symptoms range from headache, especially above the eyes
and at the base of the neck, blocked nose and hayfever to
fatigue and depression. These sometimes disappear when
the employee leaves the building, but may affect the way s/he
feels all the time.

Of course some people's jobs leave them feeling depressed
anyway, but studies have been done between people doing
similar work with the only difference being the type of building
they work in. The reasons for 'sick office syndrome' vary, but
the primary problem seems to be the lack of natural ventilation.
Buildings with airconditioning and centralized heating allow a
build up of various toxic gases in the air. Arbitrary temperature
control is also hard on people, and in many offices it is impossible to open a window or turn a radiator down.

Old photocopying machines give off ozone and many building products give off formaldehyde, a potent allergen. Smoking
bothers most people, and airconditioning systems are excellent
breeding grounds for bacteria and viruses, which are then
dispersed into the air. Biocides used to kill algae in the equipment can be dangerous too.

More subtly, the electromagnetic fields from large amounts
of electronic equipment can affect human perception, and
artificial lighting has a deleterious effect on many people.

Modern offices simply intensify problems which all of us
face in our homes, shops and schools. Recently built colleges
are often similar in design to modern office blocks, and one
wonders whether this is affecting student performance.

Cleaning products

Debra Lynn Dadd has described these as 'among the most
toxic substances encountered in one's everyday environment,

causing health problems ranging from rashes to death'. House-
wives are at risk! While packages often give lengthy warnings
about avoiding ingestion and contact with the skin, they do
not always mention the hazards of breathing the volatile fumes
given off by many products. If chlorine bleach and ammonia,
both extremely common household cleaners, are mixed they
produce a gas which can cause death within minutes.

You can make your own inexpensive cleaning products, or
buy a number of commercial products which are safe for you,
for children and pets, and for the environment.

DIY, hobby and office products

Many of these contain hydrocarbon solvents, which are so
toxic that they can cause death by inhalation. Take great care
when using them, use as little as possible, and choose alternative products when you can.

Your nose is a good guide. As adhesives dry, they out-gas
various chemicals. Sealants which stay soft will continue to do
so for years. Even paint can cause problems for sensitive
people—stay away from new paint or varnish until the smell
has disappeared, or at least keep windows open. In any case,
circulating air speeds drying more effectively than heat.

In general, the best choice is materials which are hard or
which dry hard (brittle rather than soft plastic, for example),
and which have no perceptible smell.

Pesticides

Avoiding chemical insecticides is crucial inside your home.
Indoor plants can be raised organically (see Chapter 13).
'Organic' pest control methods are quite safe, but if you are
spraying with dilute onion juice (for aphids), it is advisable to
move the plants outdoors for treatment!

Don't use fly killers, which contain dichloros, tetramethrin
or d-allethrin. Certain plants repel flies—hang bunches of bay
leaves, mint, pennyroyal or eucalyptus by your doors. Old-
fashioned sticky flypaper is safe and effective, if gruesome.
Make your own by soaking strips of heavy brown paper in a
thick sugar syrup. Let them dry until just sticky to the touch,
then hang in out of the way places. You can put the following
mixture into little cloth bags and hang them over doors: equal
parts of dried and crushed bay leaves, pennyroyal, ground
cloves and eucalyptus leaves, very slightly dampened with

eucalyptus oil. Citrus oil is another repellant and fly swatters are effective.

Moth balls simply add to indoor air pollution. Instead of using them, wash clothes before storage and air regularly. Tumbling in a dryer will kill moth eggs. Put small bags of lavender, rosemary, peppercorns, or cedar chips into drawers with woollens. And see page 232.

Air fresheners

Some commercial preparations disguise bad smells with another strong scent, while others work by coating nasal passages with a fine oil film, or by releasing a chemical which deadens your olfactory nerves. They are potentially dangerous and certainly unnecessary.

Beware of products like the 'pot-pourri' air freshener I saw the other day. The plastic case of pot-pourri decorating the front covered a disc containing p-dichlorobenzene (which mothballs are made of!). When you want to add a pleasant scent to the air, or to disguise the smell of burnt toast or a new puppy, use one of the natural air fresheners suggested on the following pages.

Heating and humidity

Electrical appliances give out no fumes, but they are less effective as a source of domestic energy than gas appliances and there is considerable scientific concern about the effects of living with high levels of electromagnetic radiation.

In a draughtproofed house it is especially important to see that gas and wood fires are properly vented. Gas ranges should burn with a blue flame—if yours has orange flames ask the gas board to come and adjust it—and the kitchen needs a vent or fan to remove combustion byproducts.

The American Lung Association advises against the use of any unvented gas or paraffin heater, and they are illegal in some US states. If you use this form of heat, consider alternatives, and in the meantime ensure that there is plenty of ventilation.

Central heating creates a dry atmosphere—some people have trouble with sore throats when the central heating is switched on, and the low humidity is hard on plants and furniture.

One solution to this problem is a humidifier, but acquiring an energy-hungry appliance to counteract the effects of an unsatisfactory method of heating seems silly. Humidifiers have the same potential for dangerous bacterial growth as airconditioning systems. Combination heating is probably the best solution: using radiant heat sources whenever possible and saving the central heating for very cold weather. A well-insulated house doesn't need a great deal of heating in milder weather, especially if there is a considerable amount of thermal inertia.

Humidity can be increased by keeping bowls of water around (the speed at which they evaporate will give you a clue as to just how dry your home gets) and by having plenty of plants inside (plants suffer as least as much as we do from central heating, but can be arranged in such a way as to add moisture to the air—see below, page 153).

Artificial materials

Many plastics out-gas toxic chemicals. You won't be conscious of this except with something like a brand new shower curtain (if you can smell it, it is out-gassing), but this still adds to the total level of air pollutants.

Synthetic fabrics continually give off fine fibres which go into the air. This has been associated with the rise in juvenile asthma and allergies—perhaps you know someone whose child cannot sleep on synthetic materials.

Needless to say, you are not going to throw away everything you have that is not made of natural materials. But when you next replace your carpets or buy new sheets, air quality is another reason for choosing natural materials.

IMPROVING THE AIR

My grandfather smoked cigars continually, and when he died after 40 years in the same house, my mother wondered how anyone else could possibly live in it, with the odour of his cigars so deeply ingrained in every room. If you've bought a house from a smoker you will know how the smell lingers, and how much work it is to remove the yellow stains on the walls and ceiling. The smell of dogs or cats can be pervasive and intractable too.

Some people live near factories which provide continuous background odour—a sensory pollutant—and the emissions from chemical plants and busy roads are actually dangerous. Most of us do not have such substantial problems to contend with, but we still want to improve the air we breathe at home.

Fresh air and ventilation

In the summer you can throw the windows open, but during the colder months the following ideas are especially important.

☛ Declare your home a no-smoking zone. If you don't feel you can go quite that far, establish that smokers can only use a particular room, and see that it is one which can be aired easily. Some people simply ask that smokers step outside with their cigarettes.

☛ Research into 'sick office syndrome' has found that still air 'feels' stuffy—we need air movement, though we want to avoid direct draughts.

☛ According to the *National Trust Manual of Housekeeping*, still air, like still water, encourages bacterial growth. Open strategic windows for a daily airing. Various essential oils, including lavender and tea tree, are said to have antibacterial properties.

☛ Don't overheat your home. Steady background heat together with specific sources of radiant heat may be the best solution to the problem of stuffiness.

☛ Use bowls of water to humidify the air. If you do this, and keep the temperature moderate, a humidifier will be unnecessary.

Ionisers

Airconditioning and heating systems, cigarette smoke, electronic equipment of all kinds and synthetic carpeting change the balance of ions in the air. Air near running water is refreshing and invigorating in part because of its negative ion charge; a positive charge is associated with increased susceptibility to illness, including hayfever and migraine headaches.

Using fewer electrical appliances and more natural materials in your home, along with good ventilation, may solve part of the problem, but an ioniser, which creates a negative charge in the air, makes a perceptible improvement in the indoor environment for many people.

In offices, they have been found to increase alertness and productivity. People who spend a great deal of time in front of a VDU screen (City traders and journalists as well as secretaries and data-entry clerks) are exposed to some 50 times the positive ion charge of someone who does not use a VDU. The screen repels positively-charged particles onto the face and into the lungs of the user—a likely reason for the increase in bronchial and skin disorders and conjunctivitis amongst VDU operators.

If you use an ioniser, point it at you, as the effect is directional. Turn it off during the day if you use it at night, or vice versa—a change in ion concentration is important for the metabolism. Ionisers are relatively inexpensive and use very little power.

- Ionisation Society, 37 Wentworth Way, St Leonards, East Sussex TN38 OXG, telephone (0424) 432523.
- Wholistic Research Company, Bright Haven, Robin's Lane, Lolworth, Cambridge CB3 8HH, telephone (0954) 81074.
- Medion Limited, 4 Beadles Lane, Old Oxted, Surrey RH8 9HQ, telephone (08833) 2641.

Plants

Plants and vases of flowers give off water and oxygen, so both will improve the air—and fragrant flowers or foliage will add their scent too. The common spider plant (*Chlorophytum*) and golden pothos (*Scindapsus aureus*) are said to absorb indoor toxins, but all plants will improve the quality of the air you breathe.

Plants stay healthier if they are grouped together. This increases the humidity of the air around them, and an easy way to see that their atmosphere stays moist as well as increasing the general level of humidity is to stand them on trays of gravel which you keep topped up with water. The plant pots should not be *in* the water—many plants will die if their roots are waterlogged—but just clear of it.

Scientists are trying to develop special air filtering systems, and suggest that you may one day keep a banana tree on your desk, in a soil bed reactor which can filter smoke and other pollutants from the air.

Natural air fresheners

The best freshener, of course, is fresh air. But throughout history people have used the scents of herbs and flowers to enhance the atmosphere in a room (as well as to disguise unpleasant odours).

Pot-pourri

The word means 'rotten pot', because pot-pourris were originally fermented mixtures of flowers and herbs. The pot-pourri many of us are familiar with is a dry blend based on rose petals and lavender. These look pretty but usually do not have a strong aroma. An occasional stirring releases the fragrance, and adding extra essential oils from time to time will increase their effectiveness. Blends vary, and you can make your own with garden flowers or purchased ingredients.

More potent mixtures are fermented with salt, and need to be kept in covered pot-pourri jars—they smell delightful but are not so attractive.

Pot-pourris do not have to be flowery. A mixture based on spices—cinnamon, cloves, vanilla pods—is an intriguing alternative. There are many books which give recipes, and you can buy ingredients from herbalists.

● Culpeper Ltd, Hadstock Road, Linton, Cambs CB1 6NJ, telephone (0223) 891196. Sell herbs and flowers through their retail shops and by mail order. Ask for their leaflet 'Making Your Own Pot-pourri'.

Cooking

Baking bread will make everyone think your home is the nicest place in the world. Freshly ground coffee is nearly as good.

A fast trick, which smells delightful and is useful if you've

just burned something in the kitchen, is to boil a few pieces of
orange or lemon rind in a small saucepan of water. Cinnamon
and cloves work equally well.

Essential oils

If I were sitting by the sea on Sark, I would not be sniffing
bottles of essential oils. As it is, I work in the basement of a
London flat and find they give me a decided, and safe, lift.
Essential oils are the distilled essence of plants and flowers—
they are also, as far as many people are concerned, quite
essential!

You'll find these little bottles of scent remarkably useful
around the house. Find the oils which suit you and your
needs, as well as your different moods. Add some to homemade cleaning products or a simple vinegar hair rinse. Put 10-
20 drops of pine or rosemary oil in a bath, a few drops of
cinnamon oil on a lightbulb to make a room smell like you've
been baking, or sprinkle a few drops of lavender oil on a piece
of cotton wool to freshen the bathroom.

A word of warning, however—be careful about what you
buy. The scented oils sold by the Body Shop, for example,
contain synthetic essences in addition to natural ones,
and their 'aromatherapy' oils are diluted in soyabean oil,
making them quite expensive compared with pure essential
oils.

● Neal's Yard Apothecary, 2 Neal's Yard, London WC2H
  9DP, telephone 01-379 7222. Herbs, oils, homoeopathic
  preparations and toiletries packaged in returnable blue glass
  bottles. Also mail order.

Aromatherapy

Aromatherapy uses essential oils to treat the skin, the whole
body and the emotions. The study is an ancient one. You may
want to consult a professional aromatherapist, but essential
oils can be used by anyone and you'll find several useful books
listed below.

You may find it easier to say that you simply like a scent
than to believe that it could lift your depression. We all have
favourite smells. If you can go to a shop which sells essential
oils, you can sniff test several dozen and start a collection.

The oils can be used in small pottery burners—the natural
alternative to chemical air fresheners. Some scents—ginger

and patchouli for example—are said to have aphrodisiacal properties, so you might keep those in the bedroom.

● *Aromatherapy, An A-Z*, Patricia Davis (C. W. Daniel, 1988).
● *The Art of Aromatherapy*, Robert Tisserand (C. W. Daniel, 1977).
● *Practical Aromatherapy*, Shirley Price (Thorsons, 1984).

Encourage your nose

After you've got rid of unpleasant or noxious odours, encourage your nose with good things to smell.

Perhaps as our food has lost its taste, our noses have lost some of their acuity. As you eliminate harsh chemical and artificially-scented products from your life, you may find that your nose becomes much more sensitive.

Modern hybrid flowers rarely have the rich smells of their predecessors. In fact, it is quite possible to raise a garden full of flowers which have no smell at all.

Grow a scented garden, concentrating on old-fashioned roses, night-scented stock, and so on. In fact, put scented plants in raised beds or near seats in your garden. Some municipal parks have put in gardens for the handicapped, beds raised to wheelchair level, with interesting leaves and fragrant flowers for the blind. There is no reason why the rest of us cannot benefit from this use of our senses, too.

Herbs have aromatic leaves. Plant them where you will brush against them or where you can run your hand over them. In John Aubrey's *Brief Lives*, he mentions how 'Sir John Danvers, being my Relation and faithfull Friend, was wont in fair mornings in the Summer to brush his Beaver-hatt on the Hysop and Thyme, which did perfume it with its natural Spirit; and would last a morning or longer.'

8
WATER

We came from the water; our bodies are largely water; and water plays a fundamental role in our psychology. We need constant access to water, all around us; and we cannot have it without reverence for water in all its forms.

Christopher Alexander *et al.*
A Pattern Language, 1977

The Beach Boys sang 'Don't go near the water, don't you think it's sad? Don't go near the water, our water's turning bad', and it is a tragedy of modern life that not only are most of us cut off from the sources of our water, but we pollute them individually and corporately in such a way that clean, fresh water is almost entirely a thing of the past.

Our earth is the water planet, with some 75% of its surface covered by water. Human beings are largely made of water too, as any schoolchild should be able to explain. A drink of water can be an exquisite pleasure—after a hard game of football or a long run or a walk in the mountains when you

finally find a small stream and kneel to drink from cupped hands.

While rivers, lakes and oceans have been dumping grounds for millenia, when the world's population was smaller and the types of waste less toxic, the water—full of animals, plants and bacteria—was able to render it harmless. Much modern waste, however, is not only non-biodegradable but highly toxic, and the ocean's natural cycles cannot clean it up.

Industrial chemicals, toxic materials of all sorts, oil and even nuclear waste is ignominiously dumped into our streams and rivers, and into the sea. In *No Immediate Danger*, Rosalie Bertell describes the US dumping of radioactive nuclear wastes off the American coasts, which went on for some 25 years after th end of World War II. When canisters failed to sink, sailors shot holes in them. Some were dropped into the San Francisco Bay because seas were rough. A study estimated that 36% of the nuclear waste drums were damaged.

Accidental spills of sulphuric acid (Cumbria, April 1988) and other chemicals wreak havoc on water life. Oil spills at sea are common, and it is thought that some 5 tons of highly toxic polychlorinated biphenyls, PCBs, were released into the North Sea when the Piper Alpha oil platform exploded in 1988.

Few people see any connection between what they pour down the drain or flush down the toilet and reports of animal deaths on the news, let alone the water they drink the next week! Yet we all contribute to the pollution of the earth's water—and our own water supplies.

WATER POLLUTION

In many areas, people can tell that there is something wrong with their water by the fact that it smells and tastes so bad. But most of the 700 or so known chemical contaminants in public drinking water are not detectable to the nose or eye or taste buds. Just because your water looks all right doesn't mean that it is good for you. The following is a summary of the major problems facing our water supplies.

Fertilizers

Nitrate fertilizers are probably the most serious threat: 3 million tons are used in the UK every year. Of this, approximately half is taken up by the crops (there are increasingly high levels of nitrates in agricultural produce), and the remainder is washed out of the soil, into our water.

In rivers and lakes nitrates contribute to excessive algae growth, which tends to choke other plant and animal life. The nitrates slowly seep into deep boreholes and formerly pure groundwater, and there is widespread concern because even now a third of British water supplies contain higher nitrate levels than the EEC maximum recommended limit.

The nitrates in the water we are drinking was probably applied to the land 20-40 years ago. Since nitrate use has been increasing since the '60s, we can expect the problem of nitrate contamination to become worse, even if we drastically cut their use now.

In the body, nitrates are reduced to nitrite (which is also used as a preservative in meats) and nitrosamines, which have been strongly implicated in stomach and oesophageal cancer. They are especially dangerous for babies because they are thought to cause the potentially fatal 'blue baby syndrome'. In spite of this, our government has fought the EEC regulations, and is only slowly facing the long-term health threat posed by nitrates.

Another worry is that water which contains a high level of

nitrates is almost certain to contain agricultural pesticides as well.

Pesticides

If you consider the vast amounts of toxic chemicals which are used each year to kill insects and weeds, it is not surprising that a substantial amount should reach us via our water supplies. A switch to organic farming methods will cut pesticide use, and in the meantime we can have little choice but to drink whatever happens to be in our tapwater. Some filtration systems, however, will remove a high percentage of pesticides from drinking water (see p 166).

Slurry

Perhaps you had a grandfather who used to race out into the street if a horse had left a sign of its passing. He was right, of course, and even gardeners who use considerable amounts of chemicals realise the benefits of old-fashioned manure. Getting hold of it is the town gardener's biggest headache.

Modern farming is usually done on a single crop basis: pigs or wheat or rape or potatoes. This does not lend itself to ecological farming practices—on a traditional mixed farm animals grazed on rough grass and ate plant stalks, while providing fertilizer for the next crop.

Intensively-reared, factory-farmed animals—pigs and cattle, as well as chickens—produce manure, but it is frequently treated as a disposal problem instead of as a rich source of fertilizer, and the waste slurry can contaminate water supplies. Routinely administered antibiotics also enter the soil and water in this way.

Detergents

Detergents are made from petrochemicals, and have a number of serious effects on the environment. As you'll see in Chapter 10, 'The Non-Toxic Home', eliminating them from your home—or at least making a big reduction in the amounts you use—is one of the basic steps of *Home Ecology*.

'Eutrophication' is a daunting word which is used a lot when talking about water pollution. It simply means 'to become rich in food', but is having disastrous effects on water life. When the water in a lake or stream becomes too rich, thanks to our input of phosphates from detergents and nitrates from fertilizers, there is excessive growth of algae, and other forms of water life, including fish, die.

Switzerland has banned phosphates because of concern about their lakes, and other countries should follow suit. Do switch to biodegradable cleaning products. You can make your own, and there are several excellent commercial ranges available.

Chlorine

The most obvious characteristic of modern tap water is the smell of chlorine, which is unpleasant at best. Some people have allergic reactions to it. Far worse, chlorine combines with with the natural acids in water from peaty soil and decomposing vegetable matter (leaves, for example) to form chloroform, a toxic compound.

It has been known for some years that there are significantly higher death rates from gastrointestinal and urinary tract cancers amongst people drinking chlorinated water, and water authorities are finally looking for new ways of eliminating bacteria.

Aluminium

Aluminium sulphate is added in huge quantities (100,000 tonnes a year, at a cost of £7 million) to UK water supplies, to settle out solid impurities such as dissolved peat. Acid rain caused by pollution has increased the amount of aluminium in our water too, because it dissolves the otherwise inert and harmless aluminium found in certain soils. Aluminium is implicated in senile dementia or Alzheimer's Disease, and experts recommend that we all cut down on the amount we ingest. Its effect is cumulative and long-term, unlike lead which affects brain development in a relatively short period of time.

Fluoride

Fluoride has been called 'the greatest medical fraud of the century', but is added to a number of public water supplies. Studies around the world link fluoride with cancer and genetic damage, and more and more countries are restricting its use. This problem is discussed on page 336, and you can contact the National Anti-Fluoridation Campaign for further information.

Plumbing

Most people know that lead water pipes are common in homes built before 1900, and many of these pipes have been replaced. Unfortunately, however, the joints in our new copper pipes are sealed with lead solder (as are tin cans), and are therefore a source of lead.

A 1981 Water Research Council report advised against the use of lead solder for pipes carrying drinking water. At present, the alternatives are mechanical rather than soldered fittings, or a special 95/5 solder (made for heating systems) which contains only a tenth as much lead as the standard 50/50 solder.

The leaching of lead into water is accelerated by the presence of chlorine and other chemicals. Soft water will dissolve more heavy metals than will hard water, and hot water more than cold.

Researchers suggest that you flush the toilet or let the water run for several minutes first thing in the morning, and use only cold water for drinking and cooking.

Water can also be contaminated by polyvinyl chloride (PVC) pipes. Vinyl chloride, which they contain, is a potent carcinogen, and Debra Lynn Dadd mentions that 'a 1980 study sponsored by the California Health Services Department showed that a wide variety of toxic and carcinogenic substances leach from the pipes into the water' (*Nontoxic and Natural*, p 209). Once again, use cold water for cooking and drinking, and let water run for a little while first thing in the morning.

Toxic chemicals

The waste from manufacturing products is often disposed of by pumping it into the nearest river or ocean. Major aquifers are now contaminated by effluents from industrial waste, and these problems have led to legislation about dumping and landfill in some industrialised countries, particularly the United States, and precipitated the new international market in domestic and industrial waste.

Waste disposal is a growing problem, and according to the authors of *Well Body, Well Earth*, 'Solid-waste disposal sites are the single most important source of groundwater contamination.' We are inevitably going to have to put our house in order, by cutting the quantities of waste we generate and by finding new ways of dealing with what is left.

Toxic chemicals get into our water in other ways, too. In

San Jose, California, there was a sudden increase in the number of miscarriages and birth defects in a small area, and residents eventually discovered that the water supply to their homes had been contaminated by leakage from underground chemical storage tanks. What made this particular alarming is that the area, the 'Silicon Valley', is known for its clean industry—there is no smoke belching into the sky from semiconductor plants. The leaked chemicals were trichloroethane (TCA) and dichloroethylene (DCE)—mutagens and suspected carcinogens—which are used as solvents to remove grease from computer microchips.

Similar leakage from underground petrol storage tanks is not uncommon, and in the same area some residents need filters to remove petrol from their drinking water.

Drugs

There have been questions raised about the danger of cytotoxic cancer drugs reaching our water supply through patients' urine and excreta. Although this fear is countered by claiming that 'treatment and dispersal would reduce even large quantities of the drugs to below detectable amounts' and that we can therefore 'assume there was no risk' (*The Independent*, 14 April 1988), the quantities of chemicals or drugs which pose a risk to human health depends on individual tolerances, and studies of risk differ a great deal. And we don't know about the effects of even minute quantities of hazardous drugs in combination.

The drugs all of us consume are eventually excreted and flushed away, and the Women's Environmental Network is concerned about water supplies being polluted with oestrogen, a human hormone, from birth control pills. This is a long-term problem which needs to be taken into account when planning water processing facilities, and when prescribing or taking drugs.

Sewage

In the past, human waste was garnered by farmers as carefully as animal waste. The soil produced food, and everything was returned to it in a beneficial and sustainable system. But as people have moved into cities, this material has become a disposal problem instead of a recycling material.

In towns and cities there is not much alternative to a

centralized system, but this could be designed to make use of waste rather than treat it as a nuisance. One advantage to a centralized system is that sewage can also be used to produce energy in the form of methane gas.

Composting at source is an even better choice because pipes and tanks and transport are unnecessary. Anyone with land can use one of the modern composting systems (instead of a septic tank, if that's what you have now) which use both kitchen/household scraps and toilet waste to make a rich, safe fertilizer. The Centre for Alternative Technology in Powys can provide information.

You may feel squeamish about this, but then you probably don't want to know just where the water which went into your tea this morning came from!

In dry climates, low-water toilets and cutting down on bulk water use is important not only to environmentalists but to every citizen.

Britain's beaches

Many of our beaches would be shut down as unsafe if they were in another country: according to Greenpeace, 'tests in Blackpool have shown a concentration of bacteria and viruses from sewage in the sea-water FIFTY times above the safety limits set by Canadian public health authorities.'

Raw, untreated sewage is sometimes piped straight from sewers into the sea near bathing beaches.

Even worse, UK regulations allow toxic industrial wastes to be discharged into the same sewers as domestic sewage (which could otherwise be treated and used as a valuable fertilizer). Contaminated sewage sludge, containing such things as cadmium and mercury, lindane and DDT, has been associated with the deaths of seabirds in the Thames estuary and Greenpeace says that London sewage is a likely contributor to the deaths of thousands of seals in the North Sea.

They suggest a three point clean-up plan: (1) all British beaches to be brought up to EEC standards immediately; (2) human waste should be treated and used as fertilizer; and (3) industry must be required to deal with its own waste.

WATER CONSERVATION

Conserving water in Britain? What a nutty idea! But it only seems that way because we equate the water which pours from the sky with the water which comes from the tap. The former is an abundant natural resource, whereas the latter has undergone considerable processing, with a wide range of ecological and environmental consequences.

In *Blueprint for a Green Planet* (Dorling Kindersley, 1987), John Seymour and Herbert Girardet point out the ways in which we affect the earth's natural water cycles. Water comes from rivers, reservoirs, and from deep underground aquifers. Valleys are flooded and villages and woods are lost in order to make reservoirs to supply our drinking water. The lowering of the water table is a problem even in Britain (and a serious one in many other parts of the world).

It's not a pleasant thought, but much of the water we drink has been reprocessed from effluent, the water and sewage we use and send down the drain. All our water, not just the water we drink or bathe in, is expensively purified, and questionable chemicals are added to it in the process.

Seymour and Girardet suggest that the present one pipe system should be replaced with a dual water system (this may not be as expensive as it sounds, because many British water systems are due for renewal). Drinking and washing water would come from underground boreholes and springs, and would not need the addition of chlorine. It would taste good! All other water, for industrial use, watering the garden, washing the car and flushing the toilet, would get a minimal filtering.

This is one possible solution, and worth keeping in mind. In the meantime, as we have to make do with an inefficient and potentially hazardous sytem, let's think about the ways in which we can use water wisely, both for our health and for the health of the environment.

Easy water savings
- ☛ Turn off taps.
- ☛ Stop leaks.
- ☛ Adjust toilet to take less water on each flush (the arm of the float can be bent, or you can put a couple bricks or a plastic bag full of water into the tank).
- ☛ Have showers instead of baths.
- ☛ Run the washing machine with a full load.
- ☛ Wash dishes by hand.
- ☛ Save rainwater and use it in the garden or to wash the car—or

bicycle. The easiest way is to run water from gutters into a barrel or water butt, which must be carefully covered to prevent animals or children going for a dive.
☛ Use plants which don't need to be watered frequently.
☛ Don't water outside during the heat of the day, when the water will evaporate. Occasional deep soakings, rather than frequent sprinkles, save work and water. A mulch will cut watering to a minimum.

WHAT TO DO

Drinking water

Anyone who has been on a diet will know that the standard advice is to drink lots of water because it fills you up and flushes you out. Eight glasses a day is a suggested target. That's about 3 pints. How much do you drink?

Bottled waters can be delightful, but they are bad news, ecologically: to package and transport water around the world is wasteful and should be unnecessary. I remember ordering a bottle of Perrier in a Sydney bar, and thinking how strange it was to be drinking a mineral water which is fashionable in California, and on every supermarket shelf in Britain.

Water bottled in plastic absorbs a certain quantity of possibly carcinogenic polymers and it is preferable to choose glass bottles (take them, minus metal neck rings, to the bottle bank) when you buy mineral water. A local source of fresh spring water in returnable bottles would be a good alternative.

Water filters

For many of us, there is little choice at present but to filter our drinking water if we are concerned about its quality. This does not remove all impurities, but gives a safer, more palatable beverage at a reasonable price.

There are a number of filtration systems on the market. The cheapest is a plastic jug which holds a disposable filter. These are easy to use and moderately effective, but less than ideal because of the plastic and the disposal filters (you need at least one a month, and probably more, as they are dangerous if over-used, releasing the filtered heavy metals and other pollutants back into the water).

If you are keen to ensure that most significant contaminants have been removed from your drinking water, you will be better off with one of the plumbed-in systems, which are expensive initially but cheaper in the long run, and have fewer disposable parts. Effectiveness, and the chemicals and pollutants which each type removes, varies a great deal. There are three basic methods of filtration, and the appropriate type depends on your water supply.

1 *Activated carbon* is inexpensive and removes chlorine, pesticides and organic chemicals, but not fluoride or nitrates. A carbon block filter may also remove heavy metals. Choose a granulated rather than powdered carbon filter as it is less prone to bacterial growth.

2 *Reverse osmosis* (R/O) uses a fine cellulose or plastic membrane to filter water under pressure, and removes asbestos, bacteria and viruses, fluoride, aluminium, heavy metals, minerals, salts and nitrates. R/O removes all minerals, even desirable ones like calcium and magnesium (which contribute to the pleasant taste of a good mineral water), and the output water is said to be very acid.

3 *Distillation* is promoted as being 'closest to nature' because rainwater, too, is distilled. The natural water we would drink by choice, however, is spring water, which is filtered through many layers of rock, absorbing valuable minerals, and flavour. Distilled water is pure but insipid, requires a great deal of energy to produce (6p worth of electricity per litre) and is slow. On the other hand, distillation is extremely effective at removing contaminants, although care has to be taken to ensure that volatile organic chemicals are not condensed along with the steam.

The purest water comes either from a distiller or from a reverse osmosis unit used in conjunction with a carbon pre-filter. The Green Farm Nutrition Centre sells expensive but carefully researched equipment by post (for address, see page 259), and magazines like *Here's Health* and *Environment Now* have advertisements for various systems.

You should get an analysis of your local water supply from the water authority before deciding on a system, and insist on having laboratory test results from any supplier (especially if you are buying one of the more expensive systems). Enquire about how best to avoid bacterial growth in the filter—the most important thing is to change the cartridge as directed. As public concern about our water supply increases, unscrupulous manufacturers are bound to get into the filter market. They can easily make unsubstantiated claims, especially as there are no British Standards for this product.

The Water Authorities Association discourages the use of home water filters, claiming that they are dangerous because there is a possibility of bacterial growth and insisting that the 'standard of public water supplies in England and Wales is high and becoming higher', although they admit nitrates are a growing problem which requires government action.

Water softening

Calcium and magnesium salts make water hard. They can also make it taste good, and provide minerals. But it is more difficult to get lather in hard water and the limescale deposits in your kettle make it less efficient. The scum on tea is not dangerous, but it isn't very pleasant either. If you use a mechanical water softener, try to have it plumbed to the hot water supply. You should not drink softened water because of its high sodium content.

Cold showers

Filtering the entire water supply to our homes would be very expensive, but some researchers believe that 50-60% of soluble contaminants that we absorb enter the body through the skin while bathing.

A report on the American Chemical Society's 192nd national meeting explained:

> Julian B. Andelman, professor of water chemistry at the University of Pittsburgh, found less chemical exposure from drinking contaminated water than in using it to wash the clothes or take a shower.
>
> Experimenting with a model shower and common water pollutants, Andelman found that the toxic chemicals evaporated—or volatilized—into the surrounding air. Increased concentrations of the chemicals build up in the shower and spread through the home, he said.
>
> The amount of the chemicals that vaporizes increases with longer and hotter showers, the scientists found.

"I tell my friends to take quick, cold showers,"
Andelman said.

Los Angeles Times,
11 September 1986

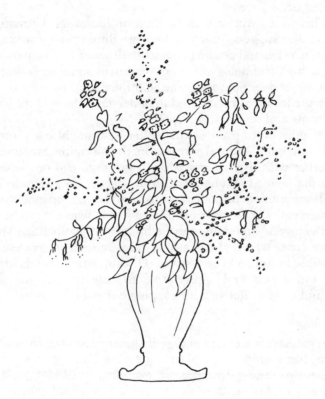

HEALING WATER

The simplest water therapy is swimming—preferably in the
open air in unchlorinated ocean or lake water. Swimming is
the exercise or sport invariably suggested for people who are
unfit, overweight, have bad backs or are pregnant, because it
gives great health benefits without putting strain on the
body.

Open water

Over the past century or so, natural sources of water have
been covered over and lost to us, in order to fit the exigencies
of 'rational' town planning. In London, where even the

Thames is only visible at a distance, dozens of smaller rivers have been routed underground (the Fleet gave its name to Fleet Street). Indoor swimming pools are heavily chlorinated and lit by fluorescent lights, and even the ponds in parks are fenced off.

This is a pity, and in *A Pattern Language* Christopher Alexander suggests that 'our lives are diminished if we cannot establish rich and abiding contact with water . . . as marvelous as the high technology of water treatment and distribution has become, it does not satisfy the emotional need to make contact with the local reservoirs, and to understand the cycle of water: its limits and its mystery.' (p 324).

He goes on to propose that water be brought back into the environment: 'Natural streams in their original streambeds, together with their surrounding vegetation, can be preserved and maintained. Rainwater can be allowed to assemble from rooftops into small pools and to run through channels along garden paths and public pedestrian paths, where it can be seen and enjoyed. Fountains can be built in public places. And in those cities where streams have been buried, it may even be possible to unravel them again.' Of course this sounds idealistic, but a new and appreciative attitude towards the water around us is a vital step in stopping our pollution of it.

Bathing

You can save water and energy by having a shower instead of a bath, but bathing has a place in our lives, too.

Consider the bath a sensual experience—ideally one to be shared. In Japan, the bathing room is a social centre. You wash in a small bucket of water, and get into a large communal bath of hot water to soak and relax.

In *A Pattern Language*, Alexander *et al.* suggest that rather than having several small and separate bathrooms, we design our homes to incorporate a single large bathroom designed for joint bathing. This would fit beautifully into an ecological home: with biodegradable soap and shampoo, the used water could go to the garden.

Kneipp therapy

Leslie Kenton gives a fascinating introduction to Kneipp therapy in her book *Ageless Ageing*. She explains that on the continent a large number of spas use water therapies developed in the last century by a Bavarian priest named Sebastian Kneipp (who is said to have cured himself of tuberculosis) to treat a wide range of ailments. The techniques include walking barefoot in wet grass or snow, and using alternating warm and cold showers sprays on various parts of the body.

Instead of cosseting ourselves and being afraid of cold water, we might start appreciating its restorative qualities. It seems that the shock of switching from warm to cold water strengthens the immune system. As an experiment, soak your feet in a basin of warm water, put them under a cold tap, then back into the warm water. This feels wonderful after a hard day at work.

Once again, water is seen to have healing, restorative qualities which are totally ignored by our current way of thinking about it. For more about this method of using water, see Chapter 22 in Kenton's book.

Looking ahead

Water authorities acknowledge that substantial improvements to our present water systems are needed to provide Britons with clean, safe, and palatable water now and in the next century. This will entail substantial costs, but we must do something now, if we want to continue to drink the water which comes from our taps. Otherwise, one prediction suggests that ¾ of the water in the UK will be unfit for human consumption by the year 2000 simply because of excessive nitrates.

There are no easy answers, and public resistance to paying more for something which we think should be free as air (and even clean air has its costs, these days) may make change difficult. The Government's plans for privatizing the water industry have focussed attention on the substantial problems of cleaning it up. These include nitrates, pesticides, pollution from sewage works, and treatment with aluminium and chlorine.

Filtering our water and using biodegradable washing powder are important steps to take, but in the longer term we need to entirely reassess our attitude to water and make substantial changes in the way it is used to fulfill our needs (including the needs of industry) without damaging the environment and adversely affecting human health.

9
HEALTH

The best measure we have for designing our future is human
health. It is here that we feel the greatest urgency to solve
problems of environmental pollution, and it is here that the
consequences of our actions are most dramatically demonstrated.
Mike Samuels MD and Hal Zina Bennett
Well Body, Well Earth, 1983

Our health provides a guide to the state of the environment we
live in, and health is an essential prerequisite to change because,
as Michel Odent writes in *Primal Health*, 'Only healthy people
can be conscious of the long-term consequences of their actions
and decisions; only healthy people can tackle the real priorities.'
He also makes a point which has profound implications for

172

anyone concerned about ecology, that the 'destruction of our planet which we are now witnessing can only be the work of a sick man.' Carol Venolia, architect and author of *Healing Environments*, writes, 'I believe that the planet cannot be healed by people who are not healing themselves. It starts with us. The self-determination you gain by increasing your awareness of your surroundings and enlivening them can eventually play out into global healing.'

Looking at our health is a way of deciding what specific things we want to change about the way we live. (Other chapters in *Home Ecology* discuss particular aspects of this.) Deciding that we want to improve our health changes our priorities—about radiation dangers, air pollution and the pesticides in modern agriculture.

Health is also influenced by social patterns: the hopelessness of long-term unemployment and the helplessness of an abused child are examples of problems which have to be dealt with. The way we care for each other, for babies and for the dying, affects the health of the society we live in.

We can look, too, at the health of the planet. Dying seals in the North Sea, acid rain damage to European forests and lakes, and the algae blooms which kill fish in the sea are evidence of our interconnected health, since human activity is causing these disasters. We prey on our environment—quite literally biting the hand that feeds us.

What is health?

If you go for a physical examination—perhaps for a new job—and get 'a clean bill of health', you may still have bad breath, flat feet, and suffer from indigestion. Health has come to mean merely the absence of an obviously debilitating 'disease'—although when we read about 'health and fitness' we have other things in mind: good diet, exercise and so on.

Think of words which describe the attributes of someone who is really healthy. Vitality, vigour, energy, enthusiasm, radiance, equanimity, confidence, adaptability and humour are some which come to mind. Health *is* fitness—fitness for the things we want to do, for growth and development and pleasure.

The doctors who ran the Pioneer Health Centre during the 1940s distinguished between 'dis-ease' and disorder. 'Dis-ease' was a state in which the member was actually conscious of a problem—but only about half of these people consulted a doctor—and they therefore found that the patient is the 'primary diagnostician of sickness'. While some people run to the doctor at the first sign of a sniffle, others stoically suffer pain and discomfort, and are limited in their daily activities by health problems.

The tribulations of the National Health Service (NHS) receive a good deal of publicity, and it is clear that people want to feel that they can depend on access to medical care. But has the NHS actually promoted health in its 40 years on the job, and can increasing expenditure make us healthy? Jonathan Porritt notes that since the NHS's success is judged in terms of the number of people treated for illness, the goal is apparently to make everyone a patient. The medical profession doesn't win praise for the people it does not need to treat.

Ecological perspectives

Human beings (and all living things) have evolved over millenia to live in a certain physical and social environment. The rapid technological changes of the past century have put us in a vulnerable position, because physically we are no different from early hunter-gatherers, whose way of life was vastly different from our own.

Our bodies need uncontaminated food, clean water and sweet air, seasons of light and dark, a supportive and stable social environment. When we ignore these simple requirements our health will suffer because our minds and bodies are being put under an impossible strain.

Allergies and food sensitivities are on the increase, heart disease and cancer are the so-called diseases of civilization, and most of us suffer from minor complaints which interfere to a greater or lesser degree with what we would like to do in our lives. Unfortunately, the assumption is that if something—say, petrochemical products or the chlorine in tap water—doesn't make us overtly ill, it must be okay. This ignores the subtle effects that these things, low level radiation or traces of toxic chemicals, can have on us.

A feeling of powerlessness leads to a weakening of the immune system, the body's ability to cope with threats to health. When we feel that there is nothing we can do to help ourselves, a physical crisis can ensue. In evolutionary terms, this will eventually lead to new ways of coping with the threat, but in the meantime deteriorating health is unavoidable.

Modern attitudes

Although there is a great deal of interest in 'health and fitness' these days, being healthy isn't necessarily fashionable, and we may feel that real vitality is the prerogative of a few lithe, young creatures in fluorescent-coloured training clothes.

Do you get pleasure out of complaining about your aches and pains, about how you are working long hours, smoking too much, not getting enough exercise? Some people don't use a bicycle because they are embarrassed about going out on one, afraid they'll look awkward or silly, or because they worry about what the neighbours—or the children—will think.

Our lives are cushioned, cocooned and sheltered in a way which our ancestors would not have been able to imagine. Fewer children die in infancy as a result, but as we grow up we lose out in becoming alienated from our bodies, as Dervla Murphy reflects:

. . . the machine-age has dangerously deprived Western man of whole areas of experience that until recently were common to the entire human race. Too many of us are now cut off from the basic sensual gratifications of resting after violent exercise, finding relief from extremes of heat or cold, eating when ravenously hungry and drinking when the ache of thirst makes water seem the most precious of God's creations. *In Ethiopia with a Mule* (John Murray, 1968), p 50.

The availability of medical attention (at no cost, in Britain) and the overwhelming demands of modern life mean that many people abdicate all responsibility for their own health, and indeed become career patients. They want access to medication and high-tech medical care in emergencies, and ignore the other indignities which come with health problems—the irritating morning cough and the breathlessness after climbing a few flights of stairs, for example, which plague many smokers.

Some three-quarters of our illnesses are caused by the way we live. Circumstances like poverty and homelessness adversely affect health, but so do many things over which we have considerable control, like what we eat and how much exercise we get. In *The Road to Wigan Pier*, George Orwell noted that the poor *wanted* bread and jam with sweet tea instead of healthier fare. We do not have to be nutritional victims, but on the other hand social change is sometimes a prerequisite for healthier choices.

Illness has become something to conquer (advertisements for aspirin talk about 'hitting back at pain') with an instant remedy, so it doesn't interfere with our busy lives. We treat the body as a machine, which needs an occasional oiling and maybe a replacement part now and then, instead of as a complex and self-sustaining system.

An entirely different approach, taken by most alternative practitioners, is to see illness as a *positive* thing because it tells us something is wrong. Fatigue is a sign that your body (and maybe your mind) needs a rest. Indigestion is a request for a change of diet. A chronically stiff neck tells you that you are tense, or that you're spending too much time hunched over your desk.

Clinical ecologists point out that disease (eczema, for example) is not the primary event, and look to the cause (perhaps a sensitivity to milk) and try to treat that.

The connection between the mind and body cannot be underestimated either. Continual colds may mean that you aren't eating well and your immune system isn't in top form as a result, but they may also be a way of avoiding a job you don't like, a way of asking for sympathy and support from those around you. Headaches and back pain are frequently related to stress or emotional problems.

Getting well naturally demands action from us, and cultivating our natural heritage of health is a personal responsibility, and decision.

Drugs

The pharmaceutical industry and the medical profession have disturbingly close links. Magazines aimed at GPs have pages and pages of advertisements for pharmaceutical products, and all drug companies have reps who try to convince doctors to use their brands. It is estimated that the industry spends an astonishing £30,000 per GP each year, promoting its products (*Blueprint for a Green Planet*, p. 109). GPs get all this attention because they write three-quarters of the annual 400,000,000 prescriptions.

Some £2,000 million is spent on drugs every year (£70,000 per GP)—12.5% of the NHS budget. The percentage is gradually rising. Britons are taking five times more prescription drugs than they were when the NHS was established in 1949. Are we five times as healthy? Britain has one of the highest rates of heart disease in the world. What a scandal for the NHS, and for all of us.

Doctors claim that patients demand a prescription and they sometimes write one on the assumption that taking something—or anything—will make the patient feel better. (There have been fascinating studies done on the effects of placebos, where patients are given plain sugar tablets but told that they are drugs. The placebos often have the same success rate as the drug!)

Patients, on the other hand, often feel frustrated when the doctor pulls out the prescription pad as soon as they begin to describe their symptoms.

Drugs are powerful chemicals, and have side effects which are not often enough taken in account. (Thalidomide is an infamous example, a drug which was given to relieve nausea in early pregnancy and which caused gross deformities in many babies before being banned.) New government legislation will require doctors to inform patients about possible side effects when they prescribe a drug, but some doctors feel that this would unnecessarily alarm people and interfere with the trust a patient should feel for his or her doctor. What it will require is greater patient involvement in treatment, more time spent discussing alternatives, and quite possibly a reduction in the quantity of drugs we take. Many patients, as well as doctors, won't like the idea!

Even alternative remedies can be used irresponsibly because of our desire for instant relief without responsibility. I have seen the mothers of young children handing out tiny homoeopathic pills for everything from whinging ('he must be teething') to a bruised knee ('arnica for shock'). This is the nutritional equivalent of polo mints because the pills are almost entirely sugar, but a potent lesson is being given.

Vitamin pills can be used irresponsibly, too, and substituted for positive changes in the way we eat.

IMMUNITY

Health, or even the absence of disease, does not depend on an absence of germs. Germs are simply types of bacteria, viruses, fungi and protozoa, which are with us all the time and some of which we *need* (bacteria in our digestive tract help to digest food, and organisms on our skin protect us from potentially harmful bacteria). A strong immune system is what will keep you well, not a sterile environment.

Michel Odent suggests that health is a capacity for adaptation, and without both bacteria and stress we become incapable of adapting to new stimuli and new challenges—physically and mentally. Resistance to disease is a natural phenomenon, not a result of vaccination (though vaccination attempts to encourage the body's natural defences). This is easy to see if we just think of the common cold. I'll bet you know someone who suffers from colds and flu nearly all the time, while another friend is smug because s/he hasn't missed a day's work for years.

'Good health', writes Carol Venolia, 'means having the flexibility and the inner resources to respond to both assaults and opportunities.' (*Healing Environments*, p 7). Diet, exercise, mental attitude, happiness at home and work are all involved in whether or not we get ill. Think about the times you have been sick recently, and whether this has coincided with special pressure at work, or coming back from holiday, or a time when you'd been living on hamburgers and diet cola. (The last couple of years I've fallen sick at Christmas, which tells me something about preparing for the holidays next time they come round.)

The plight of seals in the North Sea has important lessons for human beings. Like us, seals eat at the top of the food chain, and industrial pollutants like PCBs concentrate in their body fat. The poisons are released when they are under particular stress, when breeding and giving birth for example, depressing their immune systems and making them vulnerable to a deadly virus. Analysis showed 5,000 different man-made toxic chemicals in the fat of dead seals!

Some of the research into AIDS—the Acquired Immune Deficiency Syndrome—is coming up with interesting information about the role of the immune system in human health and disease. Instead of concentrating on developing drugs, we can concentrate on strengthening our natural resistance. Enormous sums have been spent trying to find a 'cure' for cancer, while methods of treatment which concentrate on restoring the body's natural defences receive relatively little attention.

Cancer is a prime example of the neglect of basic preventative care, even though it is commonly agreed that some three-quarters of all cancer is caused by food, smoke and chemicals. Substances which have been shown to cause cancer in laboratory animals can be detoxified by enzymes in healthy human cells.

By cleaning up our environment, in the home and outside, and by concentrating on building up our health, we could eliminate the majority of cancers without any more research, without any need to find a 'cure'.

Even animals get heart disease in stressful situations, and while every life is bound to have its share of difficulties and grief, the way we deal with painful situations has an important impact on our immune systems, and on whether we or not we get ill. How do you cope with disappointment or loss? A desire to improve our health requires some thought about the social support network we have available—and about how willing we are to offer support to friends in need.

● *Maximum Immunity*, Michael A Weiner (Gateway Books, 1986).
● *How to Fortify Your Immune System*, Donald Dickenson (Arlington Books, 1984).

ENVIRONMENT

Unhealthy living

Although it is often difficult to connect specific aspects of the way we live with a particular health problem, there are many aspects of modern life which affect our state of health.

The amount of time we spend indoors under artificial lighting, in sealed buildings, uncomfortable seating, a long and stressful commute to your job, electrical wiring and appliances, soulless architecture and traffic noise all affect the way we feel.

Social factors such as crowding, noise, and 'tough culture' are important too. A tough culture, as explained by Mike Samuels and Hal Zina Bennett in *Well Body, Well Earth* is one where the supportive dimensions of the social environment have broken down, where you are on the defensive as soon as you step outside your door. People let their dogs mess there. Car windows are smashed and neighbours share stories about the latest bag snatching ('in broad daylight, my dear—just over there!'). These things are part of everyday life for many of us, and until we recognise this 'street pressure' we may suffer without the slightest idea of why.

Clinical ecology

This study is also called environmental medicine, and concentrates on the way in which foods and food additives, chemicals, radiation and other pollutants cause disease, allergies, depression, fatigue, and plain old feeling below par.

Finding the cause of a particular problem, and then removing it, is the work of the clinical ecologist. An allergy is an over-reaction of the immune system to some element in the environment and may be fixed early in life, but improving the environment you live in can make them less of a problem, and strengthening the immune system is a way to help yourself.

● *Clinical Ecology*, Dr George T. Lewith and Dr Julian N. Kenyon (Thorsons, 1985).

● *Chemical Children*, Dr Peter Mansfield and Dr Jean Monro (Century, 1987).

Stress

Many people live beyond their bodies' real capacity—rather than on renewable energy—and when they relax and let go, their body's defences crash. Peter Nixon, Consultant Cardiologist at the Charing Cross Hospital in London, has developed what he calls a Human Function Curve, which is used in his work with cardiac patients but has intriguing implications for the rest of us. Each of us has a homoeostatic balance—a comfortable range in which we can function efficiently and happily—which is difficult to maintain in the face of life in 'a hard and urbanised society', or without adequate social support and appreciation.

For someone who is healthy, 'physical recreation brings pleasure and does not cause guilty reactions. Burdens and pressures that would cause loss of sleep and ill health are rejected.' As stress builds, 'disciplined effort, youthful conditioning for competition, social pressure and mild stimulants such as tea, coffee and cigarettes play a greater part in sustaining performance'. When the point of exhaustion is reached, we may continue to operate, but judgement and discriminatory power deteriorate, there is a reduced ability to adapt and a loss of stamina and increasing feelings of resentment and paranoia. Common symptoms of being on this 'downslope' are (1) loss of the recuperative power of sleep and (2) the harder we try to improve performance the more severely it deteriorates. (*Cardiological Aspects of Human Function*, International Symposium on Exercise, Fitness and Cardiovascular Health, Toronto, 1980.)

Although some people claim to thrive on stress, early burn-out is recognised as a consequence of too much pressure. We thrive on it only so long as it is there—in fact growing to need it in order to keep going (Nixon calls this 'adrenalin-addiction').

In the short-term, this takes its toll in quality of life, human relationships, emotional stability, and even ability on the job, while eventually a price will be paid in physical health.

A curious phenomenon is the way some people suffer depression and physical illness when they go on holiday or shortly after getting home. This can be a reaction to the removal of pressures which normally keep you going—with no adrenalin fix, you may find yourself unable to function effectively, and is a clue that you may be heading for the downslope. Running on sheer will power, instead of real energy, is asking for trouble.

Noise

Whether you live in the centre of a large city or well outside the city limits, the volume of sound in your environment will have increased substantially over the past 70 years or so. In the country busy roads and motorways, farm equipment and aeroplanes are probably the main sources of noise, while in town our ears receive an onslaught from traffic, street repairs and construction sites, trains, sirens, loud music and more aeroplanes.

Steve Halpern, an American sound researcher and musician, has pointed out that the siren volume used by police and fire vehicles in urban areas has risen to 122 decibels, louder than a jet engine. Before World War I, a brass bell was sufficient to clear the road.

As a result, we do not hear as well as our ancestors. Loud sounds destroy sensory hair cells in the inner ear, and these do not regenerate. The process of hearing loss is gradual and cumulative, and we have come to expect it as a normal part of ageing. Carol Venolia, however, cites studies which compared the hearing of Western city dwellers with that of Africans from remote areas. One study found that West Africans in their 70s had considerably better hearing than Londoners in their 20s.

Sound, for our ancestors, provided useful information about the environment. Loud noises—the crack of thunder or falling rocks—were signals which helped them to deal with the world around. Most of the noise (which is simply defined as unwanted or undesirable sound) in our modern environment tells us nothing meaningful. Besides that, we rarely hear pleasant sounds in the city.

Noise has profound effects on both body and mind, and is a surprisingly important source of environmental stress. Our bodies instinctively treat loud sounds as warning signals—our hearts beat faster, breathing speeds up and muscles tense. This reaction can lead to a wide range of health problems— from high blood pressure and headaches to ulcers, cardio- vascular disease and disturbed sleep. Noise interferes with concentration, makes us raise our voices or turn the television up (increasing the overall noise level!).

People who live near airports or busy motorways suffer from even louder 'normal' environments than inner city dwellers. European studies have shown that people living near an airport visit the doctor two to three times more often than average, suffer increased rates of high blood pressure, heart disease and psychological problems.

Of course, many of us claim to be able to 'tune out' distract- ing or irritating noises, but this places a strain on our systems which can lead to long-term problems. Although with time one might be able to sleep through almost any amount of noise, sleep patterns are disturbed and this affects the way we feel during the day. David Rousseau has noted that 'The most insidious effect of chronic noise exposure is that we are able to eventually accept and adapt to very dangerous conditions.'

The question is, what can you do about it? Traffic noise is an important aspect of road schemes for the people affected by them, but is not taken into account by planning authorities, whose only criterion is physical safety. Consciousness of ex- cessive noise as a form of pollution is an essential long-term strategy.

There are four main ways of dealing with unwanted noise:

Avoidance

Let noise be an important consideration when you choose a place to live. Visit your prospective home at different times of day, and during the week as well as at weekends. Motor vehicles are an omnipresent source of modern noise pollution, and you will want to know whether heavy lorries use your new street during the night.

Building and landscaping

Vegetation—hedges or rows of trees—and fencing can do a great deal to muffle traffic noise, and buildings can incorporate such things as sealed double pane glass, shutters, and solid doors, walls and floors. Closets and cupboards built between rooms provide excellent soundproofing. Energy-saving insulation cuts down on noise, as well as heat loss.

Dampening

Soft furnishings are a help: carpets, rugs, wallhangings are all effective. Choose quiet appliances, eliminate unnecessary and noisy ones, and place rubber mats or pads underneath fridges, typewriters and other sources of domestic noise. Separate 'quiet' and 'noisy' rooms as much as possible. Heavy furniture, like old-fashioned wooden wardrobes, placed against shared walls are a good way to reduce noise. Turn down music (insist on the use of headphones if necessary) and wear protective ear covering when working with loud equipment (even an electric drill, if you are at it all afternoon). In shared houses negotiate a noise agreement—times of day and maximum levels on the the volume control.

Pleasing sound

Sometimes your best defence is to use something pleasant to cut out undesirable noises. Music, falling water (even an aquarium pump can make a pleasant background sound), wind in trees, chimes and birdsong are all possibilities. Try to become conscious of how sound and noise influence you, and think about practical ways of increasing or highlighting desirable sounds.

PRIMAL HEALTH

The Black Report (HMSO, 1982) concluded that the social conditions before birth and just after birth were the most important guide to future health. Michel Odent, the well-known French obstetrician, has explored this idea in his book *Primal Health*.

Odent defines primal health as the body's basic capacity for adapting to the environment—essentially, the strength of the immune system. He explains that each person develops a particular *terrain* (a word not translatable into English), a fundamental temperament and ability to cope with disease, and shows how this is determined to a large extent by our experiences during the 'primal period': in the womb, during birth and the early months of breastfeeding. Learned helplessness—when a baby is left to cry, for example—depresses the immune system, and, claims Odent, to some extent determines that child's capacity for health for the rest of its life.

This is not to say that other factors do not influence our health. Odent is emphasizing the importance of the 'primal' period in order to show that the way we give birth and look after our children while early neurological and immunological development takes place is crucial to their future well-being.

This early period also influences our ability to love and respond to other people, and the way we in turn give birth (or support our partners in giving birth) and handle our children, as well as allergies, weight problems and sexual health.

While we cannot change our own 'primal' experience, finding out something about that time can help us to understand ourselves better. And primal health can be cultivated; Odent explains, 'The way each person regards his own health and the way society regards public health may be compared to the way a gardener tends his plants.' There are specifically therapeutic ways of using dance, music and laughter, but we can all find ways of incorporating these things in our lives. Not by going to a concert or the ballet, of course—make your own music, and get up and dance!

● *Primal Health*, Michel Odent (Century, 1986).

SELF CARE

Making a healthy home

Home Ecology puts the home at the centre of health and healing. Interestingly, the writers of *The Peckham Experiment* suggest that 'health is not merely a genetic characteristic; it is also a *nurtural characteristic* and, as such, is inevitably handed on from parent to child. So, a healthy family is more likely than an unhealthy one to create an intimate environment favourable to the acquisition of health, and in that sense the odds are in favour of an inherited *tradition* of health.'

This doesn't apply only to families. People who live together are bound to be affected by each other, though they tend not to spend so much time together. Notice how you feel with different friends: some may leave you feeling excited and enthusiastic about life, while others make you feel deflated and inadequate.

The other chapters in *Home Ecology* will help you to make your home a healthier environment. Don't forget that a healthy environment is more than the sum of its parts—carefully filtered water and good ventilation do not make a place a home. Think hard about what makes your home (or other places you love) *alive*, rich and stimulating and pleasurable. A really comfortable private place to sit down and read, or paint or frame pictures, may do more for your health than changing the heating system.

Eating well is easier if you have the right foods on hand and get rid of unhealthy temptations. Move toxic cleaning and DIY products outside, into a garage or storeroom if possible, and get rid of cans of insecticides.

Go through the bathroom cabinet, return old drugs to the chemist and separate non-prescription drugs you'd be better off without: laxatives, antacids (often high in aluminium), diuretics and aspirin. You won't necessarily feel happy about getting rid of these all at once, but you might put them in a box and see whether you can do without them for a month.

An estimated 9 out of 10 headaches are caused by tension, anxiety and other emotional states, and over-the-counter pain relievers have little or no effect on them (except in that you may start to feel better simply because you have 'done something' by taking an aspirin). Try a cup of hot sage or peppermint tea, a nap or a short walk. Ask someone to rub your neck, or do some stretching exercises. Or sit down and sort out why you feel anxious, and decide on some constructive step you can take to resolve the problem.

Start a safe medicine cabinet. I've found the following of value: aloe cream (or an aloe plant) for burns, calendula cream for cuts and skin irritations and Olbas oil for colds. An adequate supply of bandages for emergencies is important, but taking a course in first aid is of more value than a vast range of gear.

Health assessment

A professional health assessment can be very useful, but even more important is your own assessment. Arrange an hour or so to yourself, and settle down comfortably with a piece of paper for some quiet reflection. Remember that health should be our normal state, and what you want to consider are the barriers to health in your life.

Ask yourself questions (it may help to close your eyes and mentally examine yourself from head to toe): what condition is your hair in, your eyes, your skin? How is your hearing? Are you overweight or underweight? What about aches and pains, creaky joints? Don't restrict yourself to big worries which you would take to a doctor. What about athlete's foot or mouth ulcers, or even general stiffness? Don't assume that these things are the inevitable result of being human, or of growing old, and don't forget to look at good signs too.

Make a list as you go along. Do you feel tired all the time, or get depressed easily and for no particular reason? Trouble sleeping? Feelings of anger or aggression? Allergies or hay fever? Nervous mannerisms?

Consider your job, the place you live, your relationships, your way of life. How satisfied are you? Can you laugh at yourself? Or do you want to cry?

At the end of this you may have filled many pages. Of course you can't solve all these problems at once, and you may need professional help for some of them. The key is to decide on one or two you really would like to sort out. List these on a separate sheet of paper and start thinking about what you can do about them (put the other list away for future reference).

Lawrence LeShan, authority on alternative cancer therapy, emphasizes the importance of finding and concentrating on the things which you *like* in your life. An interesting addition to a health assessment is to follow his suggestion to make two lists, one of things which make you feel old and another of things which make you feel young. Simply becoming conscious of these distinctions can help you to make more satisfying choices, and improve your health in the process.

If you are being treated by a doctor, find out as much as you can about the problem and about any medication you are taking. Make a list of questions in advance and take it with you when you go to see the doctor, especially if you find the office intimidating. Change doctors if yours is reluctant to answer questions, and don't assume that s/he will give you the full facts. Medical treatment is usually undertaken on 'best guess' about what is wrong, but doctors still prefer to have you put complete trust in them and their diagnoses. Making an informed choice about the type of treatment you get is your right, and responsibility.

If you are taking a course of prescription drugs and do not feel satisfied with the information you get from your doctor, go to a reference library and consult the *British National Formulary* (*BNF*). This lists all drugs used in the UK, with indications for use, contra-indications, effects and potential side effects. The *BNF* includes over-the-counter drugs, and can help you make an informed choice about any of these you take.

Consulting an alternative practitioner can be an essential source of information about a chronic or serious problem.

Practical sources of information—about nutrition, exercise, relaxation and other ways of improving your own health—are:
● *Here's Health* magazine. Available on newsstands and at many wholefood shops.
● *The Whole Health Manual*, Patrick Holford (Thorsons, 1988).
● *The Joy of Beauty*, Leslie Kenton (Century, 1983).

Stress management

Virtually everyone who reads this is likely to be suffering from at least one stress-related symptom. Stress seems an inescapable part of modern life. A lot of minor stresses can add up to a large total stress burden, and are just as hard on you as a serious catastrophe.

Yet, as we have seen, stress is not necessarily a bad thing. Much depends on how we respond to it—in fact, on our capacity for responding. The reason modern stresses seem to have an adverse effect may be that they are things outside our control (radioactive emissions from Sellafield or ICI's dumping of toxic chemicals into our water supply), or which we don't know how to change or cope with.

The standard stress tests focus on life changes—the idea is that any change puts us under stress and that too many within a short period may well do us in. But Don Ardell sees this as negative and unrealistic, asking 'Who's to say that divorce is a 73-point event? . . . *Not* getting a divorce could be a 73-point

event, day after day after day! It just depends on who is
divorcing you, or vice versa.' (*High Level Wellness*, p 308.)

Everyday hassles and irritations—a partner who never telephones when s/he is going to be late, the way the TV volume
goes up when the adverts come on, your neighbour's choice of
music—may affect you far more than losing a job or going to
jail (events which happen infrequently in most of our lives).

If you are stuck in a traffic jam, you can beat your head on
the steering wheel, heckle other drivers and send your blood
pressure soaring, or you can resign yourself to being late. Use
the time to hunt for Russian broadcasts on the medium wave,
or make faces at the children in the car next to you. (Better
yet, think about finding a job closer to home, plan to start
cycling, or take the train next time.)

Taking action depends on increasing our awareness of what
goes on around us. Many of us find that we 'become exhausted
from living out of sync with ourselves, and we can no longer
tell how our environment is affecting us. We tell ourselves that
any adverse effects are either inconsequential or unavoidable
and that we must be doing okay because we're getting by
somehow. This shut-down state produces apathy and alienation,
increasing our susceptibility to disease.' (Venolia, p 24-5).
Alertness—the sort of environmental awareness which was
instinctive and necessary for our ancestors—helps to restore
both our health and our capacity for making positive changes
in the world around us.

Diet

A mostly organic diet, high in fresh foods and low in meat and
dairy products, is a healthy one—ecology and health go hand
in hand. See Chapter 2.

Supplements

Some nutritionists say that we get all the nutrients we need
from a well-balanced diet, and that the only thing which gets
healthy as a result of our taking vitamin tablets is the pocket-
book of the manufacturers and health food shops.

No doubt that there is plenty of hype in the health
food industry, but vitamin and mineral supplements may
compensate for some of the poor quality food we eat and can
actually help our bodies cope with some of the stresses and
pollutants of modern life. Leslie Kenton's books are a good

source of information about this. She recommends the following in particular:

- Vitamin C is a detoxifier and helps the body to eliminate lead.
- Vitamin E is a natural antioxidant and offer some protection against the effects of carbon monoxide, pesticides and solvents.
- Seaweeds prevent the body from absorbing radioactive materials and protect us from other environmental pollutants too.

Kenton lists a number of 'environmental' food supplements in her *Ultrahealth* (Century, 1984): bioflavinoids (from the white pith of citrus fruit), yoghurt, brewer's yeast, pectin (which is found in apples), lecithin, and beetroot. Here are a few points to consider when choosing supplements:

1 First, eat a healthy diet. Pills aren't going to make up for a lack of fresh, nutritious food.
2 Use garlic, wheatgerm, liver (preferably organically-reared) and seaweeds as ingredients. Go to a Japanese restaurant to get some ideas for cooking with seaweeds and look for recipes using traditional British seaweeds like laverbread and dulse.
3 Take products in simple forms whenever possible (codliver oil rather than tablets—if you can bear it—and nutritional yeast stirred into water or juice instead of swallowing dozens of tablets). Tablets are more expensive, and need excipients and binders to hold them together.
4 Look for sympathetic packaging when you buy vitamins and minerals. This means glass and paper rather than plastic.

- The Sea Vegetable Co Ltd, Pitkerrie, Balmuchy, Fern, Ross and Cromarty IV20 1TN, telephone (0862) 87272.
- *Cooking with Sea Vegetables*, Peter and Montse Bradford (Thorsons, 1985).

Exercise

I once read a suggestion that we should have joggers run on machines which would turn some of the energy they expend into electricity! Think how ridiculous an aerobics class must seem to someone who gets all the exercise she needs hauling water from a well three miles away and growing enough food for herself, her husband and half a dozen children.

We have to allocate special time for exercise because we lead

sedentary lives. A simple switch from driving to walking or cycling can provide an adequate amount of exercise, probably enough to substantially lower your chances of dropping dead of a heart attack at 55.

Instead of passive forms of recreation, why not think of hiking, cross-country skiing, swimming or cycling? 'Rambling' refreshes the mind as well as the body, and provides us city dwellers with much needed contact with the earth. (Driving through the countryside does *not* count as outdoor recreation!)

Otherwise, find a sport or sports which you enjoy, preferably outdoors so that you get light and fresh air along with the exercise. Sports centres are a discouraging development, with their artificial lighting and plastic food, and are geared to car owners, just like out-of-town shopping centres.

Aside from positive physical effects, regular exercise is one of the best ways of improving your emotional health. Researchers have found that exercise, even walking, can have profound effects on people who are seriously depressed. Leslie

Kenton cites a number of US studies which have shown remarkable results with cases of paranoid schizophrenia, alcoholism and drug abuse. A 15-minute walk every day has proved to be more effective at combatting stress than taking tranquillizers! (*Joy of Beauty*, p 138). These effects are attributed to increased levels of a hormone called noradrenalin and to improved blood supply to the brain.

Not only does exercise improve the way a person looks and make everyday burdens seem less heavy (perhaps partly because you are strong enough to lift them!), but leads to inner changes: more energy, increased resistance to disease, better disposition, sounder sleep, better sex, less susceptibility to injuries and easier menstrual cycles.

Eyes

Instead of buying stronger and stronger eyeglasses or contact lenses, you may want to try improving your eyesight. Ophthamology places little or no emphasis on preventative treatment, although eyes, like teeth, have regenerative capacity. Bates eye therapy has been around for many years. Like many healing methods, it requires action on the part of the patient. The following books can guide you, or you can consult a Bates teacher.

- Bates Association of Eyesight Training, 126 Merton Road, London SW19, telephone 01-874 7337.
- Nutritional Eye Health Centre, Sanctuary House, Oulton Road, Oulton, Suffolk NR32 4QZ, telephone Lowestoft (0502) 83294.
- *Better Eyesight Without Glasses*, W. H. Bates (Grafton, 1979).
- *The Art of Seeing*, Aldous Huxley (Panther, 1985).
- *Natural Vision Improvement*, Janet Goodrich (David & Charles, 1987)

Natural family planning

Birth control is a knotty issue, which no one has satisfactorily resolved. The Pill has been associated with a wide range of health problems, IUDs still in use in Britain have been the subject of dozens of court cases and massive settlements in the US, and the alternatives are often inconvenient, messy and require the use of chemical spermicides, with their attendant health risks.

A completely safe alternative is called 'natural family planning' (NFP), in which a woman charts her ovulation cycle by keeping a record of her temperature, cervical shape and vaginal mucus. These change very regularly throughout the menstrual cycle. Opponents claim that there are too many other factors involved, but if you get to know your body you will be well aware if there is any exceptional change affecting you, and most women find that they can recognise their own patterns with great accuracy after several months' practice.

The method requires some diligence and concentration, especially in the first year or so, but when one considers that most women have to think about birth control for some 30 years of their lives, in the long-term this method could not only be healthier and safer, but a lot less trouble than other forms of contraception. Its success rate is roughly comparable to using a diaphram with spermicide. Otherwise, condoms are probably the healthiest, most environmentally-sound method (as long as they are properly disposed of).

The Wholistic Research Company has a wide range of books on NFP, thermometers and other specialized aids, and offer a correspondence course in the method. *Foresight*, the pre-conceptual care organization, is also a good source of information and advice, and can refer you to an NFP teacher in your area.

● Wholistic Research Company, Bright Haven, Robin's Lane, Lolworth, Cambridge CB3 8HH, telephone Craft's Hill (0954) 81074.

● *Foresight*, The Old Vicarage, Church Lane, Witley, Godalming, Surrey GU8 5PN.

HEALTH CARE

While specialized operating facilities are necessary for a small percentage of patients, innovative doctors and other health practitioners have been talking and writing for many years about the need for decentralized, community-centred health services.

Money does not buy good health; in fact the more doctors and the more numerous the remedies, the iller we seem to become. Ivan Illich, social critic, points out:

> The fact that the doctor population is higher where certain diseases have become rare has little to do with the

doctors' ability to control or eliminate them. It simply means that doctors . . . tend to gather where the climate is healthy, where the water is clean, and where people are employed and can pay for their services.

Limits to Medicine, p 30

The essential problem is not money, and which party will put in more of it, but the whole structure of the health care system.

These suggestions run counter to the trend towards ever greater centralization, but will ring chords of sympathy from many people who use the health service. People in Shropshire have been campaigning against the closure of their cottage hospitals ('Fighting for Life', BBC 2, 21 March 1988) and the closure of maternity wings and GP units is fiercely contested in many areas.

It goes without saying that the larger a hospital is the less personal it can be, and the less accessible the staff is. A friend commented on the indignity of being examined by doctors he had never seen before, who did not even bother to introduce themselves. Architect Carol Venolia points out that 'Most hospitals are good examples of how not to create healing environments. They seem to say, The power here resides with the institution; the important people are the doctors; you represent an illness, and we have tests, drugs, and machinery to control it' (and you).

This must be discouraging and disheartening for people who spend extended periods in hospital. A study showed that patients who were able to look outside at a tree while convalescing got well faster than patients stuck in a room will nothing but bare walls to look at (in fact, seriously ill heart patients have a better chance of recovery when they are nursed at home). The personal quality of the care they get is going to be equally helpful, as is a nutritious and appetising diet (that hospital food should remain as appalling as it is shows that the NHS has not focussed on current thinking about the role of nutrition in health).

National health

One of the worst aspects of the NHS is that there is no provision (or, presumably, funds) for regular physical check-ups. Sadly, doctors get credit for specialization and ever more complex procedures, rather than for their success in cultivating a

large number of healthy people. Jonathan Porritt aptly remarks,
'It would seem that the less healthy we are, so much the
greater is the success that may be claimed on behalf of the . . .
NHS. The ultimate goal, presumably, is to make patients of
us all.'

When you visit a doctor with a 'minor' ailment, a sports
injury for example, you are almost certain to be told to take it
easy, lay off the exercise, and take painkillers. As long as we
can walk, talk and—most importantly—go to work, a harassed
GP has little interest in dealing with the cause of the problem.
It seem that there is no time, no money and no inclination to
keep people in a state of positive health (even though the
potential long-term financial savings are staggering).

If you want to start an exercise programme, would you go to
your doctor to ask his/her advice? How many women feel
really free to ask about small worries when they find out they
are pregnant? Sadly, most doctors are far too busy to get to
know patients, and find prescribing drugs easier, and faster,
than trying to understand a human being. If a man comes in
with a bad back, pain relief and bed rest are standard treatment.
The fact that he is unemployed and having problems with his
teenage children isn't taken into account, and this lack of
caring may actually make the suffering worse.

Our attitudes towards doctors is at fault too, because many
of us want a instant cure—we don't want to make any changes
in our lives and simply want some help in the process of
compensation for ill health. Illich talks about the physician's
role being to exonerate the sick from moral accountability. If
this is true only *we* can change it by taking responsibility for
our own health, and by seeing the medical profession as our
consultants.

The Peckham Experiment

In the years before and after World War II, an experimental
Pioneer Health Centre was run in Peckham, south London. It
combined the facilities of doctors' surgery, antenatal and post-
natal clinics, nursery school, youth club, family planning clinic,
neighbourhood cafe, sports centre and citizens' advice bureau,
and was called a club.

Families who lived in its catchment area were able to join by
paying a weekly fee. Members organized their own activities
and had a swimming pool and gym available. Mothers shared

in the cooking of the nursery teas, and families spent many of their free hours at the Centre.

The doctors who ran it, George Scott Williamson and his wife Innes Pearse, described it as an experiment into the nature of health. The emphasis was on cultivating health, as well as catching disease at an early stage by regular examinations.

It closed during the War, but public demand brought it back afterwards, until it was forced to close shortly after the founding of the NHS. Perhaps now is the time to look at its principles again. Instead of focussing attention and praise on curing rare diseases and on treating ever-increasing numbers of patients, we would all benefit from a decentralized service which catered for a wider interpretation of human health. The possibilities are so enormous and so appealing that a change in public consciousness could bring about a total change in the way the state provides a health service.

● The Pioneer Health Centre Ltd, 3 Tangier Lane, Frant, Tunbridge Wells TN3 9HD.

● *The Peckham Experiment, a study in The Living Structure of Society*, Innes H. Pearse and Lucy H. Crocker (Scottish Academic Press, 1985—first published in 1943).

● Templegarth Trust, 82 Tinkle Street, Grimoldby, Louth, Lincolnshire LN11 8TF, telephone Louth (0507 82) 655 or 227. A similar experimental scheme, which has been endorsed by the World Health Organisation. Offer seminars and a substantial literature list.

Maternity services

The Association of Radical Midwives (ARM) set out its Proposals for the Future of the Maternity Services in *The Vision*, 1986. Decentralization and personalization of the maternity services are at the heart of their proposals.

They suggest that midwives should be the acknowledged primary carers in pregnancy and childbirth, and that 60–70% of them should work in community-based practices and should be totally responsible for the 85% of women who have no complications during pregnancy or labour.

The other 30–40% of midwives would be hospital-based and would care for the 15% of women who need special care (this allows for a much higher midwife/mother ratio in hospital, where more intensive care is required—a better allocation of resources).

They say 'Midwives will be seen as the professionals to consult in all matters relating to childbirth.' Traditionally, women have always supported other women in childbirth, and a return to this state of affairs is to be welcomed. Under the present system, working within hospitals, the midwife becomes an adjunct to the doctor rather than an independent professional.

Ideally, midwives would work in the community within local health centres, where they would see women before and during pregnancy, attend them in childbirth at home or at the health centre. This plan would, in addition to its other virtues, save a great deal of money.

● The Association of Radical Midwives, 62 Greetby Hill, Ormskirk, Lancashire L39 2DT. *The Vision* costs £1.

Dentistry

Dental philosophy, and dental care, is changing. Instead of treating decay as a cancer to be eradicated as quickly and thoroughly as possible (even when this meant drilling out surrounding areas of sound tooth), the Department of Health is now advising dentists to leave teeth alone whenever possible. Teeth are not dead; they can remineralize and heal themselves. If left untouched, small patches of decay will sometimes disappear, especially with improvements in diet and brushing.

Of course most dentists have not yet converted to this benign approach. Even today's students get insufficient training in preventative care, nutrition and concepts of whole patient treatment. Nonetheless, the trend is a welcome one.

One of the most important areas of debate is about metal amalgam fillings. Dental amalgam contains up to 50% highly toxic mercury, and some dentists think that slow release of this recognized poison is responsible for long-term debilitation of the immune system. If you have a mouthful of fillings you will know how they gradually wear away, and sometimes even fall out. Mercury also vapourizes. It is not enough to say that metal fillings have been used for a long time, so they must be safe; lead was used in pipes for over a thousand years!

There are suggestions, too, that electrical activity between the fillings can cause physical imbalances in sensitive patients. Metal fillings have been known to act as long distance radio receivers, so there can be little dispute about the possibility of electromagnetic receptivity. This may interfere with the body's nerve impulses and circuits, and lead to ill health. Applied kinesiologists actually manipulate teeth to correct certain muscle problems.

Metal fillings can be replaced with white bonded material, which is inert, looks nice, and has other advantages. Because it bonds, or sticks, directly to the tooth there is no need to drill away sound tooth in order to place a filling, and your dentist will not need to use X-rays to check for hidden decay under existing fillings because no room is left for the growth of secondary decay.

● British Homoeopathic Association, 27a Devonshire Street, London W1N 1RJ, telephone 01-935 2163. Will send a list of holistic or homoeopathic dentists (enclose SAE).

● *The Natural Dentist*, Brian Halvorsen (Century Arrow, 1986).

ALTERNATIVE MEDICINE

You may want to consult an osteopath or some other alternative practitioner—the real problem is just how to find a good one. Even finding a GP you feel reasonably contented with can be difficult, let alone tracking down a suitable homoeopath or acupunturist. Most of us depend on recommendations from friends, or simply look in the Yellow Pages.

Because seeing one of these people is going to cost some of your hard-earned cash, it is all the more important to make a careful selection. And, even more difficult, is how to know which of these specialists is going to be able to help with your particular problem. GPs will occasionally refer patients to osteopaths when they have had no success in treating back pain, and homoeopathy is sometimes available through the NHS. Otherwise you are on your own, and in any case you may well wish to try the 'alternative' first.

First, however, let's look at whether these various techniques work.

Hocus-pocus?

Once you start to understand the complexity of our bodies and the myriad influences upon them, the all too common dismissal of any form of treatment which does not depend on medication starts to look unreasonable, if not positively stupid.

Vaccination against smallpox was used before it was fully understood, because it clearly worked. Acupuncture, too, works, even though a generally agreed scientific explanation has not been established, and indeed may never be established.

Instead of considering these forms of treatment to be useless or fraudulent, the problem is with our means of testing, our whole acceptance of the idea that nothing is true until it is proven in a particular way. Subtler and more sensitive methods of dealing with problems in the human body and mind are likely to need subtler means of testing.

The 'scientific method' is difficult to use on human beings (and it is impossible to replicate the complex demands and pressures of our lives when doing tests on laboratory rats) because this sort of analysis requires an untreated, generally equivalent control group, and a way of isolating a particular treatment. With drug testing this is easy: one group gets the drug and the other does not. Establishing whether complementary techniques work is far more difficult. As one osteopath asked, 'How do you *pretend* to treat someone?'

Broad health comparisons are intriguing: middle-aged Cretan men eat just as much fat as your average Britisher, yet heart disease, our primary cause of death in this age group, is virtually unknown. Researchers do not know why. It's interesting to look at the way medical advice about the role of cholesterol in heart disease has changed over the past fifteen years. There now seem to be two different kinds of cholesterol, one good and one bad (see page 32). Another surprising fact is that cot death is virtually unheard of outside the industrialized West. Michel Odent has observed that in these other countries children sleep with their parents, and spend almost all their time being carried close to an adult.

These phenomena are not scientific evidence of specific cause and effect, yet they offer us useful information.

When loaves of French bread are baked in Britain or America from ingredients which are, according to chemical tests, exactly the same as the ones used in Paris—even when the ovens have been imported at great expense—the end result is different. No one knows exactly why although we can think of possible explanations (the air is different, the water harder or softer, the bakers less skillful), but no one denies that the bread doesn't taste as good.

Similarly, the way each person responds to his or her environment—physical and social—is different. Holistic medicine aims to treat the whole person, and not just a symptom. Many holistic practitioners do not like to think in terms of 'disease'. Instead, they describe a particular set of symptoms as a common pattern of coping responses. The actual cause, which is what they want to deal with, may be different for each person —every treatment needs to be individually tailored.

Of course, this sort of analysis takes more time that a typical office visit to your doctor (or the five minutes you are booked with a hospital consultant), and a first visit to an alternative practitioner is likely to take an hour or more because s/he will want to discuss your health history and way of life.

- *Green Pages*, John Button (Optima, 1988). Contains a very helpful section on alternative therapies, explaining principles and giving contact addresses.
- *The Whole Health Manual*, Patrick Holford (Thorsons, 1988).

Finding a practitioner

In many alternative fields, there is no legal restriction on who is qualified to practise. For example, anyone can put up a brass plaque saying 'Osteopath'. There are, however, bodies which accredit schools and award particular qualifications, and you would be well-advised to consult one of these before choosing a practitioner.

Going to a group practice, if there is one in your area, is a good idea, because you can easily be passed to someone else if the person you first consult feels that this is appropriate. A good alternative therapist will be aware of other disciplines and happy to make referrals—beware of anyone who seems to think that their own speciality is the only way.

Look for a practitioner who makes you feel comfortable, who is enthusiastic and encouraging, and who clearly takes an individual approach to your health problem. S/he should consider different aspects of the headaches or leg cramp and offer treatment on all levels. A willingness to explain the treatment and to enlist your support is important, as is confidence in the body's ability to heal itself (treatment frequently consists of removing impediments to that natural healing, rather than a direct treatment of symptoms).

This may sound daunting compared to a quick trip down to the local surgery, and long-term improvements in health care depend on improved access to various alternative therapies. For now, the following books should point you in the right direction.

- *The Handbook of Complementary Medicine*, Stephen Fulder (*Coronet, 1984*).
- *Your Life in Your Hands, An Alternative Natural Medicine*, Dr E. K. Ledermann (Green Books, 1988).
- Research Council for Complementary Medicine, Suite 1, 19a Cavendish Square, London W1M 9AD, telephone 01-493 6930. A general source of referrals.

AGEING AND DEATH

Michel Odent closed the first International Conference on Home Birth by saying that we also have to understand the importance of home death.

It's easy to make fun of American attitudes to death, the Hollywood piped music crematoria and cemeteries for cats and dogs, but we have come to accept a medicalized death in hospital as usual, and even desirable.

Dying is a part of living, and the way people end their lives should be part of all of our lives—marked by dignity and within a community of friends and family. Tragically, this is not the case for many people, who end their lives alone in a hospital bed, strapped to monitors, with none of their own things to look at and cherish, with no familiar face to offer comfort and to communicate with.

Our care of the elderly says a great deal about attitudes towards ageing and death. Carol Venolia explains how we could change this:

> Old age can be a time of flourishing and fulfillment in a social and physical environment that acknowledges the uniqueness of the later years of life. For most, it is a time of increase personal maturity and decreased responsibilities—a fertile combination. If we don't relegate the elderly to deadly institutions, and if we consider the full span of life when we create our homes, public buildings, and outdoor spaces, the potential vitality of the elderly can be available to enrich everyone's life.
>
> *Healing Environments*, p 162

This is not an abstract, unimportant question—it is part of the future faced by each of us.

Why has death become institutionalized? Because we want to give the dying 'every possible chance'—or because we do not want to have to come to terms with death, with our own future deaths? Rosalie Bertell quotes a little boy who was dying of leukaemia, who said that 'Days aren't important unless they're good ones.' But this is a problem with our dependence on modern medicine—we want it to solve every problem, including death.

The hospice movement is an excellent sign of better understanding about the needs of the dying, when being at home isn't possible. Pain relief and nursing care are often all that someone needs as he ends his days, along with a homelike atmosphere, the care and attention of friends or family, and perhaps spiritual succour.

A proper environment for dying, and a restoration of the dignity of those who are near to death, is an important part of understanding and accepting ecological life cycles, an essential part of human health.

10
THE NON-TOXIC HOME

We've been hearing a lot about toxic contaminants—in our water supply, in our food, in our air. It is becoming increasingly clear that our health is integrally related to the toxicity of our environment, but while television newsreels and daily newspapers run stories about chemical spills, toxic waste, and industrial pollution, little attention is given to positive, immediate actions we as individuals can take right now.

Debra Lynn Dadd
The Nontoxic Home, 1986

Since World War II there has been a vast increase in the number of chemical substances in common use (a 1978 estimate was 63,000, and the number is rising by at least 1,000 per year), and the majority of them have not been adequately tested for risk to either human health or the environment. Products we use every day, and even the building materials which our homes are made out of, contain chemicals which are known to be carcinogenic (cancer-causing), mutagenic (mutation-causing) and teratogenic ('monster'-causing—that is, leading to birth defects).

We cannot underestimate the consequences of this. Toxic chemicals from industry, accidentally released into the environment or 'disposed' of, pose a constantly increasing threat. A number of scientists, including a Committee on Science and Public Policy of the US National Academy of Sciences (1970), have pointed out that the genetic hazards from chemicals is probably of even greater importance than those from ionizing radiation, barring nuclear war.

Chemicals cause cancer, miscarriages and birth defects, and in the longer term affect the human gene pool. They also have subtle, low-level effects which we may not be aware of or be capable of analyzing. The problem of chemical sensitivity is an inevitable consequence of the array of products which each of us comes into contact with, from food additives and colourings to chlorine bleach and enzyme detergents.

This chapter can be no more than a brief overview of an increasingly complex subject. I've chosen to concentrate on the practicalities of choosing non-toxic alternatives, rather than explaining the potential hazards of every product. My thanks go to Debra Lynn Dadd, whose excellent *Nontoxic and Natural* and *The Nontoxic Home* have provided invaluable information. Although her product references are, in general, to American sources, anyone interested in pursuing the switch to non-toxic products should get copies of these books, either through your bookseller or from Genesis Books at the East West Centre (see page 237).

Ecological connection

What does drycleaning have to do with *Home Ecology*? Cleaning and DIY products affect our home environment, and things which are hazardous for us are almost always hazardous to the outside environment.

The detergents, bleach and brush cleaner we pour down the drain find their way into our lakes and rivers (where their 'powerful cleansing action' has a devastating effect on water plants and animal life), and some eventually ends up back in our food or in the water we drink.

Toxic waste is a growing problem in the industrialized world, and domestic rubbish too has its share of toxic contaminants. Think how casually we throw away used batteries, an old box of moth balls, or a couple of cans of dried-up paint. A few councils have special toxic waste collection points, but most of us have no choice about how to discard these items.

By-products of chemical production are, at present levels, impossible to deal with safely. According to Professor Barry Commoner, '99 percent of the [petrochemical industry's] toxic wastes are now put into the environment, half of them into underground wells and the rest on the surface.' He points out that incinerating the present annual output of toxic waste would cost three times the total profit of the petrochemical industry.

In *The Turning Point*, Fritjof Capra comments that 'In the long run the problems generated by chemical waste will become manageable only if we can minimize the production of hazardous substances, which will involve radical changes in our attitudes as producers and consumers.' The main thing we can do, individually, is to stop using as many toxic products as possible, and to encourage the producers of environmentally- and humanly-benign alternatives.

We also need to make clear to manufacturers and government that industrial processes which result in the dumping of toxic waste are unacceptable and that adequate waste disposal is a necessary cost of production.

Chemical sensitivity

While our bodies are able to deal with a certain quantity of environmental poisons, each person's chemical tolerance point is different. Once it has been passed, severe and debilitating illness can result.

Sometimes removing a proportion of the environmental toxins can enable coping mechanisms to function again, but it seems that certain people become permanently sensitive even to things which they were previously able to tolerate. This is an area of research which has received considerable attention in the United States over the past 10 years by toxicologists, clinical ecologists and consumer groups. Possible symptoms include asthma and eczema, depression, chronic fatigue, skin rashes and migraine headaches.

Debra Lynn Dadd worked as a classical musician until 1980, when she was diagnosed as having a severe breakdown of her immune system, caused by stress and heavy chemical exposure. She had no occupational exposure; all the chemicals which made her ill were things she used at home.

Sensitive individuals find that pesticide residues on fresh fruits and vegetables, traces of detergent and solvents in and on many products, and a wide variety of additives make them ill. Reactions to petrochemical products are common.

It is very difficult to test the effects of individual chemicals on human beings. The so-called 'chemical cocktail'—the wide variety of chemicals we are exposed to in our food, air, water, building materials and domestic products—may well have serious consequences. There is no way to test the effects of each possible combination of chemicals.

Judging safe levels is equally difficult, and official standards are frequently lowered as scientists discover more about the way particular chemicals affect human beings. For example, a high rate of miscarriage and infertility amongst hospital operating room staff, resulting from exposure to anaesthetics, has led to improvements in ventilation.

Low-level chemical exposure influences each one of us. Do you feel light-headed when you use spray adhesives, or queasy in a newly-painted room? Many people are sensitive to washing powders and 'original formula no enzyme' detergents are promoted almost as vigorously as their 'biological' cousins.

Children and pregnant women

Children take in more air and more food for their body weight than do adults, and are more vulnerable to environmental toxins, just as they are to ionizing radiation.

Allergies, including asthma and eczema, are more and more common, and children's reactions to chemicals can include hyperactivity and even psychiatric disorders. Dr Jean Monro of the Lister Clinic has been successfully treating chemically-sensitive children, and recently co-authored a useful guide for parents, *Chemical Children* (with Dr Peter Mansfield). Pregnant women, and their unborn babies, are also particularly vulnerable to chemical toxins. Whatever they consume or come into contact with will affect, to some degree, their baby. If you are pregnant, make a special effort to avoid contact with strong household chemicals, particularly aerosols. Watch out with cosmetics as well. Chemical hair colourings and hair sprays, and of course smoking, are thought to be the greatest danger to the foetus.

Alternatives

Take a look at the variety of cleaners you have in the house right now. How many do you actually use? Spray polishes and carpet fresheners are enticingly packaged and expensively promoted, and advertisements about laundry powders are inescapable.

I suspect that one reason we are so prone to try new products is that few of us want to devote substantial amounts of time to house-cleaning, and we're eager to try anything that might make the job easier and faster. We buy the promise rather than the product, and end up with a cupboard full of fat, luridly-coloured plastic bottles—each used once or twice and then superseded by the next bright container to catch our eye.

Rather than buy *more*, why not keep a supply of basic cleaning products which will harm neither you nor the environment? Virtually all cleaning chores can be efficiently tackled with nothing more than soap, vinegar and bicarbonate of soda (I know this sounds extreme, but please read on). You can also buy a number of safe commercial cleaners.

Switching to nontoxic toiletries is even simpler because there are more commercial products available. It is also possible to make your own non-toxic alternatives, and I've included a number of simple formulae.

Look behind the chemist's counter: you'll probably see a range of old-fashioned products which are a delightful change from complicated modern concoctions and work just as well. These include surgical and camphor spirits, almond oil, tincture of benzoin, rosewater and glycerine.

Don't think that anything which calls itself 'natural' will be.

'Natural' wild-mountain-honey-and-herb shampoo may contain
exactly the same ingredients as any other detergent shampoo,
with the addition of a little honey and a different fragrance.
Full product labelling is an important step towards offering
consumers an informed choice.

Finding substitutes for potentially hazardous building and
decorating materials is a more difficult issue, but there are
several sources of information and safe products.

CLEANING

Household products are designed to clean, to disinfect, and to
deodorize. To achieve these aims we use vast quantities of
detergent, bleach, air fresheners and other dangerous products.

None of us wants to go back to great-granny's day, of
scrubbing clothes on a washboard or scouring floors with
ashes. But non-toxic cleaning is easy, with fewer supplies to
think about. Non-toxic products seem to take far less rinsing
(and one doesn't have to worry about traces of bleach or
ammonia left behind).

Less work

Peg Bracken wisely pointed out in her *I Hate to Housekeep
Book* (Arlington Books, 1963), if something is worth doing,
it's worth doing badly. Don't wait till you have a can (a CFC
aerosol spray at that) of the latest wallpaper spot cleaner
when a quick wipe with a soapy dishcloth would have done the
trick.

Cleaning expert Don Aslett has many useful tips about
saving time and energy in his book *Is there life after housework?*
(Exley, 1982), though the cleaning supplies he does recommend
are not ecologically sound. He says that we use too many
cleaning products and far too much of them. The first and best
cleaner is water, and his rule of thumb is 'eliminate—saturate
—absorb'. Rather than grinding away at the pudding batter
that has dried onto your cooker, simply wet everything with a
soapy dishcloth and leave it alone for ten minutes (while you
mix a drink, or feed the cat, or close your eyes and reflect on
higher things). *Then* wipe it up. If there are a few spots left,
you can always scrub them, rather than the whole surface.

This principle works on clothes (soak overnight) and
floors (wet the floor and leave for half an hour—you'll be

amazed at the amount of dirt which comes up), as well as on dishes.

Another useful hint, for all of us who want to avoid both chemical cleaning products and cleaning in the first place, is to use good doormats at every door. Carpets last longer if they are kept clean—it's the abrasiveness of dirt, rather than traffic, which does most of the damage. Aslett says that this will save the average household 200 hundred cleaning hours a year. In addition, mats will cut down on the pollutants, including lead and canine parasites, you bring into the house. (But don't shake them onto the garden or you'll end up eating the lead in next year's lettuces. Burning scrap timber which has traces of paint on it—even modern paints contain some lead—and using the ashes as a source of potash for your potatoes is something else to avoid.)

Taking your shoes off when you come in works the same magic. The Japanese have always done this, and you can buy inexpensive straw slippers to keep by the door, for guests as well as yourselves.

The ecological cleaning cupboard

Take those shiny, colourful aerosols, and powerful, potentially dangerous cleaners off your shopping list. Instead, here is a list of basic supplies which should get you through every domestic task. Some non-toxic and biodegradable commercial products are listed at the end.

1 Soap
Household soap or plain soap flakes will do the trick for many cleaning tasks, perhaps with the addition of a little washing soda. A constant refrain in books on housekeeping and saving money is the Soap Jar. This is where all those slivers of hand soap go (while you start a fresh bar). Pour on a little boiling water and you'll get a soft jelly which can be used for washing dishes or tights or diluted as a spray for the aphids attacking your Zephirine Drouhin. Another way to use soap scraps is to keep them in a metal tea ball or strainer, which you swish in your washing up water.

2 Washing up liquid
You may not need this, if you become a soap jar afficionado. But Ecover's biodegradable version smells delicious, is effective, and truly easy on hands (unlike the advertised brands, which cut the natural oils on your skin as efficiently as the grease on dishes). Faith Products' Clear Spring washing up liquid is another good one (it contains lemon grass and citrus extracts to cut grease, and is completely vegan). In a hard water area, add a little water softener to the wash basin—you'll need less soap.

3 Laundry powder
A number of biodegradable washing powders are available from wholefood stores and by mail order, and Swiss Filetti is sold at some supermarkets (Switzerland, determined to protect its lakes, has banned phosphates in detergents). In my experience these need the addition of a water softener to get clothes clean in hard water.

People used to air clothes overnight and get another day's wear out of them—you'll know yourself and whether this will work! Brushing (with a good natural bristle clothes brush) is the butler's trick for reviving garments. Machine washing and tumble drying make clothes wear out more quickly. See pages 217–22 for more on clothes care.

4 Bicarbonate of soda
Almost infinitely useful around the house. Buy a 500g box from the chemist rather than the tiny ones you get for baking (I've seen large bags of bicarbonate of soda at a Chinese supermarket). It is a partial water softener, can be used as a

scouring powder on sinks and bathtubs (effective, and very easy to rinse away), as a coating on ovens (to make them easier to clean next time), an excellent polish for chrome, and a neutral cleaner when dissolved in water.

Bicarbonate of soda also makes a good plaque-fighting toothpowder, and can be used in solution as a garden fungicide for mildew on roses and other plants (2g per litre of water, applied every 7 days).

5 Table salt
Salt is mildly disinfectant, and makes an abrasive but benign scouring powder. Keep drains clear (if this is a problem for you) with a weekly handful of salt and kettleful of boiling water.

6 Borax
This can be bought from the chemist and is a possible substitute for chlorine bleach, recommended in a number of lists of non-toxic cleaning products. It should however, be used with caution as it is a persistent poison. Some people feel that the only problem with chlorine bleach is that we use far too much of it, but the environmental problems caused by the chlorine bleaching of paper pulp (see page 69) would suggest that we should avoid chlorine bleach at home too.

An oxygen bleach—like hydrogen peroxide or sodium peroxide—would seem to be the ideal alternative, but these are not commercially available for domestic cleaning (the hydrogen peroxide you buy at the chemist can, however, be used as a gentle clothes bleach).

An American hospital tested a borax solution as a disinfectant and found that it satisfied their germicidal requirements. Use it to soak nappies, whiten clothes, soften water and increase the effectiveness of plain soap. It is also good at keeping down mould and preventing odours.

7 White distilled vinegar
From the supermarket or chemist. Mix 50/50 in a spray bottle for cleaning glass and tiles. Use to descale your kettle or remove stains from a teapot. Mixed with salt or baking soda, it will polish brass and copper.

8 Water softener
The major commercial water softener is simply scented sodium hexametaphosphate. Scented products are often implicated in

allergic reactions, so buy a softener with no added fragrance (Boots makes one which is a blend of sodium bicarbonate and sodium carbonate, ordinary washing soda). Large chemical supply houses might even sell you sodium hexametaphosphate, which Debra Lynn Dadd highly recommends. It is, however, a phosphate, and should be used discreetly.

A softener will improve washing results and enable you to cut down on the amount of powder you use. (When you switch to a biodegradable powder, run your clothes through a wash cycle with a double dose of water softener to remove detergent residue.) It can also be used as a bath salt, with the addition of a scented oil or fresh herbs.

9 Washing soda
This is a water softener, and cuts grease. Used sparingly, it makes a good heavy duty cleaner for walls and floors, and a few tablespoons added to your regular washing powder will help with really dirty clothes.

10 Trisodium phosphate (TSP)
TSP is a powerful and moderately toxic cleaner sometimes available from paint shops. Try to buy it 'straight' rather than mixed with detergents and fragrance (this is the mixture you buy to clean walls before painting). It is a phosphate and therefore has a harmful effect on water supplies, but chemically sensitive people find it useful as it gives off no fumes. Use only when absolutely necessary and wear rubber gloves.

11 Furniture polish
The National Trust Book of Housekeeping (Penguin, 1985) advises against the use of cream polish because of its emulsifiers and says that you should *never* (their italics) use aerosol polishes, especially those containing silicone. Aerosols give instant shine but do not fill in scratches, they make the furniture surface slippery, and continued use leads to a milky finish (because of the solvents they contain), which can only be removed by stripping and refinishing the piece of furniture.

The book is, of course, primarily about the care of fine furniture, but ordinary tables and chairs will benefit from this advice. The authors advise using National Trust Furniture Wax (available at NT shops) once, or at most twice, a year. In between, just dust or rub with a soft cloth—not a feather duster.

A slightly dampened cloth will remove sticky marks, and a little vinegar in the water will cut old polish film.

Make your own beeswax polish by grating beeswax (from the chemist—or your own beehive) into a jar and covering it with natural turpentine. Shake occasionally until the beeswax has dissolved.

A revitalising liquid polish can be made by combining 2 parts boiled linseed oil and 1 part turpentine. Buy both at the DIY store (don't try boiling your own linseed oil). Applied sparingly and rubbed in well, this is suggested as an alternative to refinishing a piece of furniture.

12 Floor polish

A hard, traditional carnauba wax is appropriate for fine wood floors. The West German firm Livos is a good source of information about caring for wood floors, and sell wax polish.

Many people get by perfectly well without waxing or polishing their floors at all. Linoleum will survive nicely with an occasional mopping with soapy water. Ecover's Floor Soap is nice to use and according to the bottle 'the small pores in the floor are filled with saponified oils so that with regular use a deep natural shine will develop'.

13 Cleaning cloths and scourers

David Stephens of *Practical Alternatives* (see page 108) is keen on those round knitted nylon scourers, which last virtually forever. Choose cellulose rather than plastic sponges (you can cut the large ones sold for cars into manageable pieces), and start accumulating good cotton cleaning and polishing rags (linen is useful for glass). A metal scourer can stand in for a lot of scouring powder. Use plain steel wool rather than steel wool pads—you can tear off the small piece which is all you really need, and choose your own soap.

Packaging

Look out for containers which can be reused to conveniently package your basic cleaning supplies. Shakers are useful for bicarbonate of soda and borax, and spray bottles are good for a window cleaning mixture.

Commercial products

Many wholefood shops stock the Ecover range, which comes from Belgium (but will soon be manufactured in the UK) and includes washing up liquid, cream cleaner, toilet cleaner, floor soap, washing powder, fabric conditioner, wool wash and heavy duty hand cleaner. They are fairly expensive but generally effective, safe, and extremely pleasant to use (the natural scents, like lemon, eucalyptus and pine, are delightful). An Edinburgh firm, Faith Products, make several excellent cleaning products—primarily Clear Spring washing up liquid and liquid laundry soap—and plan to expand the range.

Chemico is an odd name for a range of British cleaners which are marketed in the U.S. and Italy as safe for 'both health and the environment'. The original Chemico Household Cleanser Paste has been around since the '30s, and the range is extensively used in hospitals. It includes a creamy cleaner, cleanser paste, carpet cleaner and disinfectant. They are available through wholesalers, cash and carries and janitorial outlets, but I have also found the cleanser paste at a John Lewis branch.

A mail order source is the Allergy Shop in Brighton. The owner developed a range of non-allergenic and biodegradable cleaning products, toiletries, vitamins and minerals as a result of his own sensitivity to all commercial products.

Products aimed at people with sensitive skin are worth looking out for. Boots, for example, has introduced a range of cleaning supplies which contain no perfumes or colourants, and the ingredients have been selected for their low-irritancy.

- Ecover, Full Moon Distributors, Charlton Court Farm, Mouse Lane, Steyning, Sussex BN4 3DG, telephone (0903) 815614.
- Faith Products, 52-56 Albion Road, Edinburgh EH7 5QZ, telephone (031) 661 0900. Cleaning products available by mail order and from retail outlets including Holland & Barrett.
- Chemico, The Country Chemical Company Ltd, 553 Stratford Road, Shirley, Solihull, W Midlands B90 4LB, telephone (021) 744 2294.
- The Allergy Shop, 2 Mount Place, Lewes, East Sussex BN7 1YH, telephone (0273) 472127. Mail order only. Send SASE for free catalogue.
- Little Green Shop, 16 Gardner Street, Brighton, E Sussex BN1 1UP, telephone (0273) 689011.

● Shaklee (UK) Ltd, Norfolk House, 92 Saxon Gate West, Central Milton Keynes MK9 2LS. Basic-H household cleaner.

Specific tips

Brass—according to *The National Trust Book of Housekeeping*, brass fittings on furniture should not be shiny—just well rubbed along with the wood. Lemon juice or white vinegar mixed with bicarbonate of soda will polish brass articles, as will ketchup and even Worcestershire sauce!

Burnt pans—fill with water and add a good handful of salt. Soak overnight, after bringing to a boil if the burning is very bad. Or use potato peelings instead of salt (soak overnight and then boil)—I don't know why this should work, but it does! Avoid scouring stainless steel pans, as this is thought to release toxic heavy metals in later cooking.

Carpets—combine 1 part washing up liquid with 4 parts boiling water. Allow to cool and whip to foam with an egg beater. Sponge into carpet and wipe away with a damp cloth. You can use a steam-cleaning machine with plain water. For gentle cleaning and deodorizing, sprinkle carpet with a mixture of 1 part borax to 2 parts maize meal, or with plain bicarbonate of soda (use lots). Leave for an hour or two, then vacuum. Chemico makes a non-toxic carpet cleaner.

Disinfectants—use a water and borax solution to wipe down the bathroom if you are concerned about germs (perhaps adding a few drops of pine oil), or very dilute bleach. The Golden Health Centre in San Francisco recommends a strong solution of thyme leaves. Or buy a safe commercial product from Chemico or the Allergy Shop.

Heavy-duty cleaners—use washing soda or TSP, but cautiously. A completely natural and non-toxic product is available through catering suppliers: a simple pumice bar which is said to work on all durable surfaces, including tiles.

Ovens—first, try to keep the oven reasonably clean (glass-fronted ovens are a disaster for the casual housekeeper). Use steel wool after thoroughly wetting the oven walls and allowing the dirt to soften. Wipe the newly cleaned oven with a solution of 1 heaped tablespoon of bicarbonate of soda to ½ pint water, to make the task far easier next time.

Scouring powder—instead of the commercial products, which contain bleach, use plain bicarbonate of soda on a sponge. It words beautifully and is good for shining chrome fittings. (It can, however, scratch plexiglass or perspex; if in doubt, test on a corner before scrubbing the entire tub.) Fine wood ash can be used, and horsetail is an excellent natural scourer. This plant grows in the wild (railway embankments are a good place to look) and its very fine silica does the work—grab a handful and use as you would a hank of steel wool.

Silver—can be soaked for 10–15 minutes or gently simmered in a saucepan containing hot water, a few aluminium milk bottle tops or a piece of foil, and 1 tablespoon washing soda. A little toothpaste will polish jewellery, but for really delicate pieces try pure alcohol (or surgical spirit) on a fine paint brush.

Tiles—if you apply a wax polish to clean tiles, they will be easy to wipe down. Scrubbing with bicarbonate of soda on a sponge is effective on water spots as is a 50/50 vinegar and water mixture.

Toilets—Cleaning expert Don Aslett advises against using bleach. It oxidizes or whitens toilet stains rather than removing them, and is hard on chrome and Formica. Use plain white vinegar to remove stains, a mild borax or bleach solution to disinfect (if you must). Ecover's Toilet Cleaner has to be allowed to stand overnight, and needs to be used often, perhaps twice a week.

The ring in your toilet comes from hard water (just the same as the limescale in the kettle) and can be removed with an acid, like vinegar, left to stand. I find that the easiest solution is occasional scrubbing with a piece of wet-and-dry sandpaper, although this does scratch the ceramic glaze.

Windows—mix white vinegar and water 50/50 in a spray bottle and keep on hand. Polish with clean, lintfree cotton or linen rags, or ordinary newspaper. This works beautifully, but if you've been using commercial glass cleaners you may find that it smudges the first time because there is a waxy buildup from your old spray. If this happens, wipe the windows down with a little surgical spirit or washing soda to remove the film.

Washing up

This is worth dwelling on because if you cook at home and don't have a dishwasher, you'll spend more time at the kitchen sink than at any other household task. Everybody has his/her method, which often looks quite unhygienic to a fussy flatmate or girlfriend. Some people never rinse the detergent off dishes, which horrifies everyone else.

If you don't wear rubber gloves, it is especially important to choose a mild liquid—in spite of the television advertisements, a soap which strips grease from plates is going to do the same to the natural oils which keep your hands soft.

The dangers of eutrophication are discussed in Chapter 8, but it's worth repeating that the use of washing up detergent has serious environmental consequences. The usual liquids also contain colourings and fragrance which can irritate sensitive skin, in addition to a drying agent which can increase the body's absorption of hazardous pesticides, including DDT. This substance remains on the dishes even after rinsing.

Some people like to wash under hot running water, with no detergent at all. This works pretty well, but consumes a lot of energy and water. As an alternative, here's my method for getting dishes clean with a minimum expenditure of time, heat, and soap or detergent:

- You'll need a small pan or bowl, Ecover or other washing up liquid, and a brush or scrubber.
- Soak or rinse any really dirty dishes or pans in cold water first.
- Put the bowl in your sink, squirt a little washing up liquid into it and fill with very hot water. Wash glassware, then cutlery, plates, and pots and pans last of all, by dipping your brush or scrubber into the hot soapy water. Set the washed but unrinsed dishes aside.
- Rinse the whole lot at once in cold running water. Allow to dry in the dishrack.

Each dish gets hot soapy treatment, but you need only a small bowl of washing water. For lots of dishes, just do this in batches. And make sure you enlist help—washing up needs to be shared!

Air 'fresheners'

Don't equate the smell of bleach or other harsh cleaners with freshness. Try these ideas:

1 Plenty of ventilation. Open windows, at least once a day, are the best way to clear stale or offensive odours, as well as any toxic fumes which might build up. An extractor fan can help in the kitchen and bathroom.

2 Keep things dry and reasonably warm. Clothes should be

aired thoroughly. Borax inhibits the growth of mildew and mould, so you can sprinkle it around or wipe surfaces with a borax solution.

3 Empty your rubbish frequently and sprinkle a little borax or bicarbonate of soda in the bottom of the bin. (Once you start composting, your rubbish bin stays dry and is very unlikely to smell.)

4 Compost buckets should be emptied every couple of days, and probably every day in the summer. A cover keeps flies away.

There are a number of ideas for natural, and delightful, air fresheners in Chapter 7. Quite a few people seem to regard commercial air fresheners as part of good hygiene around the house (80% of UK households use them), but they work by masking unpleasant odours, coating your nasal passages with an oily film, or numbing your sense of smell with a nerve-deadening agent. Debra Lynn Dadd points out, 'Most air fresheners do nothing to freshen the air—they only add more pollutants.'

CLOTHES CARE

Washing products

Modern washing powders are detergents, with a variety of additives including optical brighteners, enzymes and fragrances. All of these have environmental and health effects. Instead, there are biodegradable, enzyme-free products available from Ecover, Faith Products and other suppliers (see page 213).

Before you switch to a washing powder which does not contain optical brighteners, Debra Lynn Dadd suggests running your clothes through a wash cycle with a double dose of water softener. Otherwise they can turn slightly yellow because of detergent film. (On the other hand, they may simply be returning to their natural colour.)

To make your own washing powder, combine 1 cup soap flakes and ½ cup washing soda. In soft water areas you can use a higher proportion of soap flakes, and in hard water areas you'll need more washing soda. (I don't expect many people to go this far, but add the information in the interest of thoroughness! And you might want to experiment some rainy day when you have time on your hands.)

If you're hooked on spot spray, try rubbing clothes with a damp bar of household soap. In her *Cheaper and Better* (New York: Shadow Lawn Press, 1987), Nancy Birnes recommends the following mixture as a homemade spot spray: ½ cup ammonia, ½ cup white vinegar, ¼ cup baking soda, 2 tablespoons liquid soap and 1½ pints of water.

Better yet (avoiding the ammonia in this mixture), try presoaking in plain water or in soapy wash water. Use the prewash cycle or just switch the machine off after it has filled and leave it for a couple of hours or overnight. Then wash as usual.

Whiteners

Find alternatives to bleach, because it is a dangerous product which should not be used routinely. I've been trying to find an oxygen (rather than chlorine) bleach for clothes, but with no success. These have been on the market in the US for a number of years, and we may see them in the UK before long.

Water softeners are useful alternatives. Add a couple of tablespoons of sodium hexametaphosphate, sodium sesquicarbonate or washing soda (sodium carbonate) to particularly grimy loads of washing. With very delicate fabrics, presoak for 10-30 minutes in a mixture of 1 part hydrogen peroxide to 7 parts water.

Hanging on a line in the sunshine is good for whitening clothes, and an old method was to spread them on green vegetation—a lawn, for example—the oxygen produced by the plants is said to be helpful. Stanley Ager, author of *The Butler's Guide* (Papermac, 1980), suggests that the easiest way to keep white clothes white is to wear and wash them frequently. He also mentions that frequent dry-cleaning can cause white clothes to pick up a grey tinge.

Boiling sounds prehistoric to anyone who wasn't raised in an era when teatowels were boiled daily. But as long as you have a large soup pot, it is easy enough and certainly effective. I'm not suggesting that we go back to routinely boiling clothes, but as an occasional treat for white cottons, why not? Allow to cool, drain off most of the water, and spin in your washing machine or spin dryer. (Remember that this will only work with 100% cotton or linen—not polyester blends!)

Fabric conditioners

Conditioners, or softeners, were designed for use with synthetic fabrics, to prevent static cling. If you are using natural fibre fabrics, this shouldn't be a problem. In a hard water area they do seem to give softer handwashed woollens, but a little white vinegar (soak a few dried herbs in it if you want a pleasant fragrance) should do the trick—and running a warm iron over the dry jumper also softens it.

Or mix 1 part bicarbonate of soda, 1 part white or herbal vinegar and 2 parts water. Use as you would a commercial fabric softener. Ecover's fabric softener is made of natural fatty acids, water and lemon oil, and is biodegradable.

People often use softeners to make clothes smell 'fresh'. Hanging them outside does a far better job, and you don't have to worry about possible allergic reactions. Artificial fragrances do not freshen anything. If you cannot dry outside, how about herbal bags in your drawers and closets?

Ironing

Rather than use spray starch in an aerosol can, with their inherent dangers, why not try one or more of the following ideas:
1 You can still buy old-fashioned starch, which you mix up with cold water, then add boiling water and stir to a smooth paste. This is obviously more complicated than using an aerosol spray. But just how many of your clothes really need to be starched? It's fun to give linen napkins and lace collars an occasional stiff starching, but 100% cotton and linen have a naturally crisp finish after ironing. It is synthetic fabrics which tend to need perking up with starch.
2 Mix starch powder (or even ordinary cornflour) with water in a sprayer. Add a little cologne or a few drops of an essential oil if you want it scented. A rounded tablespoon of starch to 1 pint of water will give an average hold. (I prefer to mix the starch with boiling water, according to package directions, and then dilute.) Shake before spraying and wipe the nozzle with a damp cloth when you finish—but don't keep for long or it will grow amazingly mouldy!
3 Try taking your freshly laundered garments to a drycleaning establishment for pressing-only with their special high-temperature equipment. Many cleaners will do this—ring around.

Drycleaning

'Dry' cleaning is done by using a solvent instead of water to wash clothes. The industry has a history of fatal worker illness as a result of the chemicals used. Carbon tetrachloride was used until it was recently found to cause cancer. The most common solvents at the moment are two organo-chlorines, trichlorotrifluoroethane and perchloroethylene. They, too, are toxic, and the former is a chlorofluorohydrocarbon, one of the CFCs which are causing the deterioration of the ozone layer. Short-term, acute exposure can cause giddiness, nausea and unconsciousness. Chronic exposure is even worse because the compounds accumulate in body tissue and lead to organ damage and cancer risk.

Although drycleaning chemicals evaporate after a short time, the environmental consequences of manufacturing, transporting and disposing of them mean that we should avoid drycleaning as much as possible. A government report shows that the drinking water of up to 1½ million British people may be contaminated with carcingenic drycleaning solvents. We should also consider whether we want to pay for other people to spend their days working with such hazardous chemicals.

Drycleaning machines are common at laundrettes, and are considerably cheaper than professional drycleaning. These machines generally use the stronger perchloroethylene, and people have been known to pass out after driving off with still-damp drycleaned clothes in the car. (It is essential, should you use one of these machines, that you do not overload it and that the clothes are completely dry when the cycle is finished. If they are not, close the door and call the manager for help.)

According to an article in *Mademoiselle*, 'William Seitz, executive director of the US Neighborhood Cleaners Association (a national trade association of dry cleaners), says the best possible advice is to be a smart consumer and not to buy clothes that are difficult or even hazardous to clean.' (September 1981). Better yet, avoid drycleaning entirely, since drycleaning *is* hazardous. Most garments can be handwashed. 'Dry clean only' labels sometimes mean that the manufacturer does not want to be held responsible for careless washing by the customer.

Wash cotton garments in the machine, and silk and wool by hand (silk in cold and wool in cool or lukewarm water). Use a mild soap—Lux Flakes or Ecover Wool Wash, for example, or soft soap made with soap scraps. Add a little vinegar to the rinse water to cut soap film. Sweaters should be squeezed out in a towel then dried flat, and silks should be allowed to drip dry, then ironed while still slightly damp.

If you do have clothes drycleaned (and it's hard to imagine coping with men's suits any other way, although we should be looking for an alternative), ensure that they are thoroughly aired, outdoors or in an unoccupied room, before being put away.

Stains

Drycleaning fluid, like drycleaning, should be avoided as much as you possibly can. Complicated advice on dealing with stains is lost on most of us modern housekeepers, but a simple range of products should enable you to deal with most domestic crises.

The most important thing to remember is to start with COLD water, particularly on protein-based spots like blood, egg or gravy. Hot water will cook and set the stain, and you'll probably never get it out.

1 The standard trick of pouring **salt** on a wine stain is usually effective, and is also worth trying on fruit and beetroot stains.

2 Getting out the **soda syphon** (or just a bottle of whatever fizzy water you drink, or plain soda water) works on many stains.

3 A **borax** solution—1 part borax to 8 parts water—is worth keeping around (out of the reach of children) for treating a wide range of stains. Debra Lynn Dadd suggests it for blood, chocolate, coffee and tea, mildew, mud and urine. Sponge it on and let it dry, before washing with soap and cold water.

4 Plain old **boiling water** is good for fruit and tea stains— preferably poured on taut fabric from a great height (centre the spot over a bowl and stretch it tight with a rubberband, put it in the bathtub and start pouring).

5 Rub grass stains with **glycerine** (from the chemist) before washing. Brilliant on cricket trousers and worth trying on cosmetic stains. You may need to follow with washing soda to remove the oily element of the stain.

6 **Eucalyptus oil** will deal with nasties like tar and oil and grass stains. Get it at the chemist. Rub it in well, then wash as normal. An effective tar remover is lard (or another solid fat), thoroughly rubbed in and then washed out—use some washing soda to cut the grease.

7 Soak perspiration stains in water with a good dollop of white **vinegar** or a handful of **bicarbonate of soda**—try both and

see which works for you. This apparently depends on your
particular body chemistry.

8 Try **lemon juice** and **salt** on rust stains, then lay in the
sunshine (let's be optimistic) for a couple of days. Women
used to 'bleach' clothes in this way as they dried over bushes
or on the clothesline. It both whitens and deodorizes, and
the clothes smell wonderful. Worth trying on even the most
impossible of stains (friends used it in the south of France
for ink marks on a white silk shirt, with great success), and
essential for cloth nappies.

TOILETRIES

Petrochemicals

Many people are sensitive to petroleum-based chemicals—one
estimate suggests that ⅓ to ½ of the population may have
some reaction to them. Toxic waste from the petrochemical

industry is a leading source of world pollution, and Barry Commoner comments that 'You need to regard the products of the petrochemical industry as evolutionary misfits and therefore very likely to be incompatible with the chemistry of living things. The failure to understand this basic fact has caused the whole problem in chemical pollution. We keep being surprised that chemicals that were perfectly nice and simple to make turn out to have very serious biological consequences.' ('Highrisk high tech: Who decides how it is used?', Cambridge, MA: *Science for the People*, March/April 1987, reprinted in *Utne Reader*, March/April 1988).

It isn't easy to avoid petrochemicals in everyday life, as they include plastics, synthetic fabrics, newspaper print and a nearly infinite array of other common items. You can, however, cut out at least some of the petroleum products you use on your body.

Petroleum jelly and mineral oil are the obvious things to look out for; many cosmetics, lotions and creams contain them. In the body (absorbed through the skin) they take up oil-soluble vitamins A and D. Ordinary 'baby' oil is simply a scented mineral oil, and many years ago the nutritionist Adele Davis advised parents against using it. A plain vegetable oil works beautifully—olive oil is traditional in many countries.

The same goes for adults. Try using an unrefined vegetable oil for removing makeup. If you don't want to smell like a salad, choose a mild oil and add a few drops of your favourite essential oil.

You can also look for vegetable-based products at wholefood shops. Faith in Nature is one skin care range. Every Body Shop has a file for customer reference listing the ingredients for all their products, so you can make an informed choice, but they have no policy about avoiding petrochemical ingredients.

Animal products and animal testing

You'll want to avoid cosmetics and toiletries which have been tested on animals. Beauty Without Cruelty was the first to emphasize this issue, but many companies are now responding to consumer concern, most notably the Body Shop. John Button's *Green Pages* and the *Green Consumer Guide* are good sources of information.

Fragrances

The most common cause of allergic reactions to cosmetics and beauty products is their fragrance. Natural essential oils are derived from plants, and many people who cannot tolerate artificial scents find that they have no problems with natural fragrances.

Unscented products allow you to *choose* how you are going to smell, instead of having your deodorant, shampoo and face cream all competing. With a small range of essential oils, you can concoct your own distinctive scents, as well as experiment with their subtle psychological and physical effects (see 'Aromatherapy', page 155).

Specifics

Soap

- ☛ Choose a plain, mild soap for general use, with no deodorant and no fragrance.
- ☛ Buy good quality, naturally-scented soaps. This sort of soap is expensive, but luxurious. If you store it with your shirts or underwear for a couple of months, the bars will last longer (having dried out), and in the meantime your clothes will smell wonderful. This also keeps moths away.

Bath products

Although I am not especially sensitive, ordinary bath salts (from the supermarket or chemist) make me itch. The Weleda herbal baths are heavenly, and you can easily make your own bath mixture.

Here are a few ideas: a couple of handfuls of sea salt; bicarbonate of soda or Epsom salts for a mineral bath; oatmeal and powdered milk in a muslin bag for a soothing bath; vegetable oil beaten with an egg and some milk for a creamy rich bath (store this mixture in the refrigerator). Add your preferred scent to any of these. Or try a therapeutic bath with dried seaweed.

Body powder

Talc can be contaminated with asbestos fibre, and some people are allergic to the fragrances used. Ordinary cornflour and arrowroot are soft and absorbent, and you can buy powders made from cornflour, colloidal oatmeal and even silk powder!

Antiperspirants and deodorants

Antiperspirants generally contain aluminium chlorhydrate—which blocks your pores and prevents perspiration—as their active ingredient, and can contain other heavy metals. Deodorants use bactericide and fragrance, but do not actually stop perspiration. Both can irritate delicate skin, and antiperspirants may cause severe and painful rashes. Blocking sweat glands is a bad idea anyway, and concern over the biological effects of aluminium suggest that aluminium salts should not be applied to the skin on a regular basis.

Aerosol deodorants have an added danger, in addition to their effect on the ozone layer. A teenage boy died as a result of 'excessive but proper use of an aerosol in a confined space' (*The Independent*, 5 August 1988): the propellant gases in his deodorant had caused cardiac arrest.

As long as you wash frequently enough with soap and water these strong chemicals should not be necessary, and there are very effective alternatives—giving up your antiperspirant is not the antisocial step you might imagine! Try one or more of the following:

- That old standby, bicarbonate of soda, can be patted on with a piece of cotton wool. Apply after your bath or shower, while skin is still slightly damp. Even heavy perspirers find this effective, and the packaging couldn't be simpler!
- Some people can get away with just a little essential oil—rose or sandalwood or whatever you like—mixed with a little vegetable oil or body lotion and rubbed under the arms after bathing.
- Non-toxic commercial products by Weleda (lemon juice base), Tom's of Maine (with coriander as its active ingredient) and Cosmetics To Go (bicarbonate of soda, Singhalese dendrobe and essential oils) do the job and are very pleasant to use.

Toothpaste and mouthwash

Excellent natural varieties, available at wholefood shops, will not contain ammonia, ethanol, artificial flavours and colours, formaldehyde, mineral oil, saccharin, sugar or carcinogenic PVP plastic, as commercial brands may. British-made Hollytrees toothpaste is especially nice. It comes in lemon and orange flavours—the orange is ideal for children.

You may or may not want your child to have fluoride (see

page 336). If you do, rather than haphazard intake from toothpaste, why not give fluoride drops or tablets? Some children make a habit of eating toothpaste, which is not a good idea.

You can also brush your teeth with bicarbonate of soda (perhaps mixed with a few drops of peppermint oil). This has been shown to help prevent the buildup of plaque.

Mouthwashes contain some of the same germ killers which go into bathroom disinfectants, and a persistent problem with bad breath is likely to be a sign of other health or dental problems.

Good oral hygiene—frequent brushing and using dental floss—and a healthy diet low in sugary food will do more for your teeth and breath than any number of cleaning products.

Shampoo

Shampoos contain a variety of additives which cause problems for some people and add to the chemical burden we live with. Products you use to fight dandruff may in fact aggravate the problem, according to Laurence Falk, who founded the Crimpers salon group and is marketing a range of additive-free hair products (called 'Pure' and available at some chemists and hair salons).

Anti-dandruff shampoos contain highly toxic chemicals, primarily selenium sulphide, which can, if swallowed, cause the degeneration of internal organs. Not a nice thing to use on your body regularly. Another dangerous chemical is recorcinol, which is easily absorbed through the skin. Many people think they have dandruff who don't (32% of the shampoos sold in the UK are medicated), and once you start using an anti-dandruff shampoo it can be very difficult to stop.

If you have a dandruff problem, the first things to look at are your diet and general health. Thorough brushing and regular scalp massage are preferably to chemical shampoos. Dandruff is sometimes stress-related, another possibility to consider.

Debra Lynn Dadd recommends a method which she promises will clear up dandruff forever: instead of shampooing, massage handfuls of bicarbonate of soda into your hair and scalp, then rinse thoroughly. Do not use anything else. Your hair may look like a haystack at first, but apparently the treatment works a treat after a couple of weeks—dandruff gone and hair in good condition. You then alternate the soda treatment with a natural shampoo. Faith in Nature's seaweed shampoo, used on its own, has proved a successful treatment for some people.

Hairspray

Hairsprays contain toxic polyvinylpyrrolidone (PVP) plastic resin and propellant gases. When these are finely dispersed, as they are in an aerosol, they can cause a lung disease called thesaurosis (which is, fortunately, reversible). They don't do much for your skin and eyes either. Instead, try using a safe commercial gel, or make your own:

Lemon hair spray

This gives good hold, shine and body—and it smells nice. Try it. Slice or chop 2 lemons and put them in a saucepan with 2 teacups water. Simmer until the lemons have become very soft. Cool and strain through a piece of cheesecloth or fine sieve. Put in spray bottle and store in the fridge (or add a tablespoon of vodka to preserve it at room temperature). Dilute with water to suit your hair. If it seems sticky, add a little more water.

Other ideas include a mixture of honey and water (experiment with proportions), a gel made from ordinary gelatin powder (try 1 teaspoon gelatin to ½ pint water) or vegetarian alginic gel (available from wholefood shops).

Hair colouring

Laboratory tests have shown hair dyes to be mutagens and suspected human carcinogens. These chemicals can easily penetrate the scalp, and *Consumer Reports*, the American equivalent of *Which?*, advises against their use by pregnant women or women of childbearing age.

This is a good example of casually used products which have potentially damaging effects. Fortunately there are a variety of safe plant-based products around—the Body Shop sells a range, and a West German brand is available from the Green Farm Nutrition Centre.

You can also try homemade mixtures, ranging from lemon juice and chamomile for blond hair to black coffee or an extract of walnut hulls to cover grey in dark hair.

If you must use chemical dyes, try to avoid contact with your scalp—hair painting and foil-wrap highlighting can be done in a salon.

Nail varnish

Acetone solvent not only has a strong and pervasive odour, but can cause skin rashes, dry out nails and dissolve plastics. Nail varnishes are based on formaldehyde resin and any beauty book will tell you that nails need to be left unvarnished from time to time to allow them to 'breathe'.

Nail buffing kits will give you an attractive natural shine with no chemicals to worry about. If you use varnish, ensure that the room you are in is well-ventilated—better yet, sit outside until the nails are thoroughly dry.

Nail hardeners are also made from formaldehyde. A general improvement in diet is a better way of strengthening your nails.

Cosmetics

More and more cosmetic houses are becoming aware of skin sensitivities, and are cutting out irritating ingredients, particularly scents. Some ingredients in lipsticks have been shown to cause cancer in animals (PVP plastic, saccharin, mineral oil and artificial colours).

Choose unscented products which have not been tested on animals, and avoid artificial fragrances and colours. The Body Shop and Cosmetics to Go both do interesting ranges, and you will find other brands in whole food shops.

Over-packaging is a problem with most cosmetics. The amount you buy is small, the price large, and the elegant plastic compact makes the exchange seem less unreasonable. A few firms sell refills, but on the whole there is not much you can do except use as little as possible. Write to the head office of your favourite firm about this.

● The Body Shop, Dominion Way, Rustington, West Sussex BN16 3LR, telephone (0903) 776151. Write for a mail order catalogue or to find out where your nearest shop is.

● Cosmetics To Go, 29 High Street, Poole, Dorset BH15 1AB, or telephone 0800 373 335 (no charge) for free catalogue, printed on recycled paper. Highly packaged, unfortunately.

HOME BUILDING AND MAINTENANCE

Building materials

Asbestos is a well-publicised danger, but asphalt, plastics and even particle board also pose a threat to human health.

You have little choice about the materials your house is built of, but when making any additions you could consult one of the books listed below. New homes are likely to have large amounts of plastic and pressed woods (bound with urea-formaldehyde resin) which it would be both difficult and expensive to replace. This is another incentive for improving old housing stock whenever possible.

Formaldehyde is particularly hazardous because it seems to act as a trigger for acute chemical sensitivity. After exposure to high levels of formaldehyde (with the installation of new particle board cupboards, for example) quite a number of people have become chemical cripples—unable to tolerate even small quantities of the many other man-made chemicals which surround us.

In general, sticking with natural and biodegradable materials is the safest course of action (though of course some natural materials are hazardous too: lead and asbestos for example).

● *Hazardous Building Materials, A Guide to the Selection of Alternatives*, ed. S. R. Curwell and C. G. Marsh (E. & F.N. Spon, 1986).

● *Your Home, Your Health, and Well-Being*, David Rousseau, W.J. Rea M.D. and Jean Enwright (Berkeley: Ten Speed Press, 1988).

● *Well Body, Well Earth*, Mike Samuels M.D. and Hal Zina Bennett (San Francisco: Sierra Club Books, 1983).

● Debra Lynn Dadd's books also mention hazardous building materials and suggest alternatives.

Timber treatment

More than 20 families are demanding compensation from Rentokil, the wood preservation firm, for serious health damage attributed to Rentokil chemicals and timber treatments. They include people whose homes were treated by Rentokil,

former Rentokil employees who now have acute health
problems, and Welsh council workers who used Rentokil
chemicals.

The firm's head office told me that they are researching
non-chemical ways of treating wood—by heat and electrical
processes and with carbon dioxide—but they currently use
Lindane, Permethrin, tributyltin oxide (TBTO) and various
pentachlorophenates. Lindane is a broad spectrum insecticide
and organochloride and a suspected carcinogen. Permethrin
was developed for use in places with bats, and is an analogue
of pyrethrum, a natural insecticide used by organic gardeners.
It has become popular because people think it may also be less
toxic for humans. Rentokil claims that there is no evidence
to support this, but there is, in fact, plenty of data
available.

TBTO is an extremely dangerous chemical, now banned as
an antifoulant for boats and banned in many countries for
home wood treatment. German work suggests that it causes
psychosis, anxiety and other central nervous system disorders,
but most general wood preservatives contain it.

Rentokil will, if requested, use a non-chemical method for
treating fungal decay, by cutting out all rotten timber, removing sources of damp and then carefully monitoring moisture
levels. This sort of treatment is more expensive than chemical
treatment, and they refuse to give the standard 30 year guar-
antees which almost all building societies, and councils, require
(the Ecology Building Society is the single exception—contact
them for more information).

Research into alternatives is being done by the Building
Research Establishment, the Timber Research and Development Association, the National Trust and a number of uni-
versities, and there seems to be considerable commercial
interest in safer methods.

Heat treatment (in a sauna, for example) can be used to
treat woodworm in small pieces of furniture. But I wouldn't
suggest it for a valuable item, or anything with glued joints.
Woodworm cannot lay eggs through a painted or polished
surface, so they can be stopped before they get in.

● The Ecology Building Society, 8 Main Street, Crosshills,
   Keighley, West Yorkshire BD20 8TB, telephone (0535)
   35933.

Decorating

Paints, varnishes, and the various solvents we use to mix them and to clean up afterwards can be dangerous, and also present disposal problems.

Good ventilation is the first thing to consider when using any product containing solvents. Plenty of fresh air will dry paint more effectively than heating the room.

Special paint techniques have become popular, and there is now interest in making your own paints as they have more interesting finishes and subtle colours than commercial paints. Ingredients include sizing, whiting and artists' pigments. (For a booklet about preparing your own paints, write to fine arts suppliers L. Cornelissen, 105 Great Russell Street, London WC1B 3RY, telephone 01-636 1045.)

A fascinating range of completely natural and non-toxic decorating products is available by mail order from two West German firms. Both will send information in English on request.

● Livos Pflanzenchemie, Neustdter Str. 23, D-3123 Bodenteich, West Germany, telephone 058 24-1087. (Their US distributor is Livos Plantchemistry, 614 Agua Fria Street, Santa Fe, NM 87501, telephone (505) 988-9111.)

● Biofa Natur Produkte GmbH, Dobelstr. 22, D-7325 Boll, West Germany, telephone (049) 07164 4825.

PESTS

Insecticides are poisonous and should be avoided both because of their effect on the environment and on our health. First, remove whatever is attracting the pests. Food should be stored in airtight containers (like glass jars), and you'll need to take special care with cleaning. Wash up dishes immediately after eating, don't leave crumbs in bed, and empty wastebaskets frequently. Dirty disposable nappies attract pests, another reason for avoiding them (see Chapter 15).

Then try the following ideas (there are dozens more in Debra Lynn Dadd's books and in more easily available books of household hints like Moyra Bremner's *Supertips to Make Life Easy* and *Supertips 2*).

Flies

They do not like the smell of orange and lemon peels, cloves or mint. You can also use a flyswatter, or sticky fly strips.

Ants

Sprinkle dried mint, chili powder or borax wherever they are coming in—of course, your first step should be to block the hole, if possible. Plant mint outside; ants don't like the smell. Or learn to love them! They are a fascinating introduction to colonial life.

Cockroaches

You could try baking them out—heating the house as hot as it will get for a couple of hours. Easier, and safer, is to leave out a mixture of flour, cocoa and borax, or bicarbonate of soda and powdered sugar, or flour and plaster of paris (out of the reach of children, of course). All of these should lead to a quick death for the noxious creatures. Another method is to make a 'fall trap' by putting a few sweets in the bottom of a glass jar, with a bit of wood for a ramp. They climb in but cannot get out.

Moths

Mothballs are made of paradichlorobenzene, a volatile chemical which is a respiratory irritant and can cause depression, seizures and long-term damage to kidneys and liver. Although the packet may warn 'avoid prolonged breathing of vapour', the way mothballs are used (distributed amongst your clothing) makes prolonged exposure unavoidable.

Cedar wood, lavender and natural camphor are natural, traditional moth repellants. The most important thing is to ensure that woollens are cleaned before being stored. Pressing with a steam iron or tumbling in a dryer will also kill any moth eggs.

Insect repellants

Rather than apply commercial repellants—which contain Deet (diethyl toluamide), a strong irritant which can eat through plastic and dissolve paint—rub your skin with vinegar (on a cotton wool ball) and allow to dry. The smell disappears as it dries, but this makes you taste nasty. Oil of citronella or penny-royal can be diluted in a little vegetable oil and rubbed on. Eating lots of garlic is also said to repel insects! Cosmetics To Go makes an African herbal mosquito repellant with no chemical insecticides.

MISCELLANEOUS

Plastics

In Chapter 3, we looked at the ecological problem posed by our excessive use of plastics. Plastics also pose a problem for human health. Many are suspected human carcinogens.

PVC (polyvinyl chloride) plastic is extremely common, used for everything from tablecloths to shoe soles, credit cards to squeezy toys. It contains vinyl chloride, which is recognized as causing cancer, birth defects, skin diseases and liver dysfunction as well as many other health problems. It is relatively unstable, especially if it contains added plasticizers (which are often PCBs), and small quantities of vinyl chloride are given off. NASA has banned the use of PVC in its space capsules because it out-gassed and condensed in optical equipment.

The list of proven and suspected health effects of different sorts of plastic is a long one. While none of us can avoid plastics entirely, we can reduce the amounts in our immediate home environment. American organization expert Stephanie Winston says, 'I've made a fairly serious effort to get along with a minimum of plastics and synthetics. This is not so much for philosophical reasons as that I feel better when there's not too much synthetic stuff floating around.'

Avoiding plastics
- Choose alternatives to plastic whenever possible.
- Let new plastic items (such as a shower curtain) air outside or in an unused room until any noticeable smell has disappeared.
- Avoid food coming into direct contact with plastics, particularly soft plastics.
- Buy food packed in glass, paper or natural cellophane in preference to plastic.
- Do not drink hot drinks from polystyrene cups.
- Use plasticizer-free food wrapping.

Paper products

While a few people react to the dyes and fragrances in commercial toilet paper, all of us need to be aware that bleached paper—white loo rolls, kitchen towels, facial tissues, coffee filters and so on—has been found to contain traces of the highly toxic chemical dioxin. This is the result of standard pulping and bleaching operations, and because the chemicals are also released in large quantities into lakes and rivers, paper mills are one of the most polluting of industries. For more about what you can do, see page 70.

Fabrics and furnishings

Attention has been focussed on urea-formaldehyde cavity insulation as a source of formaldehyde in the home, but the resins used to bind plywood, chipboard and furniture are also significant sources of this vapour. A 1979 study at the Lawrence Berkeley National Laboratory in the US found that 'the concentration of formaldehyde vapour in the air tripled once furniture was installed in an otherwise empty house' (*New Scientist*, 5 December 1985, p 35).

Clothing and furnishing fabrics receive a variety of chemical treatments. Even natural fabrics can be loaded with dyes and chemical residues. 'No-iron' fabrics are treated with formaldehyde resin (a well-known allergen), as well as with other chemicals. Choose natural fibres in preference to synthetics, and beware of any special fabric treatments. (It's a good idea to wash all new clothes before you wear them.) Look out for untreated cotton 'nature shirts' from West Germany.

Futons provide excellent bedding for sensitive individuals, and latex foam is a possible choice for pillows and cushions.

According to Drs Peter Mansfield and Jean Monro, cheap expanded polyester furniture stuffing can 'release irritant vapours for a large part of their lives'. The slow accumulation of volatile chemicals interferes with detoxification mechanisms and can lead to other health problems. They suggest that you choose feathers or horsehair, and say that if you are allergic to these, you can probably be desensitized.

Wool carpets are sometimes treated with mothproofing and soil repellants. If anyone in your household is chemically sensitive, new rugs or carpets should be steam cleaned with plain water immediately after installation.

Office supplies

Watch out for office products which contain toxic solvents. In general, you can tell by sniffing: try to stick to items which are odour-free.

NCR (no carbon required) paper is a hazard, and photocopying machines contain toners and solvents which you should avoid (this equipment can be sited in another room).

Car maintenance

Anyone who is keen on DIY should know about Ecover's heavy duty hand cleaner, which works a treat on engine oil and black underseal.

If you are the sort of mechanic who takes the carburetor to bits and cleans it in a bowl of petrol, please take care about breathing the fumes, which contain toxic benzene. A few garages offer self-service engine steam-cleaning equipment, which not only saves many hours of labour but does a terrific job.

A world shortage of ethylene glycol has led to a drastic increase in the price of conventional anti-freeze. As a result, anti-freeze based on the non-toxic propylene glycol is now cheaper than the normal type. (The non-toxic product was previously more expensive, and used only where it could come into contact with food or water.)

PROPOSITION 65

In 1986 the voters of California approved a 'nontoxics initiative' which came into force early in 1988. A $6 million campaign against Prop 65 was sponsored by vulnerable business interests, and they were able to get the original list of notifiable chemicals reduced to a mere 29. Nonetheless, this initiative represents a significant victory for the environmental lobby.

It is now illegal for businesses to knowingly dump chemicals which cause cancer, sterility or birth defects, and individual citizens can more easily sue violators. The listed chemicals will eventually include the approximately 200 known carcinogens identified by the National Toxicology Program.

Unfortunately, warning labels are not required on all products containing known toxins; instead, consumers have to telephone a free hotline to ask about particular items (not very useful when you are out shopping!). But warning signs will be posted in shops, restaurants and workplaces, reading something like this: 'Chemicals known to the State of California to cause cancer, birth defects or other reproductive harm may be present in foods or beverages sold or served here.' Imagine that at your local café!

As more people become aware of the danger chemicals pose to our health and to our environment, legislation like this will become the rule rather than the exception. The idea is not to spoil our fun but instead to increase consumer awareness of the chemical dangers around us, and to enable us to protect ourselves and our children. In addition, there will be a considerable incentive for businesses to clean up their products.

SAFETY

We all need to use hazardous products on occasion. Take a close look at warning labels. Here is one: 'Contains: methylene chloride, hydrocarbon propellant. Highly flammable. Harmful by inhalation. Possible risk of *irreversible effects* [my italics] from vapours or spray. May cause eye irritation.' (3M Aerosol Auto Adhesive). This could even produce carbonyl chloride, an infamous war gas, if burnt. Frankly, after reading the label I think I'd look for a safer product.

Here are some precautions to take:

1 Buy only what you need.
2 Read warning labels and follow directions. The information on labels is often sparse. Err on the side of caution.
3 Don't use more than the directions call for, and you might even start with a bit less.
4 Close containers tightly.
5 Work outside if possible, and try not to breathe fumes— take ventilation seriously. (Wear a thick sweater and keep the windows open.)
6 Do not mix chemicals (bleach and ammonia are a potential deadly combination, and many cleaning products contain one or the other).
7 Wear protective clothing and a mask if necessary, and protect your hands with rubber gloves.
8 Avoid wearing soft contact lenses while working with any solvent.
9 Clean up carefully, both yourself and your work area.
10 Store in the original container (don't leave white spirit in an unlabelled jam jar, for example).
11 Try to use up what you've bought. Dispose of any leftovers through a hazardous waste programme, should your council have one, or carefully sealed and wrapped in the dustbin— not down the drain!

12 Keep dangerous chemicals well out of children's reach.

Further information

● *Nontoxic & Natural: How To Avoid Dangerous Everyday Products and Buy or Make Safe Ones* (Los Angeles: J. P. Tarcher, 1984) and *The Nontoxic Home: Protect Yourself and Your Family From Everyday Toxics and Health Hazards* (J. P. Tarcher, 1986), by Debra Lynn Dadd. Stocked at Genesis Books, 88 Old Street, London EC1V 9BT, telephone 01-250 1868.

● *Chemical Children, How to Protect Your Family From Harmful Pollutants*, Dr Peter Mansfield and Dr Jean Monro (Century, 1987).

● *Living Dangerously*, Hilda Cherry Hills (Roberts, 1973)— available from Henry Doubleday Research Association, see address page 306.

● *Supertips to Make Life Easy* (Andre Deutsch, 1983) and *Supertips 2* (Andre Deutsch, 1985), both by Moyra Bremner. These books are full of ideas for simple cleaning products and toiletries, as are other books of household hints.

● London Hazards Centre, 3rd Floor, Headland House, 308 Gray's Inn Road, London WC1X 8DS, telephone 01-837 5605. An excellent source of information about home and workplace hazards.

11
RADIATION

Not that I wish in any way to belittle the evils of conventional air and water pollution; but we must recognise 'dimensional differences' when we encounter them: radioactive pollution is an evil of an incomparably greater 'dimension' than anything mankind has known before. One might even ask: what is the point of insisting on clean air, if the air is laden with radioactive particles? And even if the air could be protected, what is the point of it, if soil and water are being poisoned?

E. F. Schumacher
Small is Beautiful, 1973

For several weeks after the Chernobyl disaster in 1986 we were suddenly conscious of our vulnerability to radiation and of its peculiarly frightening nature. We wondered whether it was safe to go outdoors or to drink the innocent-looking milk on our doorsteps, and whether we could trust the government experts who sallied forth on every news bulletin to reassure us that all was well.

238

Chernobyl made it abundantly clear that distance provides us with no safeguard. Welsh, Cumbrian and Scottish sheep farmers have probably suffered more than anyone else, with loss of income and fears for their own families' health. Even two years later, many sheep were not being passed as fit for human consumption. It is estimated that several thousand Britons will eventually get cancer as a result of the radiation released from Chernobyl, but as with almost all deaths resulting from radioactive contamination of the environment, the victims will be anonymous.

Attitudes

Why is radiation so unnerving? Like cancer (which it can cause), it strikes most of us as mysterious, uncontrollable and even evil. Susan Sontag, American literary critic, suggested that the solution to the demoralizing effect of cancer is to de-mythologize it (*Illness as Metaphor*, New York: Farrar, Straus & Giroux, 1978), and the same can be said of radiation. Just as most of us are trying to familiarize ourselves with computers, non-scientists also need to gain some understanding of what radiation is, where it comes from and what its effects are. Only then can we make choices about the increasing levels of radiation in our environment and about military and industrial uses of radioactive material.

We seem, however, to have nothing but a choice between cowering under our beds, helpless with terror, and shrugging off all suggestions of danger. I used to think that the scientific community *wanted* to frighten us, but finally realized that most of the time scientists are attempting to reassure us that things are *not* dangerous. (We need to keep in mind that most scientific research is paid for by government and industry.) Debates over the hole in the ozone layer and pollution in the North Sea have pointed out how supposedly scientific principles can be disastrous when applied to environmental problems. Scientists err on the side of caution, waiting until there is conclusive evidence of damage. When it comes to an ecosystem or an animal species, this may be far too late to save them. Instead, we need to apply precautionary principles—when damage is seen and there is a suspected link with human activity, that activity should be on trial—it should have to be proved safe before being used again.

Many modern dangers are difficult for the ordinary person

to understand, and Thomas Kuhn, of Harvard University, has pointed out that one of the characteristics of modern scientific research is that it is no longer 'embodied in books addressed, such as Franklin's *Experiments . . . on Electricity* or Darwin's *Origin of the Species*, to anyone who might be interested . . . Instead, it will appear as brief articles addressed only to professional colleagues.' (*The Structure of Scientific Revolutions*, University of Chicago, 1970, p 20). We non-scientists are at an increasing disadvantage, and turning this situation around is one of the biggest challenges that face us in the late 20th century.

Psychologist Paul Slovic has attempted to measure public perception of a wide variety of risks—from bridges to coal burning—with two criteria, relative degrees of dread and familiarity. Three of the five greatest perceived risks were connected with radiation: radioactive waste, nuclear reactor accidents and nuclear weapons fallout. (People fear nuclear war even more, but are more certain of its consequences.) Also in the top five was DNA technology (genetic engineering), and in that field, too, the issue of who controls science and the scientists is of the utmost importance ('The Axis of Fear', *Harper's Magazine*, New York: May, 1988).

We cannot see, touch or feel low level radiation, as we can some other modern hazards. If your family starts to itch when they put on clothes washed in biological detergent, you go back to the 'original formula', without needing any technical information at all—whereas you might eventually die from a cancer caused by radiation you were never aware of having been exposed to.

The question of whom we can trust for information about radiation is a difficult one. Many residents around Three Mile Island (TMI) in Pennsylvania complained of a metallic taste in their mouths after the accident there in 1979. TMI authorities contend that this is impossible because the symptom only occurs when millions of curies of radioactive isotopes of iodine are present, and emissions had been no more than 14 curies. Just how much radiation escaped is rather difficult to determine because the Metropolitan Edison Company (Met Ed), owner-operator of TMI, insists that records of airborne emissions for the first two days after the accident have gone missing.

Nonetheless, thousands of residents have suffered as a result of the accident, and some 2000 are suing Met Ed. Many have had malignant tumours removed, and have suffered still-births, spontaneous abortions, heart failure, stroke and hypothyroidism. Cancers are rife, somewhat sooner than would be expected after a nuclear accident, and researchers suspect that previous routine ventings from the plant 'may have set the stage for even more devastating medical damage delivered by the Unit Two disaster.' Dr George Tokuhata, Chief of the Pennsylvania Epidemiology Division, is quoted as saying that 'In the long run, it seems, people are the most reliable dosimeters.' (Harvey Wasserman, 'The Disaster at Three Mile Island is not over', *Harrowsmith*, Charlotte, VT: May/June 1987, reprinted in the *Utne Reader*, November/December 1987.)

Determining the effects of various sorts of radiation is highly contentious, and for every figure one expert presents another is thrown down to counter it. Statistics can tell us whether the rate of a particular disease in a given area is higher than average, but gives no clue as to causes. Besides this, results can be dramatically altered by simple adjustments in the boundary lines for a statistical survey.

IONIZING RADIATION

What is it?

Radiation is a form of energy, and is emitted as streams of particles or in waves of vibrating electromagnetic energy. When these particles or vibrating energy strike matter, they set up corresponding vibrations which can be strong enough to disintegrate or permanently alter the matter. What makes radiation so important is that it does not simply kill individual cells, but can alter DNA molecules and change the way cells reproduce.

Ionizing radiation consists of alpha or beta particles, gamma rays, X-rays, and part of the ultraviolet light spectrum. Radiation hazards and radiation discharges result from the decay of unstable atoms, some occurring naturally and some artificially produced in, for example, a nuclear reactor.

When cells are affected by ionizing radiation, they generally die or fail to reproduce (in fact, radiation is sometimes used to kill cancerous cells), and a healthy body can destroy sick cells. Some damaged cells may, however, reproduce abnormally, resulting in cancerous growth, and the damage can cause miscarriage or be transmitted as a genetic mutation.

Health effects

We are all exposed to some artificial radiation, at home and at work, because there are many sources of ionizing radiation in our environment. As you read through the rest of this chapter, try to get an idea of the sources which apply to you and think about ways to reduce the total load. For example, someone exposed to radiation in the course of their work should try to reduce this occupational exposure while taking care to cut down on exposure from other sources.

The effects of cumulative, low-level radiation are hard to judge because it may be 40 years or more before we see the full effects of today's dose of radiation, and it is impossible to clearly separate it from other environmental influences on our health over that period of time.

In general, we only think of severe genetic defects and cancer deaths as the consequences of increased radiation in our environment, and the odds against this affecting any single person are, it is said, greater than against dying in an automobile accident. Rosalie Bertell explains in *No Immediate Danger* that risk/benefit decision making balances 'health effects' (for you and me) against 'economic and social benefit' (this often turns out to be benefit for a particular industry or for national defence). These decisions require value judgements which misrepresent the equation, ignore long-term collective damage and often take no account of public opinion. In fact, the public has so little information to go on that most of us would be unable to make a reasoned decision.

Bertell claims that the 'early occurrence of heart disease, diabetes mellitus, arthritis, asthma or severe allergies—all resulting in a prolonged state of ill health' are part of the 'subtle widespread degradation of public health' which are never mentioned in official information about health risks from radiation.

Radiation is more hazardous to children than to adults, and most hazardous of all to unborn children, because body cells are dividing so rapidly—and because there is ultimately longer for cancer to develop. Although women are thought to be up to 2.5 times more vulnerable to radiation than men, genetic disorders can be passed on from either parent. Mild mutations can show themselves as allergies, asthma, hypertension, slight muscular or bone defects—which, says Rosalie Bertell, 'leave the individual slightly less able to cope with ordinary stresses and hazards in the environment.' These genetic 'mistakes' may be passed on from one generation to the next, made worse by increases in other hazardous elements of our modern environment (toxic chemicals, for example).

Safety levels

Any industry which has acknowledged environmental consequences and poses a risk to human health will talk of 'acceptable levels' and 'acceptable risk'. Unfortunately, researchers do not agree about acceptable risks. Estimating risk is difficult, and contentious. The authors of *Well Body, Well Earth* use three major sources of data, all of which give estimates of excess cancer caused by one 'rad' of radiation. These estimates range from 100 to 3,771 per million—because each study uses different criteria and takes different variables into account. To some extent, every estimate is a value judgement.

Dervla Murphy makes the apt point that 'this civil war is being fought almost entirely with statistics, a weapon distrusted by every sensible person. And, since no non-expert can assess the reputations of scientists, we must instead assess their *motives*', and observes that in almost every case anti-nuclear scientists 'started out happily associated with the nuclear industry, then were turned against it by what statistics seemed to reveal. Most of them have sacrificed secure careers to their principles.' (*Race to the Finish? The nuclear stakes*, p 126).

There are no cumulative records on radiation exposure to members of the public from nuclear testing and the nuclear industry, which makes it virtually impossible to get a clear picture of the consequences of our defence and energy choices over the past 40 or 50 years. Nonetheless, worker studies show that standards have been set for toxic substances for which there are no safe levels—there is no safe level of exposure to ionizing radiation (an obvious fact, apparently, to anyone involved in the controversy, but I always thought that a *little* radiation was just fine).

Risk estimates are based on cancer deaths, although this is

not entirely satisfactory. Personally, any cancer—even if completely curable—would have important effects on your life, in terms of stress, finance, relationships and career.

The permissible radiation doses for both public and workers were set in 1957 by the International Commission on Radiological Protection (ICRP), an organization which has strong links with nuclear industry (and which, by the way, has never appointed a female member). The standards were based on then-current research into the effects of the atomic bombs dropped on Japan in 1945, and although recent research has shown that these effects were greatly underestimated, the levels have not been changed, in spite of international pressure on the ICRP.

A number of environmental groups and trade unions are calling for an immediate reduction in permissible levels by a factor of 5, aiming for an eventual reduction by a factor of 10. The present levels are set at 5 milliSieverts (mSv) per annum for members of the public, and 50 mSv for nuclear employees. The UK's National Radiological Protection Board (NRPB) has recommended cutting public exposure to a maximum of 1 mSv (⅕ of the current level) and worker exposure to 15 mSv (⅓ of the current level). These recommendations are not, however, legally enforceable. (The idea that acceptable radiation doses for employees should be ten times higher than for the rest of us is rather questionable, in any case.)

SOURCES

The nuclear industry is potentially the most dangerous source of artificial radiation, but there are a variety of other sources which are less well-known and also pose a grave danger to our health. You may not be able to shut down Sellafield, but you can cut your exposure to radiation by making changes in the way you live. Increased awareness of the dangers of 'domestic' radiation will lead to a more determined attitude the next time you buy a house or go to the dentist—as well as the next time you vote.

Background radiation

Light, radium, radon, uranium and potassium-40 in the earth are natural sources of ionizing radiation. Living at high elevation, and travelling in an aeroplane, exposes people to radiation from cosmic rays. These have always been part of the environment human beings have lived in, but the term 'background' radiation is not quite as straightforward as we are led to believe. It includes naturally-occurring radiation, but also covers fallout from nuclear weapons testing over the past half century and artificial radiation from fission products after they have been in the environment for a year. This is an extraordinary state of affairs—do we consider extremely persistent and dangerous chemicals like PCBs part of the natural composition of sea water simply because they have been there for some time?

'Background' radiation levels have steadily risen over the past 50 years, giving a deceptive turn to any statistics on radiation from the nuclear industry.

Radon

The form in which natural radiation affects us at home is as radon, a colourless and odourless gas given off by the radioactive decay of elements in the earth. The degree to which radon is a hazard depends a great deal on where you live and on what your home is built of. In the British Isles, trouble spots include Cornwall, Devon and Glasgow (where radon seeps from the radon-bearing granite many houses are built of). In well-insulated, poorly-ventilated buildings radiation has been known to reach a level which is twice the legal limit set for nuclear power workers, and an estimated 100,000 homes in the UK are affected. In the United States, a recent report suggests that 20% of homes may be affected by radon.

An annual 1600 cases of lung cancer in the UK have been attributed to radon, and it is the usual cause of lung cancer in non-smokers. A 1988 public health warning in the United States compared the radon levels in many homes to smoking half a pack of cigarettes a day. Polonium-210, an alpha emitter like radon and its daughter products, is also found in tobacco smoke.

Government agencies seem happier to talk about the dangers of radon than about other radiation hazards, because it can be treated as separate from the nuclear industry. However, some of the radioactive products which produce radon have been removed from their relatively harmless natural state—by being 'blasted out of the ground with dynamite or leached with acids, and pulverised into very small particles' (Bertell, p 87)—in order to provide material for nuclear power stations or atomic weapons, and are hardly what most of us would call 'natural' radiation.

This does not, happily, apply in Britain. But according to one estimate, there are about 6 billion tons (US) of accumulated uranium mine and mill tailings throughout the world—which meant that a new term had to be found, 'technologically enhanced natural radiation' (TENR)—which is now the major source of 'individual internal radiation exposure in the USA . . . and ranks a close third, after medical and radiopharmaceutical exposures, as a source of general population dose.' (Bertell, p 878).

Glass, ceramics, bricks, cement, natural gas, phosphate fertilizers, gypsum board and even deep well water can release small quantities of radon, depending on where they come from. As radon problems increase, more care will have to be taken with the materials used in building, as well as with where we build and how homes are ventilated and insulated.

The Department of the Environment (DoE) published a leaflet on radon in 1987 and is trying to deal with radon exposure in the worst affected areas. Patrick Green, Radiation Consultant to Friends of the Earth, points out that the real issue is stopping radon entering the house (through the floor) in the first place. The NRPB has set action levels of 20 mSv p.a. for old houses and 5 mSv for new houses. These are too high, according to Green, but as a prioritising system to deal with the worst cases first he does not dispute them. He does, however, question the fact that householders have to pay for remedial action themselves—he feels that as a public health problem the government should bear the costs.

General rules for homes with high radon levels are: (1) floors and walls should be sealed with caulking and cement; (2) good ventilation is crucial, especially on the ground floor; and (3) basements can be separately ventilated with a small exhaust fan and stairs can be sealed with a weatherstripped door.

● *The Householder's Guide to Radon* (HMSO, June 1988). Or contact the Department of the Environment (DoE), 2 Marsham Street, London SW1P 3EB, telephone 01-276 3000.

● National Radiological Protection Board (NRPB), Chiltern, Didcot, Oxon OX11 ORQ, telephone (0235) 831600. For copies of UK radon surveys and other information.

Medical radiation

Medical diagnosis by X-ray is the largest source of artificial radiation that affects humans. On average we receive higher organ doses from medical procedures (which include X-rays, radiation treatment and radioactive drugs) than from any other source except rare industrial accidents.

Medical X-rays are estimated to cause between 350 and 2,000 extra cancers per year in the UK, half of them fatal, as well as some 600 serious genetic disorders in babies. It is impossible to accurately determine the number of minor genetic disorders and health problems caused by X-rays.

In spite of these facts, most people have no idea that they could be adversely affected by X-ray treatment. Only pregnant women are advised to avoid unnecessary X-rays (in the past, however, these were used for routine monitoring during pregnancy, as ultrasound is today). If it is unsafe to X-ray foetuses, what about X-raying the ovaries, which contain the eggs which will produce future offspring? And if we don't know, shouldn't we be erring on the side of caution?

Of course the benefits of X-rays frequently outweigh the risks involved. If your leg has been shattered in an accident, you are unlikely to quibble about the X-rays needed to make a decision about how to set it. The important point about this is, however, that even when an X-ray is essential the doses given in different hospitals with different policies on gonadal shielding, can vary by as much as a factor of 100.

Dental X-rays are another source of radiation exposure. Although the British Dental Association takes no official position on how often routine X-rays should be done, some US recommendations are for routine dental X-rays no more often than every 5-10 years. A full mouth X-ray can be the equivalent of 18 partial shots, and is something to be particularly wary of.

My conscientious dentist wanted to take routine X-rays after 2 years, although I have not had a new filling in 15 years, because there is a slight risk that decay could start under a metal amalgam filling, where he would be unable to see it. You may decide, as I did, that decay is the lesser of two risks—with white bonded fillings, which do not contain mercury (see page 196), this problem should not arise.

What to do

☞ Avoid precautionary and routine medical and dental X-rays.

☞ Discuss alternative diagnosis methods with your practitioner. If a doctor suggests high radiation X-rays, insist on discussing the situation to your complete satisfaction before going ahead. Be a pain—it's your DNA.

☞ Women in childbearing years should have X-rays only in the 10 days following menstruation (this is the so-called 'ten day rule', which has been officially abandoned).

☞ No X-rays during pregnancy or while trying to conceive, unless absolutely unavoidable.

☞ No X-rays for children unless genuine medical emergency.

☞ Insist that X-ray films are transferred with you if you are referred to another doctor.

☞ Tell your doctor that you want to limit X-rays to a minimum, and ask for an explanation and dose estimate before agreeing to any X-ray treatment.

☞ Do not agree to 'defensive' X-rays (a problem in litigious America, where doctors like to document every step of treatment—and a growing problem in the UK).

☞ Ask the radiologist what dose you are getting, and do not accept 'very small' as an answer.

☞ Ensure that you are wearing a lead shield to protect the rest of your body, especially sex organs, any time you are X-rayed (even at the dentist).

☞ If possible, choose a radiologist or hospital with efficient, modern equipment (which can achieve the same results with far lower X-ray doses). Most of us do not have a choice, especially after an accident.

Consumer products

There is no legislation in the UK governing radioactive materials in the products we use every day—from luminous dials, antistatic devices and smoke detectors, to camera lenses and ceramic tiles, enamelled badges and glow-in-the-dark toys. In most cases, doses are very small, and it is impossible to compute an average dose for the entire population. But the misuse of some items, particularly smoke detectors, can lead to higher exposure levels, and there is an inevitable problem with disposal and long-term contamination of manufacturing sites.

In the 1920s, female workers at the Radium Dial Company of Ottawa, Illinois, were employed to paint luminous dials on clock faces. They were told to sharpen the points of the paintbrushes by twirling them in their mouths. Almost all these women died young, of radium-related cancers. The media was alerted in 1983, when careless dismantling of the factory led to widespread radioactive contamination in the area.

The nuclear industry provides a cheap source of Americium-241, an ionizing radiation source which is used in smoke detectors. What could look more innocuous than that white plastic disc on the ceiling? They are sold without any sort of warning on the package or on the detector, but there is an increase in radiation around them for up to 10 cm. (One wonders about possible effects on shop staff who spend days and weeks working next to a stack of smoke detectors displayed at gonad height.)

Optical smoke detectors work for smouldering fires, but the common ionization chamber model is required for the flash fires which have become a hazard with the advent of highly combustible foam materials in furniture. The ionizing material is not well-protected, and a child could prise the detector apart.

Patrick Green believes that consumer goods with a health or safety purpose should be able to use radioactive materials only if there is no alternative, and only then under strict controls, and that there is no justification for using these materials in other consumer goods.

The NRPB can test and approve products, but have to charge for the service. There is no legal requirement for manufacturers to have their goods tested, however, and consumers are for the most part unaware of the danger.

While the amount of radiation given off by a luminous watch dial or a set of false teeth is generally small, the cumulative amount is substantial because there are so many potential sources; as Mike Samuels and Hal Zina Bennett write, 'We must look not at the amount of radiation emitted by single consumer products, each one of which is safe by itself, but at those amounts multiplied by the number of similar products being produced . . . if the lifetime of a radioactive element is 20 or 30 years, the accumulation of such items could present a significant health hazard.' (*Well Body, Well Earth*, p 110).

What to do

☛ If you use a smoke detector, treat it with caution. Don't leave it lying around where a child could get hold of it, and don't carry it in a pocket.

☛ You may want to avoid fluorescent materials, luminous dials and so on—or at least keep them at a distance from your body and well away from children.

The nuclear industry

The nuclear threat makes other environmental problems look inconsequential by comparison, and has an insidious effect on many people's attitude towards the environment. There is an understandable tendency to adopt the words of Isaiah, 'eat and drink, for to morrow we shall die'—not a surprising point of view if one feels that global destruction may be imminent and unavoidable.

The problems and risks of nuclear radiation are the last thing many of us want to think about, because there seems so little we can do about it. The situation isn't really quite so bad as that, fortunately. Although we have been told for years that nuclear power is our only hope for the future, public resistance has been growing, and economic pressures (including the largely unknown, but potentially astronomic, costs of decommissioning power stations) are making it look less and less likely to expand as planned. The industry's continuing insistance that all is well—in spite of the evidence—is beginning to look almost touchingly naive.

Nuclear fuel and weaponry pose risks to human beings in a variety of ways: mining and manufacture, reactor operation, fuel reprocessing, plutonium storage and waste, and fallout from nuclear testing. Indigenous populations have suffered most, both from uranium mining (in the US and Canada, Australia and Africa) and from weapons testing (particularly in the South Pacific).

The security threat from reprocessing nuclear waste was discussed in Chapter 5, but another consideration is routine and occasional emissions from nuclear power stations. Britain has specialized in reprocessing nuclear waste, from other countries as well as its own, and Sellafield (formerly Windscale) is responsible for 80% of worldwide radioactive emissions (aerial and liquid) from power stations, according to Peter Taylor of the Oxford Political Ecology Research Group. There are higher than normal environmental levels of radiation in seawater around most of Britain's coastline as a result.

The problem and eventual cost of nuclear waste storage cannot be underestimated. There is a misleading linguistic ploy being used, contrasting deep sea 'disposal' with other forms of 'storage'. The fact is that the only choice with nuclear waste *is* storage, and only the location and techniques vary. At present, nuclear wastes are stored on site near power stations and the quantities generated have already reached alarming proportions without any acceptable storage option being found. It seems incredible that nuclear power has been allowed to expand for decades, while the experts tried half-heartedly to figure out a way of dealing with the inevitable and highly dangerous waste products. In *Small is Beautiful*, E. F. Schumacher quotes an government report, *Pollution: Nuisance or Nemesis?* (HMSO, 1972), '. . . We are consciously and deliberately accumulating a toxic substance on the off-chance that it may be possible to get rid of it at a later date. We are committing future generations to tackle a problem which we do not know how to handle.'

Getting to grips with the issues involved is not easy, but I've found that I feel less rather than more anxious as a result of more knowledge—not because the facts are reassuring but because the subject no longer seems so alien and mysterious.

If you have always thought of yourself as a pragmatist who supports nuclear energy because it is the only way forward (seeing anti-nukes as woolly-hatted and woolly-minded folk who wouldn't know a neutron from a narwhal), please look back at the references in Chapter 5 and at the books mentioned below.

● *Nuclear Power* (Penguin, 1976) and *Going Critical* (Paladin, 1985), both by Walter C. Patterson. The former gives the basics on how nuclear power works, while the latter book is a fascinating history of the British nuclear industry.

● *Race to the Finish? The nuclear stakes*, Dervla Murphy (John Murray, 1981). A guide for non-scientists.

● Chapter 9, 'Nuclear Energy—Salvation or Damnation?', of *Small is Beautiful*, E. F. Schumacher (Abacus, 1974), is a good introduction.

Food irradiation

Food irradiation is not yet legal in Britain, but it is being considered and we all need to understand where it comes from and what its potential consequences are. Early research into food irradiation took place as part of the 'Atoms for Peace' programme, so the technique was developed by the US Army, not by the food industry, and the preferred isotopes which are used to irradiate food are products of nuclear reactors. Irradiation has been aptly described as 'a technology looking for a use'.

Although irradiation has been vaunted as good for the consumer, it patently is not. The beneficiaries would be the industry itself, the nuclear industry, and certain parts of the food industry. Irradiation would make it possible for manufacturers to sell low quality food which would last longer in commercial storage or on the supermarket shelf, and still *appear* fresh and wholesome. Contaminated and spoiled food could be sterilized, and some forms of contamination could even be disguised.

Rather than eliminate the need for additives in food, irradiation would require a new range of additives to deal with the effects of treatment. For example, polyphosphates would be necessary to reduce the bleeding of meats and antioxidants to offset the rancid flavours which can develop after irradiation.

One industry claim has been that the technique would cut down on food poisoning, but as Tony Webb and Tim Lang point out in their *Food Irradiation: The Facts*, if chicken is irradiated to kill dangerous salmonella bacteria (a increasingly common cause of food poisoning, thought to be connected with unhealthy and unsanitary conditions in which battery chickens are raised), the technique would also kill organisms which are natural competitors of Botulinum (a bacterium which causes a lethal form of food poisoning), as well as the organisms which would normally cause a putrid odour. It would not, however, destroy the deadly botulinus toxin!

Irradiated food is not itself radioactive, but employees in irradiation plants are exposed to the same health risks as other radiation workers. We need to ask whether we would want to buy products which carry this cost in human health. Irradiation plants would add to the amount of radioactive emissions into the environment, and to our radioactive waste 'storage problem'.

There is presently no certain means of detecting irradiated foodstuffs, which makes any idea of regulating the labelling of irradiated food impossible. The industry has come up with some amusing suggestions for irradiation symbols. One was a charming little flower, which would be more likely to suggest 'organically-grown' than anything else to the average shopper. Webb and Lang are emphatic that if irradiated food is to be sold in the UK it must be clearly labelled as such.

A group of scientists at the Christie Hospital in Manchester claim that they can detect pork, chicken and seafood which has been irradiated when these contain bone or shell, because they can pick up the presence of 'free radicals'. Although free radicals are essential to some biological processes, they can also harm cells, producing genetic damage and even cancer. They have also been associated with premature ageing. If it is true that irradiation creates free radicals in food, this is another reason to be concerned about the technique. In any case, a process which kills bacteria in fresh food will also destroy its enzymes, possibly the most desirable component in fresh, live food.

● *Food Irradiation: The Facts*, Tony Webb and Dr Tim Lang (Thorsons, 1987).

● London Food Commission, 88 Old Street, London EC1V 9AR, telephone 01-253 9513. The LFC's *Food Magazine* is a good source of information about recent research and the current legal position on food irradiation.

NON-IONIZING RADIATION

Unlike nuclear or ionizing radiation, which consists of either particles or waves and which can knock the electrons off other atoms (causing molecules to become 'ionized'), non-ionizing radiation consists only of energy waves and acts on matter by transferring energy, usually in the form of heat.

We are surrounded by electrical appliances which have potentially serious effects on our well-being. Think of the electrical equipment in your home, the power cables above our heads or running underground along our streets, as well as the TV and radio broadcasting networks which have become an essential part of our lives. Until recently it has generally been insisted that non-ionizing radiation is completely benign and could not possibly affect or harm human beings unless it actually heated tissue, but this is now disputed by many researchers.

Microwaves, TV and radar

Although most of us have a vague notion that leaking microwave ovens are a risky business and that we shouldn't sit too near the TV, the real dangers of these forms of radiation are largely uncertain. Paul Brodeur's fascinating book *The Zapping of America* (New York: W. W. Norton, 1977) details the ways in which military and industrial interests have prevented biologists fully researching the effects of microwaves and radar, in the West at least. The military depends on unrestricted use of microwave radar for surveillance, and the whole system depends on the assumption that there are no biological effects.

The Soviet authorities bombarded the US Embassy in Moscow with microwave radiation from the late 1950s until 1980, and although the embassy staff were assured that this posed no risk to their health, employees were found to have white blood cell counts which were 40% higher than normal. Two of the four ambassadors during the period of the 'Moscow Signal' have since died of cancer, and a third developed a rare blood disease.

The US government said nothing to the Russians about the beaming until the matter was made public in the late '70s, but in 1959 they established a group of scientists whose job it was to monitor the signal, try to figure out what the Soviets were doing, and study the effects on embassy staff. Only in 1976, after media exposure of the problem, did they install metal mesh screens on the windows of the embassy, reducing the radiation, they claimed, from 18 microwatts to 1 microwatt per square centimetre. Brodeur points out the irony of taking this measure to protect a couple of hundred American citizens from radiation levels which were well below what millions of others were being exposed to back home.

Civilian and military radar technicians, microwave workers, TV, radio and other communication personnel are exposed to microwave radiation. So are the rest of us, from TV and radio broadcasting stations and radar systems. FM towers pose a particular hazard because the radiation they emit is 'pulsed'.

Microwave cataracts are a well-documented health hazard to workers, but microwave radiation also seems to cause a variety of non-thermal effects. Tests with animals have shown an almost immediate decline in work performance and decision-making capacity, along with chronic stress problems, inefficiency, and central nervous system disturbance. Headaches and nausea are other observed reactions, and microwave radiation is suspected of causing cancer and genetic damage. In one case, the children of men who worked as radar technicians at a military base in Alabama had an exceptionally high rate of birth defects.

Dr Jean Monro has diagnosed patients as suffering from 'electromagnetic allergies', while US studies have found that some people are exceptionally sensitive to particular frequencies. One women had adverse reactions when she went near an airport or the Soviet Embassy in Washington, 'presumably because she was sensitive to microwave or radar frequencies' (*The New Scientist*, 23 July 1987, p 32).

Research into this form of radiation has led to some worrying conclusions. Sources are, for the most part, outside our homes and outside our control. For current information, the *Environment Digest* (see page 359) is useful, or you can contact the Radiation and Health Information Service, P.O. Box 805, London SE15 4LA.

Microwave cooking

My heart drops when I hear the 'ding' of a microwave from the direction of a restaurant kitchen, moments after I've ordered a bowl of 'homemade' soup. When the soup arrives it is searingly hot and there is a dried ring around the edge of the bowl, a dead giveaway even if I haven't heard a bell.

In the US, far in 'advance' of the rest of the world with at least one microwave oven in 70% of homes, there is an enormous market for foods designed specifically for microwaving, everything from Premium Brown 'n Serve Microwave Sausages to Microwave Crinkle Cuts (with Qwik Crisp tray) to Hot Scoop, a microwaveable hot fudge sundae. In 'Brave New Foods' (*Harper's Magazine*, New York: May 1988), Erik Larson points out that these are 'the costliest, most intensively engineered foods in history', and describes a popular microwave cake: '. . . it did not smell like cake. It did not look like cake. It had the feel of sweaty human flesh . . . If you saw it on the kitchen counter, you would try to wipe the sink with it.'

In restaurants and institutional catering, microwave ovens are used to reheat previously cooked foods (whether prepared on the premises or bought ready-made). This avoids the 'warmholding' of food, but there is conflicting information about whether microwave or conventional reheating is preferable in terms of retaining vitamins. Reheating food leads to problems with microbial growth and food poisoning. (Thawing meat in a microwave oven, however, is considered safer than thawing it on a kitchen counter. Frozen meat should be thawed slowly in the refrigerator to avoid microbial growth.)

I, along with many other people, have serious reservations about the effect microwaves have on food. In Indian yogic tradition foods have varying amounts of 'life force', and this idea correlates with the system of 'biogenics' which Leslie Kenton explains in several of her books. This term was coined in the 1920s by Edmond Székely, who ran a health centre in California where the diet consisted of organically-grown, and mostly uncooked, fruits and vegetables. In Europe, a similar food cure was promoted by Ralph Bircher, inventor of Birchermuesli. These theories, which have been successfully tested on thousands of people, may tie in with modern physics and its discovery of subtle energy patterns in matter. Certain successful cancer therapies use fresh, raw foods to fortify the immune system.

Osteopaths and applied kinesiologists can tell by muscle testing that microwaved food depresses the body's systems. In Munich, Dr Wolfgang Gerz has found that a number of patients have physical ailments which began soon after the introduction of a microwave oven into their homes, and suggests that the cause may be this additional demand on a system already taxed by other forms of electromagnetic stress, the use of VDUs and so on.

Video display units (VDUs)

There has been a considerable amount of publicity about the dangers of VDUs. These are computer monitors or screens, and workers who spend much of their time in front of one have been found to suffer from a variety of ailments, ranging from headaches, eye strain, fatigue, anxiety and depression, to repetitive strain injury (RSI). Even more serious is the suspected connection with reproductive problems.

Attention was first drawn to this when a group of women working on VDUs at the *Toronto Star*, in Canada, had an usually high rate of miscarriage. Other studies have confirmed that there is a higher rate of miscarriage amongst VDU workers, as well as a higher rate of birth defects. The extent of the risk, and the exact reasons for it, are unclear. Most VDUs do not emit more than very low levels of ionizing radiation (what most of us think of when we hear the word 'radiation'). They do give out varying amount of VLF (Very Low Frequency) and ELF (Extremely Low Frequency) electromagnetic waves, and these are suspected of causing the problems.

Many of us work in front of VDUs, not only data entry clerks and secretaries, but bank tellers, writers and physicists. Lower paid workers, however, are more likely to spend unbroken time working directly at the screen, and have less freedom to move about and take rest breaks. Their output is sometimes directly monitored by the computer, which increases stress and makes it even more unlikely that they will take sufficient breaks from the screen.

It has been estimated that by 1990 half of all US workers will be using electronic terminal equipment, and that figure is bound to increase. Computers, however, like other tools, need to be used within the constraints of human and environmental health and safety. The first US legislation on this regulates the use of VDU screens in private companies. According to the *New Scientist* (9 June 1988), employees in Suffolk County, Long Island, who use VDUs for more than 26 hours a week must have a 15-minute break every three hours, and employers must pay 80% of the cost of annual eye examinations. All new workstations have to have mobile keyboards, anti-glare screens and offices with VDUs must have diffuse overhead lighting.

These regulations are, in fact, minimal, and far more stringent safety measures will eventually need to be taken. The VDU Workers' Rights Campaign suggest that no employee should spend more than 4 hours or half the working day at a VDU, that they should take regular breaks, and that computers should be properly shielded.

What other choices are there? Most of today's computer monitors use cathode ray tubes (CRT), but radiation problems are eliminated if you can use either a liquid crystal display (LCD) or plasma screen, which are now viable alternatives (if CRT is needed, perhaps for graphics, insist on low radiation units). Protective clothing is not recommended. The 'Silver Lining' slip, made from silver-plated nylon and shown on *Tomorrow's World*, is said to protect the user from *electric* fields, but researchers suspect that it is the low frequency *magnetic* fields which cause the problems.

VDUs can be fitted with anti-glare screens, which may help prevent eye strain but do nothing about the radiation. Studies in the US have found that fine conductive mesh screens can virtually eliminate ELF and VLF emissions. The machine casing is even more important, and a screen over the monitor will do little good if most of the radiation is escaping through a plastic machine case. Magnetic fields can be eliminated by shielding specific internal components. These modifications are, not surprisingly, resisted by the computer industry, but could be done at reasonable cost on the assembly line (whereas custom modification is expensive). Shielded models are already on sale in Sweden. Unlike protective aprons, internal shielding will protect that vital part of the body, the head! Tony Webb, author of *Radiation and Your Health*, says that the low frequency fields are often strongest to the side and rear of the unit. An earthed conductive cage around all the components emitting radiation should be a standard requirement for all VDUs (controls are now in effect in Sweden).

This shielding would also eliminate the problem of static. Many computer users know to their chagrin how static can wipe out a day's work in a flash. It is also unpleasant, and can result in invisible paper dust in the air bombarding the VDU worker in the face, contributing to eye and skin problems. Some attachable screens cut out static, and it helps to avoid synthetic materials in your computer room. Choose or ask for wool carpeting. Humidity is another way to lessen static—keep plenty of plants in the room, and a spray bottle of water handy (scent it with a little lavender or pine oil). Keep the central heating as low as possible to avoid drying out the air. Many people find that ionisers improve the atmosphere too.

Pregnancy

Like many women, I am concerned about the amount of time I spend in front of a VDU because of their association with reproductive problems. A word processor makes the job of writing a book infinitely easier, but as I am pregnant I have pulled out my old manual typewriter. It needs an overhaul, but I can at least use it for drafting notes, and cut down on time at the VDU. There seems no doubt that women who are pregnant or planning to become pregnant should be extremely cautious about using VDUs, and should have the right to transfer to other work. Male reproduction may well be affected, so men should take these cautions to heart too.

● VDU Hazards Fact Pack is £2 (incl. postage) from the VDU Workers' Rights Campaign, City Centre, 32–35 Featherstone Street, London EC1Y 8QX.
● *Radiation and Your Health*, Tony Webb (Camden Press, 1988).

What to do

☞ Prevent eye and muscle strain by careful positioning of both monitor and keyboard. Raising or lowering your seat can help.
☞ Adjust room lighting and screen brightness till it suits you. Working in dim light is often less taxing than in a brightly lit room. Use full-spectrum lighting (see p 273).
☞ If possible, position your VDU so you do not have to sit in front of it while doing other work or while the computer is doing a lengthy piece of storage or correction which does not need your guidance. This could mean two desks, or placing the VDU on an adjacent table.
☞ Turn it off when not in use, or turn off the monitor.
☞ Take frequent breaks, of at least 10 minutes. Simply looking away from the screen is not enough.
☞ Convince your boss or company to buy mesh conductive screens as a start. When new equipment is purchased adequate shielding should be a prime consideration (and look at liquid crystal display or plasma screens).

If you want to buy a conductive mesh screen, the following companies sell them by mail order and can offer some advice:
● Green Farm Nutrition Centre, Burwash Common, East Sussex TN19 7LX, telephone (0435) 882482.
● Wholistic Research Company, Bright Haven, Robin's Lane, Lolworth, Cambridge CB3 8HH, telephone (0954) 81074.

Electromagnetic radiation

The effects of low-level electromagnetic radiation have been of concern to a number of biologists for many years, but only recently have they attracted much public attention. In 1985 a Texas jury ordered Houston Lighting and Power Company to pay a local school district 25 million in compensation for building a transmission line through school property, and in 1988 the Central Electricity Generating Board (CEGB) announced that it would fund a £500,000 study to look into the question.

Although the most worrying effects have been noted under high-voltage power lines, all of us are surrounded by this form of artificial radiation in our homes, from the mains currents, electrical wiring and appliances—everything from hairdryers to cookers and irons. One study showed a 40% increase in the suicide rate amongst people living under power lines, and low levels of electromagnetic radiation seem to cause depression and mood changes. Health effects include childhood leukaemia, higher rates of miscarriage and increased allergies. Several recent US studies have shown high cancer rates in people exposed to strong electromagnetic fields, and a study in New Zealand found an excess of leukaemia amongst electronic equipment assemblers and radio and television repairmen.

Electromagnetic radiation is not all bad. The earth has its own magnetic fields, which govern such things as animals' migration patterns, and human tissue has electric and electromagnetic properties (these fields are sometimes used to promote the healing of broken bones and wounds). But during the 20th century, intense and chaotic electromagnetic phenomena—some call it electromagnetic pollution—have become common throughout much of the world.

Leslie Kenton has an absorbing chapter, 'The Body Electric', in her *Ageless Ageing*, in which she discusses Russian research which suggests that the difference between living and non-living matter is electricity. Western medicine is based on a biochemical understanding of the body and its systems, ignoring the likelihood that electrical influences are equally important in growth, healing and metabolism.

It also seems likely that electromagnetic fields in the human body offer some explanation for the Japanese idea of 'ki' (vital energy which radiates from the 'hara' or centre of the body), auras, and perhaps even some psychic phenomena. It is thought that acupuncture's proven effectiveness may be dependent on a subtle understanding of these forces.

This is a relatively new area of research, and we should be on the lookout for current findings. Electromagnetic radiation is our homes may well prove to be a significant hazard, and is likely to be difficult to reduce, given our dependence on electricity and electrical appliances. Until we know more, sensible precautions might include the following:

☞ Cut down on TV time, make sure you sit at least 6 feet away from the screen when you are watching, and put the set against an outside wall of your home.

☞ Do not use electrical appliances unnecessarily.

☞ Use a hot water bottle to warm your bed instead of an electric blanket. There is already evidence of a decrease in fertility and an increase in miscarriage amongst couples who sleep with electric blankets. A cancer risk is suspected.

☞ Cook with conventional equipment rather than a microwave oven.

Peter Belt

Only hi-fi enthusiasts are likely to know about the battle which has been raging in Britain and America about the controversial views of Peter Belt of Leeds. In the '70s and early '80s Belt was a respected manufacturer of electrostatic headphones and loudspeakers. He became interested in the way we perceive sound quality, and his recent work has concentrated on the effects of electromagnetic fields.

These fields can interfere with the minute electrical potentials within each brain cell, and affect the way we orient ourselves and focus on sound, and is one of those puzzling instances when low levels of environmental interference can be more disruptive than large amounts.

Belt discovered that changing the charge on surfaces and objects in a room changes the brain's perception of the quality of sound from a hi-fi system. When these systems can easily cost £2,000, and Belt and his adherents claim that they can make a £200 system sound just as good with the right treatment, you can see why the hi-fi industry would be interested—and alarmed!

We were fortunate to have a home demonstration of this by Belt's son, Christopher. After our living room had been treated, with tiny foil squares on walls, mirrors and on the hi-fi itself, and with charged plastic coils around the vacuum cleaner and TV flexes, we were able to perceive a drop in 'muffling' and a definite improvement in sound. Many hi-fi experts have had the same experience while others remain sceptical, and articles on the Belt question promote or denounce his findings with great verve. Nonetheless, DNM (a top hi-fi manufacturer) now use these simple devices on many of their products, and KJ Leisuresound in London says that 75% of the systems they sell go out with some form of PWB treatment.

Belt's treatments have been used to help some of Dr Jean Monro's patients at the Lister Hospital in London, who are 'allergic' or hypersensitive to electromagnetic fields.

Electromagnetic charge seems to produce a sense of 'pressure' in the room which is hard to identify until it is removed. Christopher Belt says that once you become attuned to the pressure in rooms, going into a supermarket—with its fluorescent lighting and banks of fridges and freezers—is very oppressive (many of us recognize this sensation, without having considered possible reasons for it).

How does this tie in with *Home Ecology*? Although Belt refuses to speculate on just how his techniques work, it seems that they do not improve the sound itself but affect our perception of it. Listening to a familiar piece of music and judging whether the sound has improved is far easier, and more immediate, than judging whether you feel better as the result, for example, of using an ioniser, and it may be that Belt has found a way of counteracting some of the negative effects of electromagnetic pollution.

● PWB Electronics, 18 Pasture Crescent, Leeds LS7 4QS, telephone (0532) 682550.

● *New Hi Fi Sound* (especially the June 1988 issue) and *Hi Fi Answers* have published, and no doubt will continue to publish, many articles and letters about Peter Belt.

PROTECTING OURSELVES
Iodine

In 1986, Frank Cook MP and Ann Clywd MP suggested in the House of Commons that the Government should arrange to have stocks of potassium iodide or potassium iodate tablets distributed throughout the country to chemists and schools, to be taken in case of a nuclear attack or accident. These forms of iodine are absorbed by the thyroid gland, which is then less likely to take up radioactive iodine. The NRPB recommends a dosage of 100 mg per day for adults for a period of 10 days, taken on a full stomach, and half that dose for children. The Government has taken no action on this but it is possible, and perfectly legal, to order supplies from your chemist (without a prescription). They will last for 5–10 years.

Diet and immunity

Quite a number of foods are thought to have protective qualities, but the primary one is seaweed (from unpolluted waters), because it acts in the same way as potassium iodate tablets. The thyroid concentrates the ordinary non-radioactive iodine, and is not able to absorb radioactive iodine, whether from a nuclear accident or in the environment. You can take kelp tablets, as well as add seaweeds to your diet on a regular basis.

For more information about protective foods and supplements, and a source for British seaweed, see page 189, and look at the following books. In *Ageless Ageing*, Leslie Kenton makes a case for eating more eggs as protection against radiation, because they are rich in sulphur!

- *Ultrahealth* (Ebury Press, 1984), and *Ageless Ageing* (Century, 1985), both by Leslie Kenton.
- *Radiation: What It Is, How It Affects Us And What We Can Do About It* (C. W. Daniel, 1986) and *Subtle Energy* (C. W. Daniel, 1988), both by John H. Davidson.
- *The Radiation Protection Plan*, Leon Chaitow (Thorsons, 1988).
- *Health Guide for the Nuclear Age*, Peter Bunyard (Papermac, 1988).

Action

Rosalie Bertell evokes a poignant image in explaining how we have allowed radiation to become part of our environment in spite of its life-threatening nature.

During the early years of the Third Reich, the Nazis manipulated Jewish people, forcing them into the Warsaw ghetto by telling them that this was the only way police could protect them from public prejudice. Simple survival engrossed most people's time and attention, and resistance was weak because they were ill-fed and suffering from disease. Bertell goes on:

> Everyone, whether wall-builders, Nazi police, Jewish manufacturers, corporate financiers or community leaders, played a role in the death system. Although their actions ultimately bred death, they also bought a few more days of life, however uncomfortable, for each individual in the ghetto. The vast majority of people quietly resigned themselves to co-operate, and to pretend things were 'normal' . . . .Anyone who tried to sound an alarm was met with disbelief.
>
> *No Immediate Danger*, p 5

We too are faced with extremely serious threats to our health and to our futures, individually and corporately. But like the people in the ghetto, most of us prefer to ignore the dangers and pretend that things are really okay. The first step is to look at the dangers of radiation, and come to some understanding of what it is. Instead of burying our heads, we can take a number of immediate steps to protect ourselves, proceed by learning more about the problems, and put pressure on government and industry to change tack.

12
LIGHT

. . . very few things have so much effect on the feeling inside a room as the sun shining into it. If you want to be sure that your house, or building, and the rooms inside it are wonderful, comfortable places, give this pattern its due. Treat it seriously; cling to it tenaciously; insist upon it.

Christopher Alexander *et al.*
A Pattern Language, 1977

Sunshine is a precious commodity in this rainy climate. When I read recently about British people travelling abroad with suitcases full of baked beans and Angel Delight my first reaction was utter amazement: why on earth had they left home? 'To get some sunshine' is probably the first and foremost reason.

Those of us who live in northern countries have a reputation for a certain dour stoicism, while people in sunny climes are generally considered more relaxed and easy-going. But we compound the natural disadvantages of dull skies and dark winters by spending more and more of our time indoors, under artificial lighting. It is estimated that we receive at least one-quarter less natural light than did our grandparents.

Human beings are 'phototropic'—that is, we naturally gravitate towards light. This is easy to see in practice: when you take a packed lunch to the square near your office, do you

265

choose a sunny bench or a dark corner? We *need* sunlight and this need affects how we feel, how we spend our time, and even where we live.

Think of your favourite rooms. What are the characteristics of these special places? One of them, as Alexander points out, is likely to be diffuse natural light. I shall always remember the long, light bedroom I stayed in as a child in upstate New York, where there was a sunny window seat to curl up in and read.

You've probably heard of biorhythms, which biologists suggest may depend on the play between night and day. This seems obvious—after all, we wake up in the morning and go to sleep after dark. But the advent of convenient and cheap artificial lighting has changed our habits, and until recently it has been assumed that human evolution takes us beyond any dependence on the natural hormonal rhythms and cycles which affect other creatures.

A few people suffer intense depression during dark winter months. The condition now has a name: Seasonal Affective Disorder, or SAD. The characteristic symptom is severe winter depression (unrelated to other events in one's life and which lifts at the arrival of spring), accompanied by cravings for carbohydrates, weight gains, and excessive sleeping. Just like a hibernating bear!

The generally accepted explanation is that light suppresses the production of a hormone called melatonin, which otherwise causes the depression. Michel Odent, the French obstetrician, has suggested that our individual adaption to darkness may depend on cycles of light and darkness during the period immediately following birth (some babies are kept in artificially lit nurseries 24 hours a day).

While some people suffer from SAD so severely that they need specialist treatment, most of us are familiar with winter blues. It seems reasonable to assume that we too can use a little help during the darkest months of the year, whether from special full-spectrum lighting indoors or a special effort to spend extra time outside. Our Christmas celebrations sensibly fall at the winter solstice, when days are shortest. But when that excitement has passed I find myself sleeping more and waiting eagerly for the first yellow spring flowers and longer daylight hours.

Light should be our primary source of vitamin D, but we

generally need supplements or foods 'fortified' with Vitamin D because it is not formed in our skin but in the oils on it, which then need to be reabsorbed. Soap and frequent bathing washes most of what we get directly from the sun straight down the drain. Lack of Vitamin D can lead to poor calcium absorption, and in turn to osteoporosis in elderly people, a condition which cannot be entirely rectified with vitamin pills.

The dangers of too much sunlight and the ageing effects of excessive tanning are much in the news. But moderation is crucial. Modern living tends to isolate us from direct sunlight: we spend a lot of time behind glass, either windows or glasses, and even when the sun does shine we don't get the full benefit of the light. In the future, light deficiency is likely to be an accepted explanation for a variety of illnesses, as well as a contributor to general malaise.

DANGER

The ozone layer

The most alarming environmental aspect of light is the danger posed by the destruction of the ozone layer, which acts as a buffer between us and highly dangerous ultraviolet radiation from the sun.

The hole in the ozone layer over the Antarctic should come as no surprise. Aerosol manufacturers' claim that 'nothing has been proven' now looks feeble in view of substantial scientific data which has been accumulated over the past couple of years. Environmentalists have been predicting the breakdown of the ozone layer for some fifteen years. The tragedy is that whatever we do has come much later than it might have, and too late to prevent considerable ecological damage and many cases of cancer.

Ozone is a volatile gas (its molecules consisting of 3 oxygen atoms) which forms a layer around the earth, a essential protective layer which happens to be vulnerable to a number of gases which are manufactured and released by humankind (particularly chlorine compounds). Chlorofluorocarbons, or CFCs, are a group of chemicals mainly used as the propellant in aerosol cans (deodorant, hairspray, furniture polish, insecticide, etc), as well as in the 'blowing' of polystyrene packaging and in refrigerants (the liquids which circulate in refrigerators and freezers to carry heat away).

According to Friends of the Earth, we can expect to see a sharp rise in the number of skin cancers, as well as an increase in eye diseases like cataracts, damage to agricultural crops (will they have to be sprayed with sunscreen?), and a worsening of smog pollution.

Even if all CFC production was stopped *now* (and sadly, it won't be, though the manufacturers are responding to public pressure to a substantial degree), there are already hundreds of thousands of tons of CFCs hanging over our heads, and the effects of a damaged ozone layer will be with us for at least their lifetime, which is over 100 years. This is a problem which all of us are going to have to live with, though we can see that our great-grandchildren don't inherit it from us.

Sunbathing

Sunlight has exciting effects on our metabolic rate and hormones—which partly explains why we feel so wonderful on the beach. It is good for us, in moderation. We all know how healthy our skin looks with a bit of colour in it—remembering, however, that the holiday effect is also due to lack of stress and to fresh air and exercise.

Of course we all know people who seem to turn brown overnight, but if you have fair, sun-sensitive skin like many people in the British Isles, no matter how much sun you get you won't get a chocolate-coloured tan, and you are at much greater risk of sun cancer than your swarthy friends.

Have you noticed how when we do get a period of hot sunny weather everyone switches into shorts and sundresses? Shoulders are soon striped like peppermint sticks and noses are bright red. It is so tempting to strip all one's clothes off and bask for as many heedless hours as you can fit in. This is a luxury no one will be able to afford if we continue to destroy the ozone layer.

We don't feel like being sensible, rightly thinking that we get so much less sun than other people. Unfortunately, however, people of Celtic descent have a high skin cancer rate, and there is even a risk scale called 'celticity'! An EEC cancer map issued in 1988 shows that the rate of malignant melanoma, a fatal skin cancer, is high in parts of England, Wales and

Ireland (much higher than in France, but lower than Germany and Denmark). The disease is rare in Mediterranean countries. Cherish an English rose complexion, and aim to be fashionably pale. It's absolutely true that Englishwomen (and men) frequently have prettier skin than their American cousins, who suffer from too much sun, extremes of climate, and centrally-heated and airconditioned buildings. Spend time outside, but not in direct sunlight (sipping cool drinks on the terrace under a parasol, or some variation that fits in with your blue jeans and three children). Men, too, can be fashionably pale.

But if you can't resist the temptation to tan, at least moderate your goal to a pleasant golden shade, and give your skin plenty of time to achieve it.

Every chemist now stocks a wide range of sunblocking creams, numbered on a scale from 1 to 15. The lower numbers are for darker skin or faster tanning, and 15 is a complete block. But put it on before you go out. And all creams need to be reapplied frequently if you are swimming, or sweating.

Start with as little as 2 minutes on each side, and gradually increase your daily dose of *direct* sunlight. But never so much that you find your skin reddened afterwards.

Leslie Kenton, the health and beauty writer, says that sunbathing for health should be done with no oils or creams. Think of it as a bath, and wear as little as possible.

Sun beds have been heavily promoted as safer than tanning outside, but much of the information consumers receive is misleading. Shorter UV-B rays have received bad publicity because they cause superficial reddening and burning, while longer UV-A rays have been advertised as safe 'tanning' rays because they develop melanin particles in the skin and create a tan without burning.

Sad to say, these UV-A rays are probably far more damaging in the long run than UV-B 'burning' rays, because they cause premature and irreversible ageing of the skin, just as the sun does.

Protecting ourselves

1 First and foremost, do not contribute to the problem. Stop using aerosols which contain CFCs (Friends of the Earth can send you a list of CFC-free products). Better yet, switch from aerosols to pump-tops, as they are less hazardous and polluting.

2 Wear a moisturizer with sunblock in it *all the time*. This will become more important as time passes—and as you get older! (Men are just as vulnerable as women, but are unlikely to convert *en masse* to the virtues of moisturizers. Before long, however, we may all be forced to use sunscreens in order to avoid skin cancer.)

3 Sunbathe cautiously, if at all, particularly if you have fair skin. Stay away from sun beds.

4 Watch out for skin growths, which could be cancerous. These can almost always be treated successfully.

5 Write to your MP about CFC legislation and contribute to FoE, who have been campaigning to save the ozone layer for many years.

KINDS OF LIGHT

Sunlight

Before trying to improve your indoor lighting, think about how to get more direct sunlight.

1 Spend as much time as you can outside. This will take special effort during the winter: try walking to work, or at least part of the way (catch a bus 15 minutes down the road or get off early), or go for a walk during your lunch hour.

2 Choose outdoor activities in preference to indoor ones: tennis instead of squash, running rather than a rowing machine. Walk or cycle instead of driving.

3 Keep track of how much time you spend in real light each day, and how you feel as a result. An absolute minimum is 15 minutes in summer and 30 minutes in winter (when the sun is less intense), but try to get much more than that.

John Ott (author of *Light, Radiation, and You*) suggests 6 hours a day; this does not have to be direct sunlight and you do not have to be outdoors to get it. The older you are the more sunlight you need.

4 Try to work close to a window, preferably with it open.

5 Make the nearest part of your garden (or the sunniest, if you have deep shade immediately next to the building) an outdoor 'room', by equipping it with a table, comfortable chairs and adequate protection from direct summer sun (informal and permanent seats, even if only a low brick wall, make a garden very welcoming.) Even if you live in a flat, it may be possible to turn the area near a window, or near one of those too narrow balconies which are common in modern blocks, into a sunny spot to work and eat.

6 Clean windows will let more light in—a good window cleaner is worth his or her weight in gold. (Lightbulbs also need to be cleaned, with a slightly damp cloth. Make sure the bulb is cold. Lampshades gradually darken with dust, so brush or vacuum them occasionally.)

7 Check the light levels around your home. A camera with a light sensor in the viewfinder is a surprising tool—a room can be considerably duller than you think. Spectators at a cricket match cancelled for bad light often feel cheated, but our eyes are not necessarily as good at judging as a light meter is. We tend to use minimal lighting, but this increases eye strain and doesn't provide enough background lighting. One woman who suffered from SAD used to turn every light in the house on when she came in. Does this sound like you, or someone you know?

8 Experiment with different types of artificial lighting. Debra Lynn Dadd, who is well-known in America for her work on non-toxic household products, says that after trying full-spectrum bulbs she went back to ordinary warm-white bulbs from the supermarket because that's what she feels best with.

9 Do your eyes a favour by emphasizing any views you have available: one of the problems with urban living is that we seldom have to look at anything further away than a retreating bus. Or go for walks in the country at weekends, where you can use your eyes. Try counting sheep on a distant hillside!

10 Avoid wearing sunglasses, unless you are near the sea or the snow where there is excessive glare. Sunglasses have become a fashion accessory, but because they filter out specific wavebands of light they can contribute to the effects of light deprivation. Remember that you need sunlight unfiltered by lenses or window panes. If you have been wearing tinted glasses a great deal your eyes will feel uncomfortable for a few days, but they soon adjust and the sensitivity passes.

Fluorescent

Many people who have lived or worked under fluorescent lighting are instinctively aware of how uncomfortable it is, without knowing exactly why. Last year I was at a polytechnic for a series of lectures on ecology. Waiting in line for lunch I overheard a woman talking about all the Green conferences she'd been to recently. She complained, 'I wish they wouldn't always hold them at these places, under these lights, where there's no air. I always have a headache by the end of the day.'

Fluorescent lighting is standard in offices, banks, shops (it is cheaper to run than incandescent, needing only one quarter the energy in continuous use).

Recent studies show that improving the quality of light reduces absenteeism, cuts down on headaches, eyestrain and fatigue. Even though we are not consciously aware of the 100-times-a-second flicker of fluorescent lights (except with a dud bulb, and you know how irritating that is), on a subconscious level it is extremely stressful. New types of fluorescent lights are being developed which flicker much *faster* than the old ones—at 30,000 times a minute—and are supposedly to be much easier on both eye and brain.

At home, you can fit full-spectrum bulbs in fluorescent fixtures, but at the office the best option is mixed lighting sources, with adjustable lights at each work station. You may be able to use an incandescent desk lamp and turn off the overhead flurorescent lights. If not—and many workers have no choice about the continuous overhead fluorescent lighting —you might mention the new type of bulb to the relevant person, and explain that recent work done by the Applied Psychology Unit at Cambridge University shows that better lighting leads to increased efficiency.

Full-spectrum lighting

There is agreement about at least one of the problems of artificial lighting. The spectrum of light produced by artificial sources is different from natural daylight. Daylight has a more even spread of light across the coloured wave bands, with a higher proportion of blue and green.

Makeup artists know how much of a difference the colour of light makes. My mother used to have a makeup mirror with three different light settings. It was great fun to play with: our faces looked fine set on Daylight, ghastly on Office, and ghostly on Evening.

When I asked a lighting consultant which type of light he preferred he said promptly, 'Halogen, it makes things look wonderful. You should see jewellery under it.' 'What about people's faces?' I asked. 'Oh,' he said and sighed, 'Faces. Well, faces are difficult. Candlelight is good.'

You know the problem of buying a tie to go with a particular suit and finding that it is a different colour when you get it home? You are advised to 'check the colour in daylight', but in a big department store this is virtually impossible. It surprises me that makeup counters aren't lit with more care—I was told that they are always happy for customers to try a tester and go outside to look at it.

Some people need to see colours accurately for their work, while at home cooking is easier and pleasanter under natural or full-spectrum lighting (so is looking at yourself in the mirror first thing in the morning).

You won't find full-spectrum bulbs at your local Woolworths (though they do have long-life incandescent bulbs, useful for saving energy). The main supplier, to hospitals and people suffering from SAD as well as for ordinary home and commercial use, is True-Lite in High Wycombe, who offer a mail order service and are happy to answer questions about their products. They sell blemished bulbs at a reduced price over the counter.

A complete set for treating SAD is expensive (£200–300, including a special case), but individual tubes can be installed in ordinary fluorescent fittings from the DIY shop.

Another mail order source is the Wholistic Research Company, who also sell sunlight-simulating incandescent bulbs for ordinary bayonet fittings.

- True-Lite fluorescent tubes and light units are available by post from SML, Unit 4, Wye Trading Estate, London Road, High Wycombe, Bucks HP11 1LH, telephone High Wycombe (0494) 448727. Write or telephone for their information pack and price list.
- Wholistic Research Company, Bright Haven, Robin's Lane, Lolworth, Cambridge CB3 8HH, telephone Craft's Hill (0954) 81074. Send £1.50 (in stamps if you wish) for product details and price list.
- Daylight Studios, 223A Portobello Road, London W11 1LU, telephone 01-229 7812.

HOME LAYOUT

Modern buildings are designed on the principle that artificial lighting is just as good as, perhaps better than, natural daylight. But it must be said that even architects of the past don't seem to have given a great deal of consideration to the provision of light. Houses on opposite sides of a street, which have completely different sun exposures, are laid out in exactly the same way, with living rooms at the front, and bedrooms at the back. Kitchens always used to be in the basement, because no one cared if servants were confined below ground.

What surprises me is that people with an entire house often choose to use the basement as the kitchen/family room, and leave the bright rooms upstairs empty during the day.

Alistair Best suggests that 'If by placing the kitchen in the basement the family finds that most of the household duties have to be carried on under artificial light, then in my view serious consideration should be given to positioning the kitchen elsewhere . . . Indeed, it seems to me logical that if the kitchen is acknowledged to be the most important room in the house, it should also occupy space at the house's centre of gravity.' (*Putting Back the Style*, ed. Alexandra Artley, Evans Brothers, 1982).

Orientation

In *A Pattern Language* (New York: Oxford University Press, 1977), British-born architect Christopher Alexander of the Center for Environmental Structure, Berkeley, California, sets out a number of design principles which can be used by anyone in arranging rooms and lighting.

He suggests arranging rooms by the availability and timing of daylight. A southerly exposure is desirable, for house and garden; because we live in the northern hemisphere, the sun is always in the southern part of the sky. Rooms you use in the morning should face east, rooms which are used in the after-noon and evening should face west.

Artists are the only ones who seem to like a northern exposure, because they need consistency of lighting, and don't want direct sunlight with its resultant glare. Perhaps you can rent out an unused north-facing room as a studio, or take up painting!

If you are interested in rethinking the layout of the rooms in your home, it is far easier to make changes when you have just moved in, or at least before you have custom-made bookshelves installed in the study.

1 Figure out where north is—if you have my kind of sense of direction, a map is probably the easiest way (make sure the map is laid out N/S—a few are not). Or use a compass.

2 Make a 'Light' chart of the rooms in your house or flat. When is sunlight available (on a sunny day, of course)? Use 1 for bright; 2 for moderately light; 3 for dull.

3 Draw the same list for 'Room Use'. Your kitchen is probably used most in the late afternoon and early evening, but it's also nice to have a bright kitchen in the morning. Bedrooms need light in the morning, and sitting rooms in the evening. Playrooms and rooms used as an office or study probably need as much light as possible throughout the day.

4 Consider some room switching. Light is by no means the only consideration in deciding how to use rooms, but it is an important criterion, which is almost always neglected. The key thing is to get the rooms which are used most in the right position. Kitchens and playrooms should be given special priority. Formal sitting and dining rooms are often used only in the evening, and can sometimes be switched to a less light-valuable part of the house.

5 Look outside, at anything which gets in the way of the light which reaches you. There isn't much to be done about the house across street or a railway station, but trees and shrubs can be pruned, or even moved. If the problem is acute, remove them and plant replacements somewhere else.

6 Dark rooms, facing north or a blank brick wall, or with no windows at all, should be used least. Special treatment can

help: careful lighting, and lots of mirrors to break up the wall surface and reflect light.

7 If you should be buying or building a new house, a long east-west axis has been shown to minimize energy consumption by keeping the heat in during the winter and out during the summer. For details, consult Alexander *et al.*, pages 616–7.

8 Even in Britain we can get too much light, which makes a room hot and full of glare. If you have a room in which you could bake fish on a July afternoon, take this into account when deciding on layout. But it is much easier to block some of the light than it is to maximize light during dark months. Curtains and blinds can be used (an outside blind is most effective), and eaves and deciduous trees can be used to block summer sun, while allowing low winter sun to enter the house. Another appealing long-term solution is to grow climbing plants around the windows. Choose varieties which lose their leaves in winter so they don't block light when it is in short supply. Short-term, try morning glories and other annual climbers.

Windows

1 To maximize available light, curtains should pull entirely off the window, which means a longer track or rail (see illustration). Of course if the curtains are already there you'll have to try something else. Simple tiebacks can make a difference.

Also make sure that blinds are easy to pull all the way up, out of the way. Curtains and blinds should be easy to draw.

2 Shutters are efficient insulators and fold well off windows during the day.

3 Windows should open wide. Double glazing doesn't lend itself to this, of course. Window glass blocks the beneficial rays from sunlight, but with windows which open you can fling them open on nice days and have fresh air and sunshine inside. Casement windows and floor-to-ceiling French windows are the right idea. Some variation on these is easy to achieve in a new house, but if you have sash windows, just make sure they open easily.

4 Window seats and low sills (with a chair and table set in nearby) make pleasant window places where you'll probably spend a lot of time—so will your cats!

5 With whatever type of window you have, do be sure to install appropriate locks. I imagine that burglar alarms are a great disincentive to opening windows, because you have to ensure that they are all closed again properly to reset the alarm when you go out. Take this up with the company if you are having a system installed.

6 Try to have privacy and security without losing your light. And you want to be able to see outside. Filtered light is a good thing and you can sometimes achieve privacy with plants climbing around a window (something rambling and easy to grow like jasmine, or climbing roses—both will bring in wafts of scents when in bloom). These plants can grow in tubs or windowboxes.

7 You can get extra light by placing cheap, fixed windows in interior walls, and by using glazed doors between rooms where privacy is not important (they can have curtains to pull if necessary—extra insulation too).

8 Use mirrors freely, not only where you want to be able to see yourself but as if they were pictures to hang on the wall. This can be very cheap, and very pretty. I like old mirrors, the kind you can find in junk shops for a couple of pounds. The glass is bevelled, and there is something about the silvering (perhaps with a few dark spots) and the slight

irregularities in the glass which makes the light they reflect prettier than new mirror glass. Mirrors can be framed, too; old frames can be picked up cheaply—try house clearance places in seedy areas, or auctions for grander items. Have old mirrors cut by a specialist firm (look under 'Mirrors— Antique' in the Yellow Pages). Try a long mirror *between* windows.

9 A friend of mine has a small-paned window salvaged from a demolition site hanging on her hall wall. It has delicate lace curtains tied back with ribbons, and behind the glass is a print of a country landscape—this is an innocent *trompe l'oeil* which gives a feeling of spaciousness even though one knows it isn't real. This could be really useful in a room without a window (I mean to do it in my windowless bathroom, one of these days). You could put a mirror behind it instead, or even light it.

10 At Brown's Hotel in London there is a stained glass window set into an internal wall, lit from behind and heavily draped to match the rest of the windows. The impression is of windows on both sides of the room—very pleasant on a wet January afternoon while sipping tea and eating cucumber sandwiches!

Rise and shine

You know the expression 'getting up on the wrong side of the bed'? Those mornings when nothing goes right, you lose a contact lens down the sink, can't find a clean shirt, get splashed with mud by a lorry on your way to work.

Have you ever thought about how you woke up? Studies show that the way we wake really does affect the rest of our day. Using an alarm clock is the worst possible way to start the day. What our bodies and minds need is to wake naturally, and that depends to a large extent on light. You're in luck if your bedroom faces east, as you will get at least some early morning light.

If you use really heavy curtains, which are fantastic as insulation, they are not going to let much light in. If you are two and one of you is an early bird, he or she can draw the curtains to help the sleepy head.

But in the winter it doesn't get light until 8, far too late for anyone heading for the office, and in the summer the larks begin to sing at around 4 (a delightful hour, though my significant other doesn't share this view). It's reasonable to get up a little later in the winter and earlier in the summer (there's more incentive to get out of bed when the sun is shining), but from November till February you might think of a 'light alarm'. What about full-spectrum lighting set on a timer for half an hour before you need to get out of bed? (Low music is also a good way of bringing yourself gently to consciousness— the whole point is to avoid being jarred out of dreamland.)

COLOUR

Marketing men and women know how important colour is. Bright, warm colours are cheerful, but they also encourage you to eat quickly and get a move on—making room for the next customer at a fast food restaurant. Colours have associations of course: purple is regal, pink is feminine. But they also seem to have subconscious, biological effects on us. We see red, get the blues, and feel green with envy.

And most of us have favourite colours, which make us feel good, effective, attractive. There is a whole new business in 'colour analysis', helping women to choose their clothes and makeup not by what is fashionable but by what suits their particular skin and hair tones. More exotic are colour healing (by visualization) and colour therapy (where patients are treated with coloured lights, oils and liquids, and clothing). These are based on a belief that our bodies resonate to the frequencies of different colours.

Decorators and artists are intensely aware of the different qualities of colour. Jocasta Innes's writing about decorating shows her fascination with the myriad possibilities of shade and intensity and depth, and she describes how to experiment with colour and how to use artists' tints to get exactly the effect you want. (The specific techniques can be followed with the non-toxic decorating supplies discussed on page 231.)

Colour and light interact continually. Light, in fact, consists of a rainbow of colours, ranging from 'warm' reds and yellows to 'cool' blues and greens. In general, it is warm colours which make us feel good. But grass is green and the sky is blue, yet we feel wonderfully comfortable in a sunlit meadow. And a room furnished all in red can be very disturbing. Interior lighting should fall in the 'warm' range, but this means that the *total* light in a room be 'warm' in tone. A wide variety of colours can add up to a warm effect, and there are even 'warm' shades of blue. Light comes from many sources: sunlight through the windows, artificial light fixtures, reflections from walls, floor, furniture, and from outside.

How you put this into practice depends on where the illumination in your room comes from. With natural, full-spectrum lighting (whether from the sun or bulbs, or both), furnishing in 'cool' colours will still give a satisfying effect. (By contrast, think of a hospital corridor painted pale green and lit by fluorescent tubes.) This will depend on whether you use a room during the day or at night, and vary depending on the season. Under artificial lighting, especially fluorescent, try for rich, warm colours from natural materials.

(Natural materials are versatile: a wooden floor with a few rugs is pleasantly warm underfoot and to the eye in winter, but is equally comfortable in warm weather. Those rough terracotta tiles which are popular for kitchens look warm and ruddy, but have a cool Mediterranean feel in summer. Any sort of tile floor is cold in winter, so a washable cotton rug is a good idea then.)

Harsh lighting in work places is often made even less inviting by bleak, carefully neutral colour schemes (though it has to be said that this is changing—even hospitals are cheering up). You have even less control over this than over lighting, but something as simple as a bright desk pad might help.

Another aspect of colour to consider is that pale tones reflect light and make things look bigger. Instead of painting rooms brilliant white to make them look spacious and modern, try a rich creamy shade—this does the trick a sight better because of the warmer light reflected from it. (It's also kind to imperfect walls.)

None of this means throwing out your furniture—or moving house! Creative adaptation is the name of the game. You may want to try colour therapy, or have your wardrobe analysed; but the most important thing is to be aware of the choices you make and how they affect the way you feel and function. Thoughtful home design, natural lighting and sympathetic colour schemes can have a dramatic effect on our quality of life.

13
GARDENING

. . . it is one thing to sit around talking about how the balance of nature is being upset and how black the future looks because of this, to sit and discuss the tragic felling of age old trees, the hacking of chunks out of majestic mountains so that unspoiled beauty is becoming rapidly a thing of past memory; it is quite another to ask ourselves what we are doing about our own plot of ground, whether it is a little four by four foot square, or an acre, or a whole farm or forest. This is where we should be expressing some ecology in a practical fashion, where we should be doing some original landscape architecture which combines art with preservation and conservation, which produces a growing beauty, and which inspires other 'artists' to do the same.

Edith Schaeffer
Hidden Art, 1971

281

I was once chatted up by a fellow from California on the pretext of admiring the plants in my office. He told me about his, perhaps I'd like to see them some time—'and what was this beautiful creature called?' he asked, as he stroked my philodendron.

I never found out if his thumbs were really green. But some people do seem to have a knack with plants, while most of us struggle to keep a valiant little ivy alive.

Many offices have potted plants scattered about, but unless they are tended by a gardening firm (the kind who can be called out in an emergency—'the dieffenbachia is wilting!'—ghostbusters of the plant world) these are usually very scruffy indeed.

They come from one of the large chainstores, and the plastic tags giving care directions are still stuck in the soil. Every couple of weeks, when they look particularly feeble, someone throws the dregs of a cup of tea on them. Unfeeling souls stub out cigarettes in their soil. The secretary whose boss likes plants but who can't stand them herself may resort to poisoning them with nail polish remover.

Don't keep plants around because they have been given to you or because you think they are an essential in a properly decorated room. If you don't like them or don't have time to look after them, put them up for adoption.

Modern offices are hardly ideal environments for plants (or people, for that matter). The air is dry and there is little or no natural light. Small wonder most plants do not thrive.

GETTING STARTED

But I want to make a case for not only keeping those plants but adding to your little menagerie, because they really do improve the environment. They increase the oxygen content of the air, act as a humidifier, and can even filter the air to some degree. Spider plants actually remove formaldehyde, a common irritant in modern buildings (see page 229), from the air.

If you think you have a black thumb, instead of sticking with boring easy-care plants (which always die on you anyway), why not try growing something which you really like—because it's pretty or odd-looking or smells nice or is edible. Even if you have a few casualties, nursing a plant you like is going to teach you more than desultorily tending the office yucca.

Bulbs

One fun way to start is by growing bulbs which will bloom during the winter, or even for Christmas if you plant at the right time.

They can be planted in bulb fibre, but grow better in either commercial potting compost or garden soil. After flowering, find a spot for them in the garden. Hyancinths, huge heavy stalks of blossom the first year, will gradually get smaller until eventually they look like large bluebells. You'll need to buy new bulbs each year for indoor potting.

Unfortunately, some bulbs on sale in Britain have come from the wild, principally cyclamen dug on Turkish hillsides. The EEC is considering a control on their import, but at present up to 2.4 million of these wild bulbs are sold in Europe each year. Brian Matthews of Kew Gardens says that because the bulbs are generally packed in Holland there is no definite way to identify them, but if you are buying cyclamen watch out for misshapen and irregularly-sized tubers, signs that they are likely to have come from the wild.

Garbage gardening

Another way to start gardening without too much commitment is to buy a bag of potting compost—or use some (sifted) garden soil—and fill a couple of pots or cottage cheese tubs with a hole punched in the bottom for drainage. Put them in a sunny spot, if you have one, out of draughts.

Then start collecting seeds. Orange and lemon pips grow nicely, and will turn into attractive little trees (even in a dark corner they seem to stay dark green and healthy—although you won't get fruit, the leaves are nice for garnishing food). Grapes make pretty vines. Apple seeds will grow into little apple trees, and there are all sorts of other things to try, from mangoes to walnuts to avocados. Why not plant a conker, or an acorn?

Here is a kid's trick with carrots (parsnips and swedes will work too, but don't have such delicate foliage). Pack the stubby tops (leave ¾ inch) close together in a shallow layer of aquarium gravel, add water to the top of the gravel, and wait. Fine silky leaves will sprout, and look very pretty on a window ledge. (Pineapple tops will grow by this method too.)

This costs nothing and takes almost no effort, and is a form of recycling, undemanding but intriguing.

Why?

A woman I knew when I was a teenager used to say that she grew vegetables for her stomach and flowers for her soul. Architect Christopher Alexander believes that growing vegetables is 'a fundamental part of human life'. How can we appreciate the food we eat, and take proper care in choosing and preparing it, if it always comes off supermarket shelves? He suggests that this must lead to feelings of insecurity in city dwellers. Producing at least a little of one's own food provides an immediate connection with natural life cycles.

Growing things is good for you (fresh air, sunshine and exercise), and home-grown food is good for you (delicious, nutritious and uncontaminated by artificial chemicals). Even if you stick to raising non-edible shrubs and flowers, they disguise unattractive features, offer privacy, shelter and food for wildlife, and generally beautify our surroundings.

City dwellers don't have much space, tall buildings shade what little ground they have, gardens are built on heaps of builders' rubble and getting hold of manure is virtually impossible, but it is city dwellers who have the most to gain from even a tiny garden. A well-cultivated window sill might be as much room as you have and may take as much time as you can spare.

Green thumbs

Before you start a gardening project, assess your circumstances. How much ground do you have (if you have any at all)? Is it sunny or shady? Boggy or dry? What about other space to grow on: walls, patios, steps? Indoors, is there enough light to grow plants? Don't give up—growlights will transform even a sunless dungeon. See end of chapter for mail order address. If you have a conservatory or a balcony your choices expand considerably.

Just as important, how much time do you have? Who will share the work? If you are away a lot, is there someone to take over watering? And how much money do you have to spend?

If you have a largish garden and don't seem to manage to keep up with it, consider hiring a local lass or lad—perhaps a student—to help with the heavy work. A well-kept garden will entice you to use it more, and muscle often costs less than expensive fertilisers and expensive plants which die because they've gone into the wrong spot or are never watered.

A large garden could also be profitably shared with someone who wants space for a vegetable garden—you could exchange a patch for a share of the produce, or for some help in the rest of the garden.

And how much do you know about gardening? The worst problem for most of us is that we didn't grow up helping our parents maintain a garden or grow vegetables. Green thumbs can be cultivated, and depend on a combination of knowledge, instinct and keen observation.

When I read that when you move house it's best to leave the garden alone for a full year and just watch and see what comes up, I was horrified. A year seemed like forever, and I wanted results today if not sooner. Cultivate patience, along with the impatiens. The gardener becomes attuned to rhythms and signals which other people miss, and perhaps for this reason many people suffering from stress find gardening a particularly satisfying pastime.

You learn to grow things by getting your hands dirty, but there are scores of books, and several good organizations, to tell you a few things before you start, and to answer questions as you go along. Black thumbs can turn green—see 'Cultivating a green thumb', page 304.

ECOLOGICAL GARDENING

- Organic growing techniques (no chemicals).
- Native plants in majority.
- Permanent rather than disposal plantings.
- Self-sowing annuals.
- Food plants.
- Household scraps for compost.
- Spaced paving rather than concrete.
- Cater for wildlife.
- Avoid plastics.
- Plan for pets and children.

Organic gardening

Chemical fertilizers and herbicides and insecticides have no place in an ecological garden—which is what every garden should be. If you are already a 'chemical' gardener this is going

to make you feel nervous—where will you be without gro-more and rose spray?

Organic gardening really isn't complicated and peculiar. In fact, it's basically the way people always grew things until the last 40 years or so.

One benefit is that you no longer have to worry about the poisons in your garden shed. What a a relief to know that it is essentially impossible to overdose your plants with liquid sea-weed, and that you can mix it up in a juice pitcher without worrying about residues. I think that the large numbers of poisonous products we live with are a source of unidentified stress. If you have garden chemicals to dispose of, do NOT put them down the drain. Ideally, they would be taken to a special toxic waste collection point, but unless one is available you should seal them carefully and put them in your dustbin (old oil cans are ideal for this).

Organic gardening means raising your plants without chemical fertilizers, sprays or weedkillers. There's an amusing notion which I've seen in a couple of gardening articles lately, that natural fertilizers like manure and homemade compost are all right but that they cannot provide all the nutrients plants need—so hop down to your gardening centre for a big bag of N-P-K. This is not true.

Plants can get too much nitrogen, which makes for soft, leggy growth which is more vulnerable to insect damage. One of the paradoxes of chemical agriculture is that the more artificial fertilizer you use the more insecticides you need!

'Organic'?

When gardening books talk about 'organic' fertilizers what they generally mean is animal- or plant-based products rather than chemical powders and solutions. Examples are processed manure and garden peat.

Most of these will not be organic in the sense of organically-raised food. Horse manure from your local stables will contain residues of chemicals from the horses' feed and from worming products. Organic farms depend on good supplies of manure and there is some debate about whether an organic grower should use manure from intensively-reared animals, on moral grounds as well as because these manures are likely to be contaminated.

Home gardeners can have ready-to-use manure, garden and potting compost from Soil Association standard organic farms delivered anywhere in the country—contact Cowpact Products, address page 307.

Pest control

Keeping insects under control without using dangerous chemicals is not the hurdle you might think. Stronger plants are more disease-resistant, and organic gardeners make use of companion planting (tomatoes love carrots) and natural predators like ladybirds. There are a number of sprays and powders available to help you deal with any serious problems. Plain bicarbonate of soda is an effective treatment for mildew (diluted 2g to 1 litre of water, with a little soft soap to make it stick). A few well-known plant-derived pesticides—like derris and pyrethrum—are suitable for organic gardens.

Slugs and snails are probably the worst problem for the organic gardener, and there are many techniques suggested for dealing with them, ranging from saucers of beer to night hunts with a torch and a bucket of soapy water. (Or, on a gastronomic note, you could eat the enormous snails which are devastating your hostas, but only if you clean feed them for several days first.)

Chemical slug pellets are a well-known danger to birds (if they eat the dead slugs), but this form of pest control has other disadvantages. A 1986 study at the Long Ashton Research Station near Bristol suggest that methiocarb, a commonly used slug killer, leads to higher aphid populations because it kills natural aphid predators too.

Weeds are controlled by close planting, mulches, and hand weeding. You can use newspapers or old carpets to smother tough perennial weeds and clear ground for planting. Rather than burn the weeds you dig, they can be allowed to dry for a few days (to ensure they don't come to life again) and then added to the compost. Burning is a waste of nutrients and humus, and only necessary for diseased plant material and weed seeds.

Swedish tests have found that stinging nettles make a rich liquid fertilizer which has a better effect on plants than a chemical solution with the same concentration of nutrients. If you have nettles available, simply don gloves and pack them into a bucket or tub, fill with water and cover. Stir every couple of days and after two weeks you can strain off a potent (and smelly) liquid feed for all your plants. Nettle water can be made with fresh or dried nettles, and can be used as a spray to control aphids (HDRA Newsletter 112, Summer 1988).

I ought to warn you that since the Pesticide Regulations 1986 came into force only pesticides on an official list are legal for use, which rules out even tossing your washing up water over the roses to kill greenfly. Although the Ministry of Agriculture (MAFF) admits that prosecution of home gardeners for using organic pest treatments is unlikely, the situation is nothing short of ridiculous when one considers that in 1986 a senior MAFF official told the House of Commons Agriculture Committee that safety tests on older pesticides may have 'considerable deficiencies in data'. While new tests on these pesticides are being done, a process which could take 20 years, two of those older pesticides have been banned after being found to cause birth defects.

Until new safety tests are done, suspect chemicals remain legal for use, while organic plant sprays which have been in use for hundreds of years are technically illegal!

Feeding the soil

Compost, like 'organic', has more than one meaning. There is the potting compost which you buy to fill a windowbox. And, vital to the organic gardener, there is garden compost, which you make yourself from whatever organic materials you have to hand. At home this starts with all your kitchen scraps.

Some experts say not to use meat or bones because this could attract rats, while others advise burying such things in the middle of the compost pile. A middle approach would be to feed meat trimmings and fat to the birds (their droppings will add some nutrients to the garden).

I chop up the few bones which come our way with a sharp spade and dig them in. American Indians used to plant sweetcorn with a freshly caught fish in each mound as fertilizer, so don't neglect to include any fish scraps. Everything else just gets piled on. Dick Kitto's *Composting* is a help, but any organic gardening book will give you the basics of the New Zealand box and double bins.

The simplest approach is to mark an area about 4 foot square, loosen up the soil with a fork and pile on a layer of twigs to keep the bottom aerated, then add whatever you've got whenever it comes along. Sides can be built of scrap timber, if you like, and in wet weather it should be covered with a piece of old carpet.

Add grass clippings, leaves, cotton scraps, match sticks, plant clippings, manure, animal litter, anything made of natural materials. (W. G. Shewell-Cooper, founder of the Good Gardeners Association, used his old tweed jackets. I have a shabby fox fur coat from a jumble sale which I plan to cut up and put under the straw mulch around my blackcurrants.)

Make sure your kitchen compost bucket is the right size: too big and it'll start to smell, too small and you'll get sick of emptying it. Mine is a plastic bucket which a mushroom-growing kit came in, and has to be emptied about every other day.

A practical source of material is your local greengrocer. If you're on friendly terms there's no reason s/he shouldn't let you haul away good quantities of cabbage trimmings and bruised pears. Some people even manage to keep their soup pot going on the proceeds of this kind of arrangement.

Egg shells won't rot, but they are a valuable source of nutrients. Throw them into the compost pile if it suits you, or let them dry (on a tray in the oven), crumble them and sprinkle them on the soil, especially on lime-loving plants.

Compost needs to be 'activated' with something high in nitrogen. Fresh manure and seaweed work well, comfrey and nettles are both useful, but an even easier and readily available activator is urine. This is perfectly safe, by the way (urine is not the source of possible bacterial contamination in human waste).

Worm compost is sold commercially, but you can make your own in a dustbin. This technique is perfectly suited to small gardens as it takes up no actual garden space, just a few feet of pavement. Kitchen waste is added as it accumulates, and the worms turn it into rich compost. For details and a starting kit, contact the HDRA or Turning Worms Limited, who also sell an 'Ecology Box', complete with bedding and worms.

Manure can be used to 'activate' a compost heap or simply dug into the soil after it is well rotted (fresh manure will burn plants).

Leaves are a valuable source of organic matter which is generally wasted. Think of the soft dark leaf mould one finds under trees in a forest. Making your own leaf mould is a better choice than using peat, because it is richer in minerals, available locally, and because the 'mining' of bog peat has undesirable ecological consequences. If you can get hold of large quantities of leaves, simply pile them somewhere they can't blow away and leave them till they break down. Or bag the dry leaves in heavy plastic bags and stick them out of the way for a year or two. If you do this each autumn, after the initial wait you will have a steady supply. The annual burning of leaves wastes a wonderful resource.

Seaweed is available in granular or liquid form, and is a potent fertilizer. (Gather your own if you get the chance—put a bucketful of seaweed in the boot when you go to the seaside.)

Other useful additions include bracken, wood ashes and paper, hair clippings and spent hops.

A simple way to add nutrients to the soil, smother weeds and cut down on the watering you need to do is to use a **mulch**. This is a thick layer (you should not be able to see the soil) of some organic material like straw, leafmould or home-made garden compost. A layer of newspaper will help to eradicate perennial weeds.

Paraphernalia

Try to stick with biodegradable materials when you garden. The average garden centre is full of plastic equipment and tools, plants come in plastic pots or polystyrene trays and most gardening string is not biodegradable.

Grow whatever you can from seed, to avoid those plastic pots and get stronger, organically-grown seedlings with a far greater choice of variety. Yoghurt tubs and plastic packing trays are useful for this, and you can cut the bottom off plastic mineral water bottles to make mini-cloches. Net bags from the greengrocer open up to provide supports for climbing plants.

Old newspapers can be used to make a homemade version of peat pots. Wrap 6 or 8 sheets around a bottle to form a cylinder and fasten with an 'organic' glue like Gloy. When dry, cut into suitable lengths, place the rings of newspaper in a large garden tray and fill with potting soil. The whole thing can be planted in the garden—roots will grow through the paper.

While black polythene is commonly used as a mulch, it has several disadvantages. It flaps in the wind, tears at inconvenient moments and regularly clutters up the dustbin because, as a plastic, it does not break down. Organic mulches have a great advantage in that they give off carbon dioxide as they decompose, which is extremely beneficial for your plants.

Choose 'Nutscene', a biodegradable gardening string, or use strips of cloth to tie up your tomatoes (these are good because they do not cut into soft stems). Both plants and ties can go straight onto the compost pile at the end of the season.

FOOD FOR THE TABLE

Soil testing

Before you start growing edible plants, you may want to have your soil tested. Some town and city soil is badly contaminated with lead from car exhausts, and other heavy metal contamination is possible. Some councils are now regularly testing allotments, and you can send soil samples to Elm Farm Research, Britain's only research establishment devoted to organic agriculture. Farmers use their Organic Advisory Service in the process of converting from chemical to organic agriculture. See end of chapter for details.

The home test kits available at nurseries will tell you about pH, nitrogen, phosphate and potash levels, but organic gardeners recognise that a wide range of trace minerals are important to plants and to human health. This is one reason organically grown food is tastier and more nutritious than food grown with chemical fertilizers.

Raised beds

Also known as the French Intensive method, raised bed gardening is absolutely ideal for small space vegetable growing. First developed in market gardens around Paris in the 19th century, the method has been developed over the past 25 years in California and around the world. Curiously, the kitchen garden at Hatfield House in Hertfordshire, where Elizabeth I spent much of her childhood, is laid out in a similar way, in raised beds 5 feet deep and 10 inches high, edged in brick.

You divide the garden space into narrow beds which can be worked without walking on them (3–5 feet wide, depending on how long your arms are, with 12-18 inch paths in between), and plant very closely on well-composted soil. Experiments show that yields are 4 times better than by conventional techniques!

According to John Jeavons of Ecology Action and author of the essential *Grow More Vegetables*, it is possible to grow enough vegetables for one person's annual consumption on 100 square feet of ground (that's 10'x10', the size of a small bedroom). If you eat a *lot* of vegetables you might need a bit more room. Double the area and you can also grow a year's supply of soft fruit. And, he says, after the initial hard work, only 5-10 minutes a day will maintain that 100 square feet.

Sound enticing? Novice gardeners, on neglected city soil, can't expect those yields, but Jeavons recommends that you start with 100 square feet anyway. Many domestic gardens have a plot this big which could be devoted to vegetable growing. (In a magazine interview he once suggested starting with only a 3' square patch, far better than tackling more than you can handle.)

Jeavons says that it takes 10 years in the garden to produce a fully experienced food grower!

Ecology Action (address at end of chapter) is involved with projects in many developing countries, applying this intensive but soil-enriching, undemanding and unmechanized technique to some of the problems of world hunger. You can become a supporting member if you're interested in the idea.

Allotments

I was once involved in an organic gardening project started on several acres of land behind a library. It was rototilled and divided into groups of raised beds. Each section was allocated to several families who were to work it jointly.

Spring started enthusiastically, but the commitment of some members was much greater than others—and some people lived within walking distance and others didn't. A member with small children came often because it was a pleasant outing, and she'd been brought up on a farm and recognised the right end of a spade.

If you have never seen anyone gardening and never done any yourself, be cautious about taking on an allotment. For the first year or two it will be rather like a baby—needing lots of attention and feeding. This depends of course on what sort of state it is in to start with, but in any case there is bound to be a lot of work (backache, time) required.

There are lots of people who like the idea of growing their own, but my impression is that they are often stopped by two factors: they take on too much, too soon and they don't know enough about what they are doing.

Keep the following points in mind: (1) The closer your allotment is to your home, the more often you will visit it. (2) If you haven't gardened much before, try to start with a small plot, no more than 10' square if possible. (3) Share a plot or pair of plots with a friend. You can cover each other over holidays, and provide moral support during bad weather. (4) Find out who organizes and administers the allotments. Try to meet the other allotment holders, who can tell you about the soil, sources of manure and so on. (5) Look at what is growing well in other plots for clues about promising crops (but don't stick to cabbages and potatoes just because everyone else does!).

The HDRA has started an Allotments Directory, so check with them too to find out if there are any vacant allotments in your area. Local councils can be helpful or not—mine told me that there were none near me, but I found one on council land just up the road.

Remember that most allotments will not be organically run,

and you are likely to have at least some chemical spin-off from other plots.

What to grow

Gardening expert Joy Larkcom suggests three approaches: 'Economic', 'All Year Round' and 'Speciality' gardens, and she gives plans for each of these in *Vegetables from Small Gardens*, which any novice gardener should have to hand (the 'Economy Tips' section is a list of good recycling ideas).

I've always thought that as an urban farmer I should concentrate on 'specialist' crops: things which you can't buy, which need to be eaten fresh from the garden, or which are very expensive. This applies more than ever if you are trying to switch to organic produce. The available range is limited, sometimes the quality isn't too high (I don't mind a few blemishes on apples, but I object when they are expensive *and* are shrivelled and soft), and there's no doubt that an organic vegetarian diet, while wonderful, can be quite expensive.

In a sense I try to combine Larkcom's three types of garden, because of course having something available all the year round is desirable both in terms of money and taste—so little seems to be available during the winter, and what there is is often of low quality.

This ties in with advice to buy bulky organic produce, the things you use a lot of, before items which you use just a little of. It would take a lot of space to grow all the potatoes a family could get through in a year (though you might want to grow a patch of early potatoes as a treat).

When you put in trees and shrubs, consider varieties which will offer crops as a bonus. Fruit trees, grape vines and quince bushes (which have lovely pink and white flowers, and sulphur-coloured fruit which is excellent in pies and jam) are favourites. Or let the brambles grow at the bottom of the garden, and give them a little manure in the spring (you might prefer to plant cultivated blackberry varieties to get a higher yield).

Tuck herbs in amongst your flowers, in beds and in window-boxes. Try to keep some parsley, mint and other favourite herbs near the kitchen; you won't use them half as often if you have to trek to the other end of the back garden.

Good protective plants for the flower garden are clumps of

chives (especially pretty when they are in bloom), French marigolds and calendulas.

Keeping a few chickens, ducks or rabbits is a possibility, even in a suburban garden. The droppings will add a terrific boost to the compost heap.

If you have never gardened, try to imagine the pleasure of growing your own raspberries, and having so many that you can eat all you please while picking and still have big bowlfuls for supper. A high point for me was going to my allotment after the snows of February '87 had melted and picking a large bag of salad rocket.

Lawrence Hills has compiled *The Good Fruit Guide* (order from HDRA), which lists over 1,000 varieties of fruit and where to buy them, and makes a poignant plea for the delicious and pest-resistant varieties which have been replaced by more 'commercial' varieties. He describes the Golden Delicious as 'a permitted sweetener' and contrasts it with the dozens of really delicious apples which have vanished from our fruit stalls.

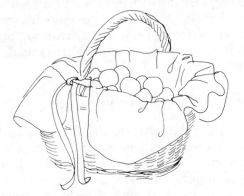

The seed scandal

Current UK legislation (the Plant Seeds and Varieties Act of 1964 and later amending Acts) has virtually eliminated many old varieties by establishing a list of 'approved' seeds. Plant varieties can be patented and royalties collected on seed sales. Unfortunately, the process of getting a seed variety onto the list and keeping it there is expensive, and the registered maintainer of a seed must sell approximately 5,000 packets a year to be eligible to stay on the list. (5,000 packets retailing at 30p apiece would gross £1,500: it costs some £800 just to keep the seed on the list.)

An estimated 1,500 seed varieties had been lost to the British public by 1985, and more are being lost all the time. One firm gives away packets of 'illegal' varieties with orders over a certain value, since *selling* the seeds would be in breach of the law.

This is a disaster on three counts. (1) Large firms with agrochemical ties are profiting at the expense of smaller, family-run seed companies. In fact, a majority of seed companies are now owned by chemical giants such as ICI. (2) The hybrids which are sold to commercial growers are the flavourless varieties discussed in Chapter 2, which require large inputs of chemical fertilizers and pesticides. Our environment is polluted and we get tasteless and less nutritious food in the bargain. (3) Genetic variety is being lost.

Lawrence Hills, President of the HDRA, helped Oxfam to found the world's first vegetable gene bank to preserve hundreds of British varieties which it has become illegal to sell. He suggests that a simple legal change would be to exempt all seed varieties older than 50 years from the regulations. What can we do? Join the HDRA and get more information about the seed scandal from them. Then write to your MP. Buy your seeds from the small firms which are campaigning to have this legislation changed.

THE DOMESTIC GARDEN

The English, like the Japanese and Persians, are famous gardeners. Old-fashioned cottage gardens are popular again, and Victorian writers like Gertrude Jekyll and William Robinson are being republished. Thank God we may see the end of gardens with regimented rows of bedding plants and spikey and unapproachable stands of roses. A traditional English garden is very much an ecological habitat for both humans and animals, rich in colour and scent, full of permanent plantings and underplantings.

Small spaces

I once nearly bought a flat which had a concreted area in front of it, and a dark, narrow paved area around the back. Until I was gazumped I spent quite a bit of time drawing garden plans, and I still feel somewhat regretful about not being able to put my ideas into practice.

You may have nothing but a small patio, or a tiny portion of shared garden, or a balcony, or a rooftop. These all present exciting challenges! You have the great advantage that everyone will rave about the transformation, no matter what you do, and the special pleasure of creating something from nothing.

There are a number of books about this sort of minimal gardening, but my favourite is *The Town Gardener's Companion* by Felicity Bryan (Penguin, 1983).

Worm composting bins are ideal because you need only a few feet of space to make splendid compost from kitchen scraps (see page 290).

In *Quantum Carrot* Branton Kenton writes about ways of growing food plants in hanging baskets, windowboxes and tubs, indoors and out. If you are operating in a very restricted space and want to grow some of your own organic food, do have a look at his book.

Flowers

Faced with a bare garden, the first thing one does is head for the garden centre to buy trays of pansies and wallflowers. Then you pull them out and plant something else the next season. This is what I call the municipal gardens approach, which is wasteful and a lot of work compared to a closely planted perennial bed.

Try to plant old-fashioned scented varieties, which are enjoying something of a revival thanks to interest in the traditional English garden. Modern hybrid roses appeal to some, but the glorious fragrances of 'old' roses will be a delight to everyone who comes into your garden.

Like vegetables, flowers have been bred for size and appearance in recent years, and more subtle charms have been neglected. But even the big seed companies offer a few of the old-fashioned varieties, and there are specialist firms with fabulous ranges.

If you have room, grow plenty of flowers for cutting. Even a small garden can offer quite a good supply of house flowers, especially if you use plenty of greenery too (prunings are fine for this). Much nicer than those plastic-wrapped bundles of imported flowers most of us depend on to add some colour to the table.

Trees

The loss of forests, both temperate and tropical, is one of this century's greatest disasters. Trees have a special place in human consciousness—in Jungian psychology they stand for wholeness. Most of us can remember a tree or two, perhaps from childhood, which played a special part in our lives. For me, there was the apple tree at my grandpa's where I could hide with a book and eat green fruit all afternoon.

In nature, trees grow where soil, light, wind and moisture suit them, but in towns they have to struggle to grow where they are planted. (As we found in the storm of 1987, many trees were vulnerable because they lacked a balancing, buttressing spread of roots.)

In *A Pattern Language*, architect Christopher Alexander suggests that urban trees need people as much as people need trees. They should be planted where they provide not just attractive greenery but shade during hot spells, a pleasant spot for a seat or a good place for children to play, because this means that the people who enjoy them will also care for them.

Lawns

Lawns are something of a dilemma for an organic gardener. Actually, women don't seem to be worried about daisies in the lawn. It's men who turn into fiendish chemists at the sight of a cheerful little creeping buttercup.

I live with a keen league cricketer whose idea of a proper lawn comes from practice sessions at Lords when he was 16, and as far as he's concerned our scruffy patch of lawn is just not up to snuff. Seaweed and blood meal are fine, but what are we doing about the weeds? He wouldn't dare suggest chemicals, so he has offered to dig the whole lawn up and replant it. Presumably we would have to sterilize all the soil in the oven to get rid of the weed seeds!

Some environmentalists concerned about famine say that we should devote the land given over to purely ornamental lawns to growing food. There are lots of attractive ways to incorporate food growing into even a front garden (*Times* gardening writer Francesca Greenoak suggests a thickly planted bed of potatoes for their lush foliage and pretty flowers).

Here are some suggestions:

1 Choose an appropriate seed blend. A hard-wearing mixture will be easier to maintain (and the weeds won't be quite so obvious).
2 Spike the lawn—with a fork or with special spiked boots available from HDRA.
3 Feed it with a high-nitrogen natural fertiliser two or three times a year. Seaweed meal is also very good and so is sifted compost.
4 Arm yourself with an old kitchen knife to dig out dandelions and dock. Or you can leave the dandelions, eat the early leaves and buds in salad and make the flowers into wine!
5 Leave lawn clippings where they fall, to replenish the soil. (Unless there are too many, in which case they will stick to your feet and get tracked into the house.)
6 Remember that worms are good for the soil. Sweep the castings around on a dry day.

Paving

If you decide to pave part of your garden, please don't concrete it. Approximately one-third of the land in an average city is already concrete or asphalt, mostly for roads and carparks, and this has undesirable ecological consequences.

Solid paving leads to water run-off because natural drainage is blocked, affects the microclimate and does nothing useful with the solar energy which falls on it. Damage can only be repaired by replacing an entire slab (instead of just a couple of bricks), and it essentially kills the soil below.

Make a surface with old bricks or paving stones, set in dirt so that mosses and plants can grow between the cracks. This sort of surface responds well to weathering—it will look better in 10 years than it does now. The delicate ecology of earthworms, plant and insect life will be preserved, while you still have a firm, dry surface on which to put a table or for children to push a tricycle.

Paths can be laid in the same way, or you can use stepping stones set in grass or amongst low-growing plants.

Traditional York stone (often advertised in the Classified section of the newspaper) is laid on a foundation of crushed stone, rolled flat, which allows water to drain away without turning the soil into mud, a good idea with any material on a damp site. Rather than point the cracks, place the stones quite closely together and allow tiny plants to grow.

The stonemason Geordie Bolan thinks that well-laid unequally sized rectangles of York stone makes the best paved surface, but considers old London paving a good second-best and, for something cheaper, reconstituted Cotswold stone slabs. But cement-based paving is not as durable as stone, which will last virtually forever. Old bricks are attractive, but you must ensure that they are of outdoor quality (or frost will crack them).

OUTDOOR LIVING

Garden furniture

Provide as much natural seating as you can, which can stay in place all year round. The lawn is fine on warm, dry summer days, but you'll use the garden a lot more if there are sheltered, sunny seats for cool weather. A bench is lovely, if your garden is big enough. Thick sawn logs are good too.

Think about shelter from the sun, and about whether you want the seat to face activity or to be more secluded.

Watch out, if you are buying a wooden bench, for endangered tropical hardwoods. The FoE *Good Wood Guide* will advise you. Avoid plastics as much as possible—an accessible storage place is vital if you have wood and canvas folding chairs, and for toys.

Shelter from wind is important much of the year, and a big umbrella will help during hot weather. Make the garden an outdoor room, connected to the house, with a table, chairs, play equipment and shelves.

White flowers show up at dusk and after dark, so if you are going to use your garden then it is well worth concentrating on white blooms. Some form of lighting will make the garden more enticing on mild evenings.

Privacy has a lot to do with how much we use our gardens. It is not rude to want privacy from even the friendliest of neighbours, but some diplomacy is a good idea. An 8-foot board fence is not. And whatever you plant, think about how it will affect your neighbours—don't cut off their light. Climbing plants are very useful, on a trellis or on wires.

Perhaps you could organize a shared back garden, especially nice if you live in a place where each garden is only a narrow sliver. This could be an open area between 6 or 8 houses, with a play area for the kids.

Child gardening

Gardening books always warn you that you'll have to choose between your flowers and your children. But why not design the garden to cope with children? Establish a part where no trespassing is allowed for your tenderer plants, put a simple fence around the vegetable patch, and watch out for prickly plants and dangerous ones if you have babies around. (I don't see why one couldn't use prickly plants as a harmless deterrent to rough 10-year-olds.)

Then plant a tough lawn, put up whatever equipment seems appropriate, a sandpit, a low table for children (those big wooden cable reels can do for this—and they're great to roll around). Hang a tyre swing or just a rope to climb.

Children love to dig and plant. You can hardly get them started too early, with plenty of help and encouragement and their own collection of pots or a designated area for their own garden.

The easiest way to protect precious flower beds is to raise them, although it will require some initial hard work and a lot of extra soil (some from digging the sand pit). Railway sleepers or bricks will make a rough seat at the front, and you'll find tending the beds a lot easier. The flowers are close so you can smell them easily, and children can look at them without scrabbling through your nicest hostas.

Winter

If you want to use your garden all year round (and, let's face it, the weather in January is sometimes better than in July), it needs to be congenial. Kids need toys which can be brought out quickly when there is a clear afternoon, and some flowers or green things will make you feel brighter too—and provide something to cut and bring inside. There are standard winter bloomers, winter jasmine and snowdrops, but for other ideas have a look at *Down the Garden Path* by Beverley Nichols (out of print, but try the library), chapters 4 and 5. Joy Larkcom's books are full of ideas for winter vegetables.

Greenhouses

A freestanding greenhouse is an efficient way of using solar energy, but if it is connected to the house you have an extra room, as well as a place to grow seedlings and houseplants (which you can tend in the winter without going outdoors). A conservatory is a sort of greenhouse, and most usefully brings the outside and inside together.

WILDLIFE

Domestic gardens can provide extra habitat for beleaguered creatures whose natural habitats are being chewed up by development. And because a certain amount of casualness is necessary to make the right environment, this type of garden should appeal to occasional gardeners. The bed of nettles is there for the butterflies, of course, not because you never have gloves on when you go into the garden.

There are a number of books on this subject available and local wildlife trusts can advise on suitable plants for your area, but here are a few ideas:

1 Set up a bird table or hang a feeder (which you can get at most pet shops). Put it somewhere you can see it from the house, but out of cats' reach. The Royal Society for the Protection of Birds (RSPB) has a number of helpful factsheets and leaflets, including 'Feeding Garden Birds'.

2 Plant native trees and shrubs, which support a wide range of insect life. This in turn attracts birds, hedgehogs, frogs and toads. An ecological cycle in the making! Hedges provide a home for many creatures, and you can prune trees which would be too big left to grow into an excellent thick hedge. Field maple and hawthorn are two to use. Try to place these as a windbreak, which will perhaps cut your heating bills as well as make sheltered spots in the garden.

(The RSPB has an information sheet on trees and shrubs for birds.)

3 Plant native wildflowers (seeds from Suffolk Herbs)—these include snowdrops, bluebells, violets and primroses, as well as poppies, cornflowers and oxeye daisies.

4 A wildflower lawn, like many native plants, grows best on poor soil. You'll need to clear perennial weeds before you start. This sort of lawn needs mowing only twice a year! While you probably want some ordinary lawn for sunbathing and the children's football games, why not allow a corner to go wild? Consult a book on the subject—it's no good just letting the weeds grow!

5 Plant to attract bees and butterflies and birds. They like old-fashioned, sweet-scented cottage flowers. Buddleia, which grows wild on decaying inner city roofs, is known as 'butterfly bush'. The *Buddleia davidii* at Sissinghurst looks like a frock covered with white bows in summer. Birds like berries and, part of your organic gardening programme, insects. (Get the RSPB 'Gardening for Birds' pack.)

6 Piles of rocks, bricks or logs will make a home for many small creatures like beetles and centipedes, and maybe even a hedgehog. Think what a wonderful garden you'll have for scientifically-minded children.

7 Leave the weeds. This is so tempting that it could easily get out of hand, but try setting aside one area for nettles, wild parsley and buttercups (or whatever grows where you are). My garden is too small to allow much of this, but I can't resist my patch of creeping buttercup. I know they're invasive, but they look so beautiful in a dark corner that I only sporadically try to uproot them.

8 Build a pond. The easiest way to line it is with a rubber sheet. You can put in a variety of water plants and either wait for the insects to come, or get a bucketful of water and mud from a friend's pond to inoculate yours with water boatmen, water beetles and snails. Apparently frogs will find their own way, but if you are in a hurry you can import some from your friend (not from the wild). Frogs and toads include slugs in their diet, another ecological boon. Their habitat is declining in the countryside, so friendly gardens are important for their survival. (Obviously you need to take special precautions with a pond if you have children.)

- RSPB, The Lodge, Sandy, Bedfordshire SG19 2DL, telephone (0767) 80551. Leaflets are free, but enclose two first class stamps.
- *The National Trust Book of Wildflower Gardening*, John Stevens (Dorling Kindersley, 1987) is probably the best, although only available in hardback.

CULTIVATING A GREEN THUMB

Or, Gradual Gardening:

1 Garden with someone else if you possibly can. It doesn't matter if they know as little as you to start with. The important thing is to have someone to show the emergent sweet peas, to commiserate over aphid damage, and to share the initial spadework.

2 Take it easy. Don't put your back out with improvident digging (make sure tool handles are long enough, bend your knees and not your back, turn to throw the spadeful of soil *after* you have straightened up—and don't try to do the whole patch in one afternoon). Wearing gloves helps to prevent blisters. Sticking your fingers in handcream or butter will make cleaning much easier (make sure the cream goes under your fingernails), and a hat and/or sunscreen will protect your neck and nose.

3 Buy or borrow decent tools and learn to care for them. Wellies aren't exactly tools but they come first (or sturdy country shoes which can take a battering and which you won't worry about). A good fork won't get bent first time out, and an expensive pair of clippers will last forever. Start with a fairly narrow spade, or a fork if your soil is really heavy (you'll want to have both eventually), a small trowel, a hoe, a pair of clippers, a mower if you have a lawn (power mowers are unnecessary for modest domestic lawns).

4 Get advice. Watch TV programmes about gardening (the popular *All Muck and Magic* on Channel Four was about organic gardening; look out for future series), and join either the Henry Doubleday Research Association (HDRA, whose work *All Muck and Magic* was based on) or the Good Gardeners Assocation—or both. You may also want to become a member of the Royal Horicultural Society for their monthly magazine, free advice and entry to shows.

5 Read—especially during the winter. Organic gardening is a popular topic, and books in print range from profusively illustrated coffee table books to small manuals on specific techniques. Many gardening writers tend towards an organic approach nowadays, and some newspaper gardening columns are excellent, and of course usefully seasonal. They often list gardens open to the public.

6 Look at other people's gardens. If, like me, you cannot get a nice lawn to grow in your front garden, observe what other people do in theirs. Every neighbourhood has a few keen gardeners, and they are often delighted to know that you admire the fruits of their labours and ready to give tips on dealing with your area's quirks of sun or soil.

There is also a National Gardens Scheme, in which people with particularly fine gardens open them to the public on a day or two a year (many are open more often than that). National Trust gardens will prove inspiring. At Sissinghurst each plant is labelled so you can write down the names of the plants you like. (The list can stay pinned to the notice board until you forget what *Campanula poscharskyana* looked like and why you wrote 'summer garden' next to it.)

The HDRA runs Ryton Gardens, which is a demonstration organic garden on 22 acres near Coventry, with a restaurant which appears in a number of food guides, and there is a demonstration organic garden at the Centre for Alternative Technology in Wales.

7 Grow your own plants from seed. This saves money, gives you a wider choice, and stronger organically-grown plants. There are a number of large seed companies with extensive ranges, but do order catalogues from the smaller family firms (starting with Chase Organics and Suffolk Herbs— there are many more). The HDRA sells seeds and a few plants by post, and you'll also find a number of smaller plant suppliers advertising in the newspaper or gardening magazines.

8 Learn to propagate from cuttings and how to layer plants. An experienced gardening friend is a great help.

9 Tackle a small area at a time.

10 Use easy techniques. The Good Gardeners Association encourages the use of the No-Dig Method, which is an especially good idea in flower beds where you probably

have lots of bulbs planted, as well as in the vegetable garden.

11 Get yourself equipped for easy watering and make a place to store tools.

12 Grow things you *love*.

13 Mix flowers and vegetables and herbs and fruit.

14 Remember to plant plenty of bulbs (deeper than you think, and put a handful of bonemeal in the bottom of each hole). They get each new season off to a happy start.

Organizations

● Henry Doubleday Research Association (HDRA), National Centre for Organic Gardening, Ryton-on-Dunsmore, Coventry CV8 3LG, telephone Coventry (0203) 303517. Membership includes a chunky quarterly newsletter, free gardening advice and unlimited entry to Ryton Gardens.

● Good Gardeners Association, Timber Yard, Two Miles Lane, Highnam, Gloucester GL2 8DW, telephone (0452) 305814. Exponents of the No-Dig Method (sounds good, doesn't it!).

● Soil Association, 86-88 Colston Street, Bristol, BS1 5BB, telephone (0272) 290661. Organic agriculture and gardening. Run a 'Living Earth' campaign and publish an informative magazine about the organic movement, *The Living Earth*.

● Elm Farm Research Centre, Hamstead Marshall, Newbury, Berkshire RG15 OHR, telephone (0488) 58298. Comprehensive soil analysis, £17.25 per sample in 1988.

● Ecology Action of the Midpeninsula, 5798 Ridgewood Road, Willits, CA 95490, USA. Support research projects in the US and Third World countries using French Intensive methods. (Ecology Action is the US distributor for Chase Organics, a British firm, and almost all the seeds in their catalogue come from Chase, because it is one of the few complete lines of untreated, unhybridized seeds in the world. Chase's address is below.)

Books

● Get the HDRA's leaflet *All Muck and Magic*—only £1.50 and a good beginner's guide.

● *Grow More Vegetables (than you ever thought possible on less land than you can imagine)*, John Jeavons (Berkeley: Ten Speed Press, 1982)—available from the Soil Association.

- *Vegetables from Small Gardens*, Joy Larkcom (Faber, 1976).
- *Salads The Year Round*, Joy Larkcom (Hamlyn, 1980).
- *The Holistic Gardener*, Margaret Elphinstone and Julia Langley (Thorsons, 1988).
- *Quantum Carrot*, Branton Kenton (Ebury Press, 1987).
- *Herb Gardening*, Claire Loewenfeld (Faber, 1964).
- *Composting*, Dick Kitto (Thorsons, 1988).
- *The Town Gardener's Companion*, Felicity Bryan (Penguin, 1983).
- *The Allotment Book*, Rob Bullock and Gillie Gould (Macdonald Optima, 1988). Emphasis on organic methods.
- *Organic Gardening* magazine: order through your newsagent or directly from P O Box 4, Wiveliscombe, Taunton, Somerset TA4 2QY, telephone (0984) 23998.

Sources

- HDRA, above, also sells fertilizers, pest control products, gardening supplies and seeds by post.
- Chase Organics (GB) Ltd, Coombelands House, Coombelands Lane, Addlestone, Weybridge KT15 1HY, tel (0932) 858511. *The* source for untreated, open-pollinated seeds and seaweed fertilizers. Much cheaper to collect heavy items, but call ahead (they do not have a shop). Send two first class stamps for a catalogue.
- Cumulus Organics and Conservation Ltd (who now handle membership of the Good Gardeners Association), Timber Yard, Two Miles Lane, Highnam, Gloucester GL2 8DW, telephone (0452) 305814. Offer an Organic Starting Kit for £27: soil test kit, composts, various fertilizers, six HDRA pamphlets and organic caterpillar killer!
- Cowpact Products, P O Box 595, Adstock, Bucks MK18 2RE, telephone (029671) 3838. Sell a variety of garden composts and manure from Soil Association registered organic farms.
- Suffolk Herbs, Sawyer's Farm, Little Cornard, Sudbury, Suffolk CO10 ONY, telephone (0787) 227247. A bit of everything, and a beautifully produced catalogue. Herbs, wild flowers, tools, and books.
- Hollington Nurseries Ltd, Woolton Hill, Newbury, Berks RG15 9XT, telephone Highclere (0635) 253908. A beautiful place to visit; 400 different herb plants in a beautiful old walled garden. Send £1.50 for illustrated catalogue.

● Turning Worms & Organic Supplies, Perthi Yard, Llanrhystud, Aberystwyth, Dyfed SY23 5EH, telephone (09746) 240. Ecology box £40 incl. carriage (1988).
● Sunlight Systems, 3 St. Mary's Works, Burnmoor Street, Leicester LE2 7JJ, telephone (0533) 470490. Indoor growlights.

14
PETS

Introduction
  Choices
Food
  Ecological eating—A better diet—Making
  converts—Vegetarian cats and dogs
Dog pollution
  Danger—Ground rules
Health
  Fleas—Worms—Health care
Animals in the city

. . . the behavioural changes in our society, with falling birth
rate and fewer people in stable marriages with children, probably
mean that there are increasing pressures for pet-keeping substitutes. This adds urgency to the need for healthier ecological
interaction between man in Britain and his pet animals.

Professor Barrie R Jones, CBE
Director of the Department of Preventive Ophthalmology,
Moorfields Eye Hospital, London

Wildlife groups have done a tremendous job of increasing
public awareness of the importance of animal habitats, in cities
as well as in the countryside, and many wildlife areas have
been preserved thanks to their efforts over the past few years.
Everyone knows that we need green spaces in our cities. But
having other living creatures around—birds, rabbits, deer,
hedgehogs, foxes, goats, beetles, butterflies and earwigs—is
just as important as open grass for sport and trees to doze
under and flowers to smell.

The ecological system of home and garden will be richer
and more successful if you have a variety of creatures in it.
Sparrows and blue tits will eat insects which would otherwise

be nibbling on your primroses. Frogs and toads will grow fat eating your slugs. Hens will eat kitchen scraps and produce wonderful manure for the garden. Domestic cats and dogs, however, '. . . are pleasant, but so humanized that they have no wild free life of their own. And they give human beings little opportunity to experience the animalness of animals.' (Alexander *et al.*, *A Pattern Language*, p 372).

The real dilemma is that our pets consume vast amounts of food (651,000 tonnes in the UK in 1987) while people are starving in other parts of the world. To see a pair of fat Siamese cats eating fresh crab from a Limoges porcelain plate (as I have), contrasted with images of dying children in the Sudan, is quite monstrous. In 1987, pet food sales in the UK were valued at £825 million, and £45 million was spent on advertising.

Cats and dogs are carnivorous, and other animals have to be raised and slaughtered in order to feed them. Since it takes approximately 10 pounds of vegetable or grain protein to produce 1 pound of animal protein—and the grain used to feed livestock is often imported from Third World countries— keeping a pet merits some serious thought. The giant Blue Bass was hunted to near extinction in order to feed American dogs and cats, and other marine life is not exempt. A lot of tuna is used in commercial catfood—because its strong flavour means that pets are likely to become 'addicted' to it—but tuna fishing leads to thousands of dolphin deaths. Since 80% of owners buy tinned petfood, packaging is another environ- mental cost of keeping them (2 billion petfood cans per year, according to the *Green Consumer Guide*).

In spite of the British reputation as animal lovers, some 350,000 dogs are put down every year (that is nearly 1,000 every day), and the RSPCA estimates that there are 500,000 unwanted dogs roaming our streets.

What role should animals play in our towns and cities? Most children are thrilled by almost any kind of animal, and Alexander suggests that there is some evidence that 'animals may play a vital role in a child's emotional development'. More than half the households in Britain have at least one cat or dog, and the more children in a family, the more pets we are likely to have. But city children (and, in these days of intensive animal rearing, country children too) seldom have any contact with wild animals or even with the domesticated animals which provide us with food and clothing.

Pets can fulfill a social need by offering companionship to people who live on their own and who do not have a supportive family or community network. A dog offers protection without turning your home into a fortress, not an inconsequential point for women or elderly people who live alone.

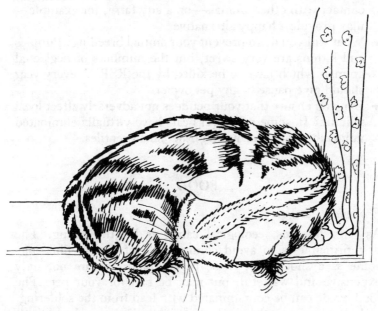

Choices

If you already have a cat or dog, your choice is made. The rest of this chapter discusses feeding and pet care. If, however, you are only thinking about acquiring a pet, the following questions may be helpful.

- ☛ How would you feed your pet? Look through the section on feeding.
- ☛ If you want a dog, have you considered how you would deal with its excrement? Please don't think that public paths and parks are suitable toilet facilities (see page 316).
- ☛ What size dog will you choose? The trend in Britain is towards larger dogs—comparable to buying large cars in both expense and ecological consequences.

☛ Why do you want a pet? Security and companionship *can* be achieved by other means.

☛ Is it really fair to keep a dog or cat in a city or town, particularly if the animal will have to spend most of its time indoors?

☛ How will your having a pet affect your neighbours?

☛ If you want a pet for the children's sake, think realistically about whether they will be able to cope with its care. Regular contact with other animals—on a city farm, for example— may provide a happy alternative.

☛ What will you do to prevent your animal breeding? Puppies and kittens are very sweet, but the numbers of neglected animals which have to be killed by the RSPCA every year should give pause to any pet owner.

☛ Can you ensure that your pet does not adversely affect local wildlife? In some rural areas cats have virtually eliminated vulnerable slow worms and other small reptiles.

FOOD

Ecological eating

As with humans, ecological eating *is* healthy eating. The first principle is to avoid commercial pet foods. This may come as a shock, but those packets and tins are not only expensive and wasteful, but may be bad for your pet. The food inside can be contaminated with lead from the soldering, and more importantly is heavily laced with chemical additives, flavourings, salt and even sugar, just like processed human food.

Dry commercial food is more sympathetically packaged, in cardboard or paper, and it can sometimes be bought in bulk. It is also lighter, which means lower transport costs (and energy consumption). However, it is still a highly processed food, which is made from the byproducts of intensive meat rearing—not something we want to support!

You may find, as we did with our two cats, that your pets seem to be addicted to their current brand of food. American veterinarians suggest that '. . . excessive—and costly—eating may be caused also by addiction to the chemical appetite stimulants and preservatives in fake foods' (Pat Lazarus, *Keep Your Pet Healthy the Natural Way*, p 15).

Semi-moist food is highest in preservatives and sugar, and the (humanly) attractive gravy which you mix with some expensive dry dog foods is actually undesirable for a dog, who should have her water after a meal. In the wild, cats and dogs would eat the organ meat of their prey first. It would, obviously, be raw. The closer you can replicate this diet, the healthier your pet will be.

A better diet

The wild ancestors of today's cats and dogs ate a very different diet from the one we expect our pets to thrive on. Most importantly, what they ate was fresh and raw—not cooked or dried or preserved with chemicals. A famous study with many generations of cats, made by Francis M. Pottenger, Jr. in the 1920s, remains an important source of information about feline, and canine, health.

Pottenger was doing experiments on adrenal cortical material, but found that the cats he used were dying young and not surviving surgery. He decided to experiment, feeding one group of cats cooked meat and pasteurized milk while giving another group the same food, raw. There were dramatic differences between the two groups of animals. The raw food cats thrived, while the cooked food animals suffered from allergies, skeletal abnormalities and a variety of illnesses. The contrast became more pronounced in succeeding generations.

Leslie Kenton mentions this experiment in her popular *Raw Energy*, and over the years Pottenger's work has stimulated much interest in the effects of raw food on human health. When we are deciding how to feed our pets, we need to take this into account. A useful book is *Keep Your Pet Healthy the Natural Way* by Pat Lazarus, who has compiled a great deal of information from nutritionally-oriented, orthomolecular veterinarians in the United States. The emphasis is on a diet of fresh, mainly raw, unprocessed foods—environmentally-sound as well as healthy. Much of the book concentrates on dealing with ill pets, but the fundamental information on diet is relevant to anyone with a cat or dog. (It can be purchased from Green Farm, address on page 259.)

In Chapter 2 we looked at the reasons we should cut our protein consumption, and pets can join us in this small dietary change. After all, cats and dogs in France live on scraps and leftovers, and in other Mediterranean countries they are treated as wild animals and expected to fend for themselves.

In fact, a dog's diet should be only ⅓ meat (a good proportion of that offal), while a cat needs some ¾ meat. The balance can be made up of grains, vegetables and the occasional egg. While cats do not need milk (or saucers of cream), and it can be positively bad for them, Lazarus suggests small amounts of raw milk or yoghurt as desirable additions to the diet.

The scraps which butchers sell for pets are often fat and gristle, not the best thing for your pet. If you know your butcher, discuss your pet's requirements with him—concentrating on liver, kidney, heart and so on. Do not aim for 'lean' meat. Cats need a fairly high intake of saturated fat. Variety is important for a balanced diet, and he may be able to set aside appropriate pieces for you, or do a special deal if you buy a large amount for the freezer. Make friends with your fishmonger too.

This diet will be cheaper than your pet's present one, as well as healthier. You do not need to buy steak for your dog! Pat Lazarus reports that animals on a natural diet eat approximately ⅓ less, and, incidentally, produce far less waste (faeces). This is because the food is more nutritious and better digested.

The most difficult thing for most of us is that fresh and unprocessed food cannot be stored on a shelf indefinitely like a tin, and needs to be cut up (but not too much—animals are quite capable of chewing fairly large chunks of meat). If you are squeamish, perhaps you'll want to consider a vegetarian diet for your pet!

Making converts

A *Which?* report on pet food in the August 1987 issue confirmed that cats are far more finicky about their food than dogs, something any cat owner knows from experience. I have no experience in converting a dog from a processed to wholefood diet, but I have struggled with a pair of cats and can offer a few observations.

Like many cats ours were devoted to a leading brand of tinned catfood, which we supplemented with dry food. Our first switch was to Safeway's premium tinned food, simply because it was nice to dish out something which was recognisably what the label claimed (most catfood looks and smells the same, whether it called prawn or kidney or lamb 'variety'). We also started offering small amounts of raw meat, along with table scraps.

We gradually increased the portions of fresh offal (mainly heart, but sometimes kidneys or liver) and reduced the processed food they got. There were some failures, when they turned up their noses at something new and simply howled when we refused to give them anything else, but after some months they tuck into their raw food diet with an enthusiasm which would do credit to a television commercial.

Hunger does seem to be the best sauce when trying to get cats to switch to something different. This makes for a difficult time if one of you is more soft-hearted than the other, when those imploring looks and plaintive meows start coming thick and fast!

Pat Lazarus's suggestion that ¼ of a cat's diet should be made up of cooked cereals (brown rice for example) and grated carrot, sounds fine to me, but I haven't figured out how to convince the cats. Many cats, however, enjoy table scraps—everything from tossed salad to boiled potatoes. Mixing the grated vegetable into something they like is a good method, at least with a dog. Cats are remarkably skillful at picking out what they want and leaving the rest.

Meat can come from the supermarket during your weekly shop, but I have a butcher nearby and find it convenient to buy a small amount every couple of days. Bulk purchases can be frozen and a small amount thawed each day (it should be near room temperature when offered to your pet). One great advantage of a butcher is that you can ask him to cut the meat into pieces for you—for freezing it could be packed in old yoghurt cartons. Some pet shops sell large bags of chopped tripe and other fresh meat for dogs.

Keep a couple of tins or a box of dried food in the cupboard for emergencies. Wholefood shops sell a few additive-free, natural products which you might want to try.

Vegetarian Cats and Dogs

If you start from birth it is possible to raise a dog as a vegetarian. Although this is against canine nature, in today's world it seems a reasonable compromise, and the Vegetarian Society will provide detailed information sheets about a suitable vegetarian diet for dogs.

They do not, however, recommend a vegetarian diet for

cats. A vegetarian diet is deficient in arachidonic acid, an essential fatty acid found in the structural fats of meat and fish. Because of this, the Vegetarian Society 'urges vegetarian cat owners to consider whether their beliefs are consistent with risking jeopardizing the health of any animal, or whether they should expect any animal to adapt its natural diet to suit the philosophy of the owner, no matter how noble the cause.'

It must be said that many pets enjoy non-meat foods. I once had a cat which liked steamed courgette, and friends have a cat which eats salad. Dogs are even more adaptable. Some dogs seem to eat absolutely anything, and most table scraps can be offered to Fido before going to the compost bucket. (Between the dog, the bird table and the compost heap, you'll have to start asking friends for their leftovers!)

● The Vegetarian Society, Parkdale, Dunham Road, Altrincham, Cheshire WA14 4QG, telephone (061) 928 0793.

DOG POLLUTION

Danger

While dogs provide companionship for the lonely and excitement for children, they are also a major social menace. The main problem is the appalling state of the country's pavements and parks. Dog faeces is not just unpleasant (and it is *exceptionally* unpleasant), but very dangerous too. According to the Hospital for Tropical Diseases, up to 100 children in Britain suffer eye damage every year as a result of Toxocara canis, a roundworm which is transmitted in dog faeces.

Take a guess at the quantities involved—*one million gallons* of urine and *100 tons* of faeces are left on our streets every DAY. Owners who allow their pets to foul public paths and parks are far more anti-social than young graffiti artists. The most aggravating aspects of this problem was summed up when I saw a neighbour walking her dog home one afternoon. She stopped to let the dog defecate on the pavement a few houses away from her own door, looking off into the distance while the deed was done. It was not her family who were going to have to look at it or watch their step when they next went outside.

Is it fair to keep a large dog confined in a city flat? An

unhappy, barking dog is a nuisance to neighbours, and a potential danger. Britain is fortunate in not having to worry about rabies in the estimated 400,000 dog bites that occur each year, but there are any number of horrifying news reports of children mauled and permanently disfigured by previously docile animals.

The League for the Introduction of Canine Control (LICC) is a national pressure group seeking changes in the law and action by local councils to eliminate these dangers.

Some councils are moving towards more stringent controls, and many parks now have dog-free areas. (I met two boys who thought this was the area where dogs could be free. Clearer labelling and explanatory signs are in order! Talk to your local councillor.) But the planned elimination of the dog licence is going to make controlling dogs even more difficult than it has been. LICC and the RSPCA are both campaigning for the licence to be maintained and the price increased to pay for a national dog warden service.

Toxocara can be carried into the house on shoes and pram wheels and survives for several days on the floor. You might think about switching to slippers and leaving shoes at the door (a good way to avoid carrying street dirt inside, in any case). Park bikes and prams just inside the door if possible, or even under shelter outside. If you have a crawling child, you'll probably want to take special care.

If you move house, find out whether dogs have had access to the garden. In one tragic case a little girl went blind after her family moved into a house which had been an RSPCA shelter.

Ground rules

Anyone who insists on keeping dogs in an urban environment, or who has a faithful Fido already, should bear in mind the following points:

1 Train your dog to defecate in a box or tray, inside the house or in your garden. LICC has a pamphlet about how to do this, and suggests that droppings be flushed down the toilet. Dogs can also be trained to go on newspaper.
2 Careful worming is important to eliminate Toxocara—get advice from your vet. Faeces should be *burned* for two days after worming. (If that isn't enough to put anyone off having a dog I don't know what is.)
3 Toxocara can survive in soil for over two years so you

should ensure that your pet does not use the lawn as a loo, especially if you have children. *Never* eat while playing with a dog, and take care to wash your hands afterwards.

4 A pooper-scooper (pet shops stock these, and a Pet Mess Pick-Up can be purchased by post directly from the manufacturer) is the answer while training your dog.

5 A dog needs a considerable amount of exercise to stay healthy and happy. If you cannot provide this, either give the dog away or find someone else to take it out. (But no messes on the pavement or in the park!)

6 See that your pet does not annoy neighbours with constant, irritable and irritating barking (see point 5). If it does, you have a responsibility to either solve the problem or get rid of the dog.

7 Use a lead, and remember that Trixie should not be allowed to approach anyone she doesn't know, no matter how small and friendly she is. You should be even more careful if your beloved is a mastiff, and particularly around children. (If someone wants to say hello to your pet they will approach you.)

8 See that your pet wears a collar and tag with your name and address.

If you are a dog owner and this seems overly severe, consider other people's small children: similar rules seem perfectly reasonable when applied to them.

● LICC (League for the Introduction of Canine Control), P. O. Box 326, London NW5 3LE, no telephone.

● Royal Society for the Prevention of Cruelty to Animals (RSPCA), Causeway, Horsham, West Sussex RH12 1HG, telephone Horsham (0403) 64181.

● Petcetera etc Ltd, P O Box 112, Henley-in-Arden, Solihull, W Midlands B95 5HD, telephone (0926) 843030. Pet Mess Pick-Up £4.95 (postfree) in mid-1988.

HEALTH

Pests

Fleas are an annual problem, but avoid using insecticides— flea sprays, powders or collars. The first non-toxic step is to vacuum thoroughly: carpets, rugs, upholstery, cushions, mattresses, everything. Then seal the vacuum bag in an old plastic bag and throw it away. Or burn it. (If the problem is acute, put your bedding, pet's bedding and rugs through a hot wash.) Do this at least twice a week.

The next step is to mix brewer's yeast into Trixie's food to make her taste nasty. Several cats I know adore nutritional yeast, which is very palatable to humans too. Garlic is also said to help (one mashed clove a day, in food).

The key herb is a mint called pennyroyal. It has tiny leaves, spreads rapidly, smells delicious (you can use it to make tea), and happens to be a fleabane. Plant it all around your garden (each plant can be divided many times as it spreads), and use the dried leaves to pack a fabric flea collar. You can also buy pennyroyal oil to dab on a collar or bedding (this seems to have caused rare cases of spontaneous abortion, so be careful if you have a pregnant pet). Rubbed on *your* arms and legs it will act as an insect repellent.

You can give your pet a rinse with strong (cool) pennyroyal tea after a bath.

● Many nurseries sell pennyroyal plants, or can obtain them for you. A good source of herb plants (retail and by post) is Hollington Nurseries Ltd, Woolton Hill, Newbury, Berks RG15 9XT, telephone (0635) 253908.

Worms are another problem for pets and their owners. Cats and dogs on a fresh, raw diet generally do not suffer from intestinal parasites, as animals eating processed food do. A daily dose of garlic is also beneficial and some breeders report using nothing but this to prevent their animals getting roundworm. Since garlic in the diet is an ancient remedy for colds and is said to increase resistance to disease, and fends off fleas too, why not give this a try? Mash or press the fresh garlic and mix it into your pet's food.

An easy way to peel a lot of garlic (for this or for a big pot of garlic soup) is to separate the cloves and pour boiling water over them. Allow to soak for a couple of minutes—the skins should slip off easily. Press a dozen cloves into a jar and mix with an unrefined vegetable oil to make a convenient paste. Stir a spoonful into Fido's dish of table scraps or chicken livers.

Health care

A good diet is the most important way of keeping your pet in prime condition. Convenient supplements are egg yolks, unrefined vegetable oils (safflower, for example), cod liver oil, onion and garlic, and brewer's yeast.

The British Homoeopathic Association can refer you to a homoeopathic veterinarian. Send an SAE to the BHA at 27a Devonshire Place, London W1N 1RJ (telephone 01-935 2163) for a list of vets and of the books they sell on homoeopathic pet care.

ANIMALS IN THE CITY

Your neighbours probably would not welcome a rooster, but if you have a large garden there's no reason you can't keep hens or rabbits. While city by-laws do not prohibit goats, they need a bit of room. But you'd better think about what you are going to do with the hens (once they stop laying) and any baby bunnies (an avoidable predicament). Can you face slaughtering them? Or can you sell them? How will you tell the children?

Domestic animals—goats, ducks, geese—could be raised on common land within communities. There are city farms all over Britain now, providing children and older people with a chance to experience something of the life of a farm. They also give people a chance to buy locally reared food. We buy delicious goats' milk and eggs from Surrey Docks City Farm, as well as honey in season and occasionally fresh meat. The animals are fed with reject fruit and vegetables (like yellowed cucumbers and slightly faded parsley) from Spitalfields market, and local children do a lot of the feeding.

Humans need contact with other creatures for emotional well-being, and we need a proper picture of the ecological balances which enable us to survive on the earth. Even in the countryside the sight of a pig rolling in the dirt or a flock of chicken scratching for insects has become a rarity: intensive animal rearing sees to that. An increase in natural habitat for native animals and the keeping of domestic animals on city farms (as well as by individuals) can help to make the city a living ecosystem instead of a concrete jungle.

● National Federation of City Farms, The Old Vicarage, 66 Fraser Street, Windmill Hill, Bedminster, Bristol BS3 4LY, telephone (0272) 660663.

- Royal Society for Nature Conservation, The Green, Nettleham, Lincoln LN2 2NR, telephone (0522) 752326. National association of 48 local Nature Conservation Trusts. Membership of any of these includes a subscription to the RSNC magazine *Natural World*.
- *City Wildspace*, Bob Smyth (Hilary Shipman, 1987).

15
CHILDREN

Despite the claim that we are seeking to leave a better world for
our children, we know at another level that we are doing no
such thing: we are eating up their future, devouring their
resources, recklessly squandering their substance in the pursuit
of our here and now . . . .

Jeremy Seabrook
The Guardian, 24 August 1987

When a North American Indian tribe had an important decision
to make, their council asked 'How will this affect the seventh
generation?' If you have children, you'll be aware of the many
choices you make on their behalf, and with their future in
mind. But even parents rarely consider the ways in which
environmental problems in the news today will have to be
faced and dealt with by our children, grandchildren and great-
grandchildren. We are only beginning to see the consequences of

air pollution from the burning of fossil fuels, nuclear contamination of the seas, and the breakdown of the ozone layer resulting from our use of CFCs.

As a society, the next generation (let alone the seventh generation) has been far from our minds. Genetic damage resulting from ionizing radiation and toxic chemicals in the environment will actually affect the physical condition of the babies which are born over the next generation, and, in turn, their children.

This no doubt sounds terribly grim and discouraging. But it is up to us, now, to start to change the way we live for the sake of the children—for the sake of the seventh generation.

PRE-CONCEPTION

Before you and your partner get pregnant, do a little self-analysis. As well as thinking about whether your home is big enough or how you will manage on a reduced income, give careful consideration to how healthy you both are.

It isn't enough to change your habits once you find out that you are going to have a baby. Animal breeders know that the fitness of the father before conception is of great importance, but at best we tend to look only at the mother, and then only *during* pregnancy. Sperm cells are vulnerable to damage, as are egg cells. Smoking fathers, for example, are known to have reduced sperm counts and their children are more likely to have birth defects.

Even people who are aware of the importance of how a baby comes into the world, with dim lights and warm baths and a loving welcome, often don't realise that parents can help the baby and themselves by improving the way they live. Eating well, getting enough exercise and rest, and not smoking or drinking are all important. Eliminating pollutants is also going to make for a healthier and happier baby.

Foresight was set up to give advice and information about the environmental factors which affect foetal health, with the aim of reducing the problems of birth defects and infant ill health. The organization provides material on nutrition, pollution, allergies and Natural Family Planning, and can refer you to a doctor who runs a Foresight clinic if you would like a full health check—and advice—before you conceive.

If you are already pregnant *Foresight* can give advice on

diet, nutritional supplements, protecting yourself and your baby from pollution and combating allergies.

Foresight also advises couples who are having difficulty in conceiving, and publishes an excellent little booklet on additives which you can tuck into your wallet, each E number colourcoded for quick reference.

● *Foresight*, The Old Vicarage, Church Lane, Witley, Surrey GU8 5PN. Send SAE for information. *Find Out*, the additive decoder, is £1.35 including postage, and *Guidelines for Future Parents* is £1.20.

PREGNANCY

Pregnancy brings many physical changes, but perhaps even more dramatic are the changes in one's plans and priorities. Everyone wants to give advice, and it is often difficult not to feel that you are being pulled backwards and forwards, with no way to get the information you want. The overwhelming feeling of responsibility for another life leaves a first-time mother vulnerable to persuasion, especially from those who are providing antenatal care. I hope that the following information and contacts will help you to resolve questions for yourself.

Chemical caution

Your doctor or midwife, as well as any good book on pregnancy will recommend a healthy diet with plenty of fresh fruit and vegetables, and will caution against tobacco, alcohol and drugs. But you are unlikely to be warned that pregnant women should also avoid hazardous household chemicals.

Your nose will tip you off about some of these—many pregnant women find that their sense of smell becomes particularly acute. Pesticides, chemical fertilizers, many cleaning products, paints and paint thinners, contact adhesive and all aerosols are best removed from your home—Chapter 10 suggests alternatives for many standard products.

These changes are also important after your baby is born, because of ingestion through your breastmilk and direct inhalation. Many babies grow up surrounded by dangerous fumes from household disinfectants, used out of misplaced concern about hygiene. Most disinfectants contain cresol, a chemical which can affect the central nervous system and cause organ damage. Even hair dyes have been shown to be carcinogenic and mutagenic in laboratory tests. Small amounts are absorbed through the scalp, and the fumes are inhaled. For several years US obstetricians have been warning pregnant women against using any chemical hair treatment (including permanent waves).

Avoid all medication (many common drugs have been shown to have a deleterious effect on the developing foetus), and make a special effort to stay away from food additives, including artificial sweeteners. Organic fruits and vegetables are not contaminated with pesticide residues so buy them if you can, and eat only lean meat because pesticides, hormones and antibiotics concentrate in fatty tissue (try to get hold of chemical-free, organically-raised meat). Tea and coffee, as well as alcohol should be treated with caution while you're expecting, and while you are planning to conceive.

Rather than think of this as restrictive, look at pregnancy as an excellent opportunity to make improvements in your diet and surroundings.

Ultrasound scanning

The use of high frequency sound waves (which cannot be detected by the adult human ear) to monitor pregnancy has become routine in Britain, in spite of the fact that there have been no long-term studies done to establish its safety. While no gross effects—such as deformities—have been seen, more subtle consequences are quite possible. US studies suggest a connection between scanning, dyslexia and hearing disorders.

The information obtained by scanning can, of course, be valuable in some cases, but ultrasound tests with rats have shown foetal abnormalities and growth retardation, and these should at least be taken as an indication of potential risk in humans.

Melody Weig, an independent midwife, points out that: (1) *no* form of technological intervention should be used on the vast majority of women and their babies; (2) dependence on information from scans means that practitioners have less incentive to really listen to women; and (3) midwives and doctors are losing their palpation skills because of over-reliance on machine data, which is only as accurate as the machine's operator. (Correct reading of ultrasound is difficult. Even in a controlled study done by the Royal College of Obstetricians and Gynaecologists one normal foetus was aborted after an incorrect diagnosis.)

What effect does scanning (with up to three ultrasound beams at a time) have on the unborn baby? In general, s/he seems to try to move *away* from the beam, and many mothers report 'my baby didn't like it'. Unusual foetal activity is common afterwards, and women sense that their baby is disturbed. (This was certainly my experience, when I was persuaded to have a scan because my doctor and midwives were 'almost sure' I had twins, which they said they would not be able to deliver at home. They were wrong, both about the twins and about the size of the baby.)

Routine scanning is expensive (upwards of £14 million a year in Britain) and no adequate records have been kept on the women and babies exposed to it. The World Health Organization has issued a policy statement stressing that 'ultrasound screening during pregnancy is now in widespread use without sufficient evaluation.'

The best sources of information about this debate are the Association for Improvements in the Maternity Services (AIMS) and Beverley Beech's *Who's Having Your Baby?*. Remember, you have no legal or moral obligation to have your baby scanned.

BIRTH

Technology has been creeping up on us in many areas of our lives, but none is more vital to our health and to the health and wholeness of society than where and how we give birth. Michel Odent, the French obstetrician, believes that the period before, during and immediately after birth affects our immune system, our ability to love and respond to other people and even the way we age (see his *Primal Health* and page 183 of this book).

Odent's first book, which has not been translated into English, is called *Genèse de l'Homme Ecologique, L'instinct retrouvé* (Paris: Epi, 1979), 'Genesis of Ecological Man'. He points out that the technologist sees both women's ability to bear children and the cycles of the natural world as insufficient and inefficient, to be manipulated and improved upon. Birth is an important 'ecological' issue.

In 1970 the Peel Committee Report (Standing Maternity and Midwivery Advisory Committee, HMSO) recommended that 100% of births should take place in hospital, and the trend towards hospital confinements which started early in the century has continued, from a total of 90% of babies born in hospital at that time to 99% in the mid-eighties.

The notion that hospital births are safer than births in small GP units or at home was uncontested until Marjorie Tew, an enterprising statistician at the University of Nottingham Medical School, decided to collate the data from two official perinatal surveys. Her results were published in *Place of Birth*, eds. S. Kitzinger and J. Davis (Oxford University Press, 1978). Tew found that the presumed connection between hospital births and reduced infant mortality did not exist, and that home birth is statistically safer, in every risk category!

More recently, Rona Campbell and Alison Macfarlane did another statistical review, once again based on official NHS figures, and amongst their conclusions is the following: 'There is some evidence, although not conclusive, that morbidity is higher among women and babies cared for in an institutional setting. For some women, the iatrogenic doctor-caused risk associated with institutional delivery may be greater than any benefit conferred, but this has yet to be proven.' (*Where to be born? The debate and the evidence*, 1987, National Perinatal Epidemiology Unit, Radcliffe Infirmary, Oxford). A woman who has a home birth is continually told how brave she must be, but those of us who have had a home birth often feel that it is having a hospital birth that requires bravery!

Perhaps the most important factor in a successful labour is that the woman in labour feels comfortable and confident about her own abilities, and at ease in her surroundings. It's no coincidence that women frequently arrive at hospital only to have their contractions stop. This is embarrassing and inconvenient, but hardly surprising. (If you were to move a labouring animal, the same thing would happen—it is a natural safety mechanism.)

Hospitals are not hospitable places. Doctors and nurses seem to bristle at this idea, but of course the hospital is familiar territory to them. Even seriously ill heart patients have been found to do better when they are nursed at home rather than in hospital. When it comes to avoiding dangerous bacteria, a hospital is surely the last place one would want to take a woman about to give birth. Babies born at home are, for example, highly unlikely to get staphylococcus, a contagious infection which sometimes runs rife in hospital.

You are far more likely to end up with what is euphemistically called a 'managed labour' in hospital. There are a number of reasons for this. A woman who isn't at ease is more likely to need intervention, hospital routine makes a timetable for labour more likely, and the simple fact that equipment, drugs and staff are available make it more likely that they will be used.

There is also an apt expression, the 'cascade of management', used to describe the way one act of intervention leads to another. If your waters are manually ruptured to speed up labour, the contractions become much more painful and you are therefore more likely to need or want drugs or an epidural. If labour is induced with a drip of oxytocin, you cannot move around freely and will probably have a more difficult and painful time, making the use of further drugs more likely. If a woman has anaesthetics, she is more likely to need a forceps delivery, and so on.

Many couples think that they aren't allowed to have their baby at home, but in fact community midwives are obliged by law to attend any birth in their area, and there are a number of organizations which will help you if you want to have a home birth.

If you need specialist care, try to find a hospital where you can get to know the staff before your baby is born. Unfortunately it is difficult, if not impossible, to arrange to have a midwife you know with you when you have your baby. Caroline Flint, midwife and author, has been running a 'Know Your Midwife' scheme in London for several years, but although it is popular with midwives and mothers, the hospital authorities are not sufficiently supportive for the idea to spread rapidly.

You can have an independent midwife for antenatal care and delivery at home, if you prefer not to use the community midwives and a GP. Do some reading and make up your own mind. Even under the National Health Service you have a choice, right up until the last minute.

Contacts

- Association for Improvements in the Maternity Services (AIMS). Send an SAE to 40 Kingswood Avenue, London NW6 6LS for their literature list, which includes an excellent leaflet on 'Choosing a Home Birth'.
- Independent Midwifery Service, 65 Mount Nod Road, London SW16 2LP, telephone 01-677 9746.

Reading

● *Birth Reborn* (Souvenir Press, 1984), *Entering the World* (Marion Boyars, 1984) and *Primal Health* (Century, 1986), all by Michel Odent.
● *Birthrights*, Sally Inch (Hutchinson, 1982). Excellent.
● *Who's Having Your Baby?*, Beverley Lawrence Beech (Camden Press, 1987). A practical, rather brusque guide to getting the birth you want.
● *Where to be born? The debate and the evidence*, Rona Campbell and Alison Macfarlane, National Perinatal Epidemiology Unit, Radcliffe Infirmary, Oxford OX2 6HE (£2 incl. postage).

BREASTFEEDING

Scandals about the selling of artificial milk products to women in the Third World, with advertising to persuade them that 'formula' is superior to their breastmilk, has had considerable press coverage.

But what about us? Only 64% of British mothers choose to breastfeed their babies at all, and of that number only 40% (26% of the total) continue to breastfeed for at least four months, the minimum period recommended by most paediatricians. A recent survey shows that there has been a slight *decline* in the number of breastfeeding mothers in the 1980s.

Breastfeeding is officially encouraged, but not nearly enough is done to make it easy for many new mothers. Midwives and nurses try to help, but hospital routine doesn't make early breastfeeding easy, and the standard advice is that 'it'll be better when you get home'.

Having your baby at home does make breastfeeding easier in the early days (a domino scheme, where the mother and baby return home a few hours after birth, is also helpful).

Virtually all women in the Third World breastfeed their babies, even women who are very poorly nourished themselves. Surveys in Africa suggest that no more than 1% of rural women and 5% of urban women are unable to nurse their babies. Yet many of us give up nursing because we haven't got enough milk. How can this be?

The main problem is extremely simple: not allowing the baby to nurse enough. The sucking is what stimulates milk production. You also need to eat well, and get enough rest. Midwives and doctors will give you advice on feeding your baby, but they still tell mothers how many minutes to nurse on each breast and how often to feed—rules which have nothing to do with *your* baby.

Take your cues from the baby, and your own feelings. Many babies like to nurse on and off throughout the day (and night), and there is nothing wrong with this! The National Childbirth Trust trains breastfeeding counsellors who are knowledgeable, friendly and supportive. Do contact them if you need help.

Taking the baby to bed with you makes things much easier. Michel Odent has pointed out that in many other parts of the world babies always sleep with their mothers. He has also observed that cot death, Sudden Infant Death Syndrome, is unknown in these countries and suggests that 'Possibly it is the cot which is the essential factor!'

Young children, and older children and adults too, often feel isolated if they sleep alone, but many parents feel a misplaced sense of guilt about the fact that their children like to climb into bed with them. A large 'family' bed is a happy option for some, and a low bed (or futon) is a great help, especially with a small baby. See the reading list below for a book about this.

Breastfeeding is physically desirable when a baby is small, but psychological benefits continue with extended breastfeeding. Michel Odent has done an informal survey amongst children who have been breastfed for at least a year, and finds that these children do not develop an attachment for a 'transitional object', the psychologist's term for that grubby cot blanket or ragged stuffed bear many small children drag about everywhere.

The other factor which prevents women breastfeeding is embarrassment about using their breasts in this way, and particularly about the difficulty of feeding in public. Social support, from partners, family and friends, is terribly important in successful breastfeeding.

Women who will happily bare their breasts on a beach are sometimes desperately shy about feeding a baby, no matter how discreetly. Perhaps this is because they feel that they are the only one! We so rarely see a mother breastfeeding that it doesn't seem normal or ordinary, and any use of our breasts is treated as something sexual. The more common breastfeeding becomes, and the more comfortable all of us (men, women and children) become about it, the easier it will be for every new mother.

(It is worth noting that women who breastfeed are less likely to suffer from breast cancer in later life.)

● National Childbirth Trust (NCT), Alexandra House, Oldham Terrace, London W3 6NH, telephone 01–992 8637.

● La Leche League of Great Britain, BM 3424, London WC1N 3XX, telephone 01-242 1278. Their classic book *The Art of Breastfeeding* is available by mail order along with a wide range of other publications. They offer advice and have local groups around the country.

● *Breast is Best*, Penny and Andrew Stanway (Pan, 1978).

● *Babies, Breastfeeding & Bonding*, Ina May Gaskin (New York: Bergin & Garvey, 1987). Especially recommended. Available by mail order from Changes Bookshop, 242 Belsize Road, London NW6 4BT, telephone 01-328 5161.

● *The Family Bed*, Tine Thevenin, 1976 (available from the La Leche League).

NAPPIES

When you have a leaky little one you get obsessed with nappies. Fathers swop notes on the best type, and friends report on which shop has your favourite brand at 50p off.

Of course I'm talking about disposable plastic-and-paper nappies, not the terry nappies our mothers or grandmothers boiled in a copper. 65% of babies are now put into disposable nappies and approximately 2,500 million are sold every year in Britain, according to an industry report. Sold, soiled, and discarded.

But unfortunately, not disposed of. The trouble is that disposable nappies simply are *not* disposable. They are an ecological disaster on a large scale, non-biodegradable and a potential health hazard to babies and to the public. They contribute to the depletion of limited timber and petroleum reserves (in the US, disposable nappies use 100,000 tons of plastic and 800,000 tons of wood pulp every year).

Anyone who has used disposables will remember how the dustbins were suddenly twice as full. Random checks in a small American town found that ⅓ of the community's solid waste consisted of disposable nappies! A general US estimate is that 4% of household solid waste is made up of soiled nappies. For every pound we spend on disposable nappies, we as taxpayers will spend 10p on disposal.

I understand why people use disposables, and I have used them myself. After all, everyone else seems to, including the maternity ward at your local hospital. This tacit medical endorsement, fortified by the free samples given to new mothers, is enough to convince many parents that disposables are the correct thing to use.

Because disposables save time and effort they can seem worth the *expense*, though it is considerable: over £1000 for a child potty-trained by 2½. But they are not worth the ecological cost, a price which our children will have to pay.

Not only is there growing public concern over the disposal problem—some US states have proposed legislation banning disposable nappies—but over the health risks they present. (The question does not involve only baby nappies. The Japanese, as well as the Americans, are concerned about the additional burden of disposable nappies worn by the incontinent aged, in an ageing society.)

Modern sanitation involves the separation of sewage from other waste, but with disposable nappies huge amounts of faecal matter are treated as part of the household rubbish rather than being processed through the sewage system. (When one considers that raw sewage is piped offshore near many British beaches, perhaps this is an idle concern.)

Nappies may be yet another source of groundwater contamination from landfill sites. 'Leachate containing viruses from human feces (including live vaccines from routine childhood immunizations) can leak into the earth and pollute underground water supplies. In addition to the potential of groundwater contamination, airborne viruses carried by flies and other insects contribute to an unhealthy and unsanitary situation.' (Carl Lehrburger, 'The Disposable Diaper Myth', *Whole Earth Review*, Fall 1988).

Many children are sensitive to the chemicals, perfumes and plastic in disposable nappies. The plastic covering efficiently holds in moisture, which causes nappy rash. 'Keeps baby drier' means that his blanket or your knee is kept dry—while the moisture is sealed inside the nappy, next to his skin. Because of the high cost of disposables they may not be changed often enough (12–15 times a day is recommended for newborns—which would cost nearly £20 a week!).

Nappy rash was virtually unknown before plastic pants became available in the 1950s, and the mother whose child has a recurrently raw and painful bottom will know that it is essential to get the child out of 'ordinary', ie disposable, nappies. Doctors suggest leaving the child bare as much as possible (a good rule for any baby) and at least temporarily switching to cloth nappies.

Another advantage of using real nappies is that they make beautifully absorbent and lintfree cleaning cloths, when your children no longer need them.

Supplies

Many people are put off by the idea of using pins. Terry nappies are very absorbent, but I've found the standard 24-inch squares awkward to handle and virtually impossible to fit neatly.

An alternative, which could convince you that using 'real' nappies is feasible in today's world, is Biobottoms from California. These are similar to old-fashioned knitted 'soakers', which went on over the nappy instead of plastic pants. Biobottoms are made from fully-felted, machine-washable wool and fasten with velcro. They make changes simple and painless—rivalling disposables—and allow baby's bottom to 'breathe'. Biobottoms are not totally waterproof, but each one will keep clothes and bedding dry through 4 or 5 nappy changes. You can use folded terry nappies inside a Biobottom or buy fine cotton flannel nappies which are designed to fit the cover.

At time of going to press, Suma Wholefoods was hoping to import and distribute Biobottoms in the UK—contact them at Unit AX1, Dean Clough Industrial Park, Halifax, W Yorks HX3 5AN, telephone (0422) 45513.

Although the initial expense of using cloth nappies and covers is much greater than buying a bag of disposables at the supermarket, in the long run you should cut costs by about half, even taking laundering into account. And subsequent babies add nothing to the total!

In practice

As the eldest of five children, I remember the deft way my mother sluiced out nappies, wrung them firmly and tossed them into a covered pail. With modern washing machines and dryers, using cloth nappies is much easier for us than it was for our mothers. The real difficulty is getting a routine established. Here's how:

1 Make sure you have enough nappies, at least 3 to 4 dozen to start with. You will also need a covered pail to hold rinsed nappies until wash time (which will be nearly every day, while your baby is small), a supply of borax and a gentle washing powder.

2 Gauze liners make cleaning easier—use them rather than disposable paper liners.

3 Half fill the pail with a mild borax solution (to disinfect the nappies, and reduce odours and staining).

4 Wet nappies can go straight into the nappy pail—you can rinse them first if you like—but soiled nappies should be shaken or scraped (with an old knife or spoon) and then rinsed in the toilet bowl.

5 When ready to wash, drain the excess solution into the toilet, and use a spin cycle to remove dirty water. Then a hot wash, and double rinse—don't overload the machine.

6 Inside, you may want to use a tumble dryer (if you have one) on high heat to help sterilization. Tumbling also makes the nappies softer than drying on a rack or over a radiator. Dry outside whenever you can: sunlight acts as a natural disinfectant and gentle bleach.

7 Try to avoid plastic pants. Terry nappies can sometimes be used on their own. 'Soakers' are knitted wool or fabric covers which offer some protection, or you may want to try Biobottoms, which you can order from California.

8 Let your baby go bare whenever you can, inside and out.

9 Take a plastic bag with you when you go out, to carry home dirty nappies. Just fold this in your nappy bag, along with the usual change of clothes, toys and so on. (Another thing to avoid, if you can, is those disposable towelettes. Instead carry some tissues and a flannel in a small plastic bag.)

10 If you use cloth nappies most of the time, don't feel guilty about using a 'disposable' occasionally.

This sounds far more daunting than it is. I've described everything in detail so anyone could start from scratch, but the process will become just a small part of your baby routine.

Why doesn't someone start a nappy service? With a budget of £1000 per child this would surely be a feasible proposition. When my mother had twins she got a year's free diaper service as a prize, and the poet Sylvia Plath used one in London in the early 1960s. A nappy service provides cloth nappies and regular pick-up and collection. You hand over your pail of rinsed nappies, and in return get a pile of bouncy fresh ones, washed and dried in high-temperature machines. What a delightful idea!

● Biobottoms, P.O. Box 6009, Petaluma, CA 94953, USA, telephone (707) 778–7945. Extremely helpful and happy to ship overseas orders.

HEALTH

Immunization

A Health Education Council leaflet on immunization insists that it is entirely safe and utterly necessary. In fact, the leaflet says that 'any child who does not have the measles vaccine is virtually certain to catch the disease . . . So there's a clear choice between having the measles or having the vaccine.'

A 1978 survey of 30 of the United States found that more than half the children who contracted measles had been adequately vaccinated against them!

A common justification for universal vaccination is that it is largely responsible for this century's reduction in infant mortality. The common childhood diseases were, however, in decline *before* many modern vaccines came on the scene. Better hygiene, clean water and an improved diet were crucial factors.

If you have a young baby, take the time to look into this question before you make up your mind. Your clinic (or GP or health visitor) will press you to have the baby's first set of shots at 5 months, but the timing is not crucial—they like to start at this age because you are still bringing the child into the clinic regularly.

The possible risks with the whooping cough vaccine have got a great deal of attention, but there are concerns about other routine vaccinations. One might think that a sickly infant would need immunization more than a robust child, but children who are already unwell are most vulnerable to ill-effects from vaccination. An American study shows a connection between the DPT vaccine and cot death—the most likely explanation being that in these cases the vaccine was the last straw for a child whose system was already under stress.

An Australian doctor has used Vitamin C and zinc supplements to boost immune function before giving vaccines to vulnerable Aboriginal children, and infant mortality in the group virtually disappeared. If you decide to go ahead with vaccination, you might want to give your baby extra Vitamin C and some multimineral drops containing zinc.

As Michael A. Weiner says in *Maximum Immunity* (Gateway Books, 1986), 'people are beginning to take a critical look at how safe these vaccines really are. It seems in some cases that the possible risks may outweigh the benefits of continued vaccination programs.'

● *Vaccination and Immunisation*, Leon Chaitow (C.W. Daniel, 1987).

● *How to Raise a Healthy Child in Spite of Your Doctor*, Robert Mendelsohn (Chicago: Contemporary Books, 1984).

Fluoride

Until the 1930s, fluoride was considered a poison. The expanding steel and aluminium industries at the time had serious problems disposing of the soluble fluoride waste which was being generated. A chemist employed by the sugar industry, which wanted to find a way of reducing tooth decay without lowering sugar consumption, noticed that small amounts of fluoride seemed to produce this effect (in larger doses it causes mottling, brittle teeth and abnormal bone formation).

Instead of being *fined* for contaminating water supplies with toxic fluoride, the aluminium and steel industries were eventually able to *sell* the waste fluoride to water authorities. Most water is used for washing and sewage, so an enormous amount of toxic waste could be disposed of, with the public convinced that this was a benefit.

One potent argument against fluoridated water is that it is involuntary mass medication. This has frightening implications—we know that Vitamin C is good for us, but who wants to be dosed with it in every glass of tap water?—and can only be explained by the fact that metal production (and the resultant consumer products made from them) would become more expensive if the true cost of fluoride disposal was borne by the industries. It seems reasonable to call it 'the protected pollutant'.

The chemical is promoted by the medical and dental professions, in spite of the fact that it is implicated in a wide variety of health problems, from allergic reactions to cancer, and even to cot death. A child who makes a habit of eating fluoridated toothpaste may be getting as much as three times the amount of fluoride officially considered safe and desirable.

A diet low in sugar and high in minerals, along with proper brushing habits, will keep your children's teeth in good condition without fluoride. If after further reading you still want your children to have fluoride, why not use fluoride drops in a prescribed dose rather than rely on random intake from toothpaste or tap water?

● See pages 33–36 of *Chemical Children* (Mansfield and Monro), and contact the National Anti-Fluoridation Campaign, 36 Station Road, Thames Ditton, Surrey KT7 ONS, telephone 01 398 2117, for more information.

Safety

The best thing about clearing our flat of harmful chemicals was the relief I felt from knowing that there were not so many things to keep out of the reach of little hands. Even the biodegradable toilet cleaner doesn't carry a warning label—it's made from acetic acid (basically vinegar), vegetable oils, and pine and lavender oils. I wouldn't want my child to drink it, but what a far cry from a bottle of bleach!

Although we worry about children getting hold of drain cleaner or methylated spirits, the most common type of 'poison' is medication. Many drugs, both prescription and over-the-counter, look very much like sweets, and until childproof caps were introduced, aspirin poisoning was common.

This is another excellent reason for cutting down on the drugs you use. Doctors often offer prescriptions because they feel that patients expect one, so make it clear that you want medication only if it is absolutely necessary.

1 Read labels and take their warnings seriously.

2 Keep dangerous items well out of reach—not on the bathroom counter or in your handbag. Because of its high alcohol content, a few spoonfuls of your cologne could lead to unconsciousness and even death for a small child.

3 Get rid of whatever you can—aerosol cans of fly killer, old medicines and unwanted aftershave. Return unused drugs to the chemist for disposal.

4 Switch to safe household products and toiletries. Even with these, care is advisable.

5 Until there are non-toxic products on the market, as there are in West Germany, DIY items are probably the most hazardous things you'll have around the house. Lock them away.

6 Be careful about dog faeces on the street and in parks—it can carry a roundworm which causes a virulent disease called Toxocariasis, blinding 100 British children each year (see page 316).

7 Take these precautions even if you don't have small children: you'll never be able to remember everything when little Cousin Jack comes to visit.

FOOD

All the principles set out in Chapter 2 apply to children just as much as to adults, but there are a few special difficulties with feeding the kids.

Getting children to eat what you want them to eat is not easy. My two-year-old son, for example, who was practically weaned on organic carrots and used to beg for kelp tablets, now sings ditties about ice cream and chips.

But things are not as discouraging as that sounds! In spite of his fascination with chips (partly because he seldom has them), he tucks into a meal at a vegetarian restaurant—or a bowl of rice and stir-fried vegetables at home—with gusto, and will try pretty much anything.

Many parents seem to think, perhaps thanks to the baby food industry, that kids need and like to eat a limited range of 'children's food'. With all good intentions they give the children an early tea of fish fingers and mashed potatoes, and later eat something far more interesting themselves. Is it such a surprise that children become 'fussy' and refuse to try anything different from the usual round?

A child's palate is more sensitive than ours, but it is easy to get into the habit of adding strong spices to food after setting aside a portion for the little ones (this takes a little juggling with some recipes).

Letting children eat with you (from the age of 6 months they can begin to join in family meals) is quite an incentive to improve your own eating habits!

Sweets

In spite of constant publicity about the hazards of sugar consumption—tooth decay and hyperactivity, for example—I am surprised at how many parents just don't bother to curtail the biscuits, sugared drinks and sweets their children eat. Even the most genteel playgroups and nurseries seem to offer sweet snacks.

Parental example will help, but the extraordinary visibility of sweets and chocolates is a hard one to deal with. Racks at every supermarket turnstile, with bright wrappers and enticing cartoon characters, beckon. Even health food shops have displays of sweets near the till.

This is a battle I'm fighting at the moment, and all I can do is suggest that you offer yourself as a good example, eliminate sweets from the house (serve fresh fruit and cheese as a dessert and have alternative snacks on hand) and *never* offer sweet things as a reward.

The sugar industry is immensely powerful, as Professor John Yudkin graphically details in a new edition of the classic *Pure, White and Deadly*. Incredibly, Tate & Lyle is one of the major sponsors of the British Nutrition Foundation! Sugar has been implicated in some cancers, liver disease, gout and eye and skin problems, as well as in diabetes. Yudkin asserts that 'If only a small fraction of what is known about sugar was revealed in connection with any other material used as a food additive, that material would be banned.'

Sucrose is not the only form of sugar. Quite a few manufacturers are now substituting other sweeteners to mislead parents trying to avoid refined sugar. Fruit syrups can also rot teeth, but they are not so concentrated as refined white sugar and provide some nutrients along with sweetening power. Dove Farm makes a range of sugar-free biscuits made with organic flour which offer a persuasive substitute for the supermarket version.

● *Pure, White and Deadly* (2nd ed.), John Yudkin (Penguin, 1988).

Crisp snacks

Double jeopardy: salt and refined fats. Both are positively bad for children's health, and spoil the appetite for real food. Advertising and constant availability is a real problem with these too. The only thing to do is to offer alternative snacks. Children are creatures of habit, and once they get used to pieces of fruit or cut-up carrots as their usual nibbles the battle is nearly won. Savoury wholegrain crackers (like oatcakes) are also good.

You can try explaining that 'store' potato crisps aren't very nice, and occasionally make some REAL ONES, at home. Crispy roast potatoes are a happy alternative (try coating chunks of potato with cold-pressed corn oil then baking in a hot oven—use organic potatoes and leave the skins on).

Scholastic ability

Recent analyses of schoolchildren's diets have shown startling cases of malnourishment. British children not only eat far too much sugar and fat but are short of major quantifiable nutrients. Vitamin and mineral supplements given in double-blind experiments initiated by Gwilym Roberts, head of the science department at Darland High School in North Wales, and reported on 'QED' and in *The Lancet*, showed substantial increases in IQ and non-verbal intelligence amongst the children who had received the supplements.

If you are keen that your child does well in school, watch what goes into her mouth. But concentrate on good food, rather than on vitamin tablets. It's just as important to cut back on junk food as to add nutritious items, and in fact you can't do one without the other.

Ringing the changes

There's no doubt that changing your child's diet is even harder than changing your own (and *you* cannot change a teenager's diet!). Move cautiously and make sure that you are willing to stop eating crisps, or whatever it might be, too. There are bound to be some 'good' foods your children like. Carrot sticks? Apple sauce? Cheese?

How about vegetables? Try chopping salad ingredients very fine and use a creamy (perhaps yoghurt-based) dressing. Or cut up raw vegetables (celery, red and green peppers, carrots, fennel, cauliflower, tomatoes, young turnips) into pieces for nibbling—it's a good idea to keep a plentiful supply of these crudités ready in the fridge. Good for adults' figures, too. Serve with a dip occasionally.

Puréeing, and carefully seasoning, cooked vegetables can make all the difference for children (and some adults!). Root vegetables like carrots, parsnips and swedes are delicious mashed half and half with potatoes.

Here are some general ideas for eating with children.
1 Let your child join in with your meals from about 6 months, with tiny tastes of suitable foods.

2 Eat a variety of foods, both cooked and raw.

3 Don't force anything on a child.

4 Aim for a balanced diet over the course of each week, not each day.

5 Don't panic if your child doesn't eat as much as you think s/he should; a healthy child will not starve himself!

6 Don't let a child who isn't eating meals have sweets and crisps—I've noticed that parents sometimes think 'at least she's eating *something*', even though the snacks will spoil her appetite for the next meal.

7 Notice which nutritious foods your children *like*, and try to emphasize those dishes.

8 Let children get involved in meal planning and preparation as early as possible.

Many older children will be fascinated by food and development issues—you can talk about additives and pesticides, visit city farms and Ryton Gardens, and discuss where our food comes from and how what we eat affects people in other countries.

Growing at least a little of your food is another way to get children involved in family meals. Do everything you can to encourage cooking skills (even when this means helping to deal with flour on the ceiling afterwards). One of the most interesting things you can do is make or bake common store-bought foods: water biscuits, for example, or piccalilli or baked beans. Enjoyment and imagination are the attitudes you want to encourage.

● *Let's Have Healthy Children*, Third Edition, Adele Davis (Unwin, 1981). A classic.

● *The Right Food for Your Kids*, Louise Templeton (Century, 1984)—good on principles, but some of the recipes sound appalling ('Real Custard', for example, made from maize meal and water!).

● The London Food Commission, *Children's Food*, Tim Lobstein (Unwin Hyman, 1988).

CLOTHES AND EQUIPMENT

How easy it is to get carried away dressing a small child. The miniature trappings are very appealing, and with a first baby you're likely to be given lots of frilly little garments. Chapter 3 has general ideas about ecological buying, and the suggestions about buying secondhand become even more relevant with kids. Tiny garments can cost a small fortune, yet have to be replaced every couple of months as a baby grows.

Shopping

You may be lucky enough to have friends and relatives who will hand over a nearly-new baby wardrobe (and it's well worth letting people know that you are not averse to borrowing clothes and baby gear). Otherwise, charity shops and boot sales sometimes throw up terrific bargains—a dozen babygros for £1. Tiny clothes get very little wear so they are often in excellent condition.

Just because a garment is secondhand does not mean it will be shoddy. You may well find you can afford far better quality—and originally more expensive—clothes by careful shopping. There are resale shops in some towns, and while the prices cannot rival those at jumble sales they are still considerably cheaper than buying new.

Choose well-made, sturdy garments, in natural fibres whenever possible. Look out for missing buttons or broken zips on older children's things. These can be replaced, but you should know what you're getting into. Encourage friends and relatives to ask before they buy presents, so they can supplement your 'finds' instead of duplicating them.

If you worry about your child looking uncoordinated because you've acquired clothes here and there, decide on a basic colour scheme and stick to it. This may seem fussy—and plenty of parents and children couldn't care less—but if you do care it makes dressing a recalcitrant and opinionated toddler, and hunting through piles of clothes at a jumble sale, a lot simpler.

You'll be staggered at the amount of money you can save by buying secondhand. (You might want to send a proportion of the savings to a children's relief organisation.) A friend of mine, who has a very well-to-do husband, sneaks off to jumble sales when he is away on business trips!

When your child has outgrown his or her clothes, and you are not saving them for another baby, either pass them on to someone or donate them to one of the charity shops.

Baby equipment, too, can be acquired secondhand. Check your NCT branch newsletter, local free sheet and notices in the newsagent's window. Place your own advertisement asking for the things you need and specifying the approximate price you are willing to pay.

American furniture manufacturers once went through a phase of trying to persuade parents that it was unhygienic to use hand-me-down articles. What nonsense! Be prepared to give your purchases a good scrub (some sellers clean and polish items first, other do not), and as with clothes check first for the small parts which may be missing or broken, and practically impossible to replace.

PLAY

Babies have cupboards full of battery-driven stuffed dogs and helicopters with revolving blades. Even good old Lego comes with ready-made detail nowadays. These toys are designed for what one box describes as 'imaginative play'—that is, play the way the designer imagines it. Not play which genuinely encourages a child's imagination.

What effect does this have on children? Some will grow up wanting an endless supply of new toys. Others will annoy their parents by ignoring their toys and pulling out all the saucepans for a jam session in the corner.

Parents are apt to lose their temper when an expensive toy is taken apart 'to find out how it works'. But if you give a small child a toy with complicated internal mechanisms, her native curiosity (the imagination we want to encourage) inspires her to set to work with a screwdriver.

Older children compare notes with friends at school, and the child with the wrong bicycle or wrong computer software feels left out and out of step. How a child copes with this depends on her own independence and self-confidence, and on whether her parents too feel the need to have every new gadget (she wants a new play kitchen and you want that new sorbet machine).

The environmental and social consequences of this are profound. The sheer quantity of raw materials used to make toys (most of which don't last for long) is one aspect of the problem. Even more important are the lessons children learn before they can walk about ceaseless consumption, ready-made entertainment, and disposability.

Basics

The following list is probably not complete, but I find it useful when I want to come up with something new to do or make or buy:

water	animals (real ones, or soft toys)
leaves, rocks and sticks	riding toys
earth	tools
sand	homemaking things
seashells	beads to string
blocks	paper and paste
balls	paint, crayons, pencils, chalk
boxes	playdough
dolls	real cooking
	things to climb (especially trees)

Toys and playthings

Buy for durability. Considering the price of even the flimsiest toy, you might as well spend a little more and get something which will last. Durable toys made of good, solid materials *are* expensive, but even if you have only one or two children, toys can be passed to friends, sold through small ads, or saved for the grandchildren! Well-made stuffed animals and wooden toys will last nearly forever. (You might be lucky enough to find old toys or children's furniture in grandma's attic, or even at a house clearance store—I'm always hoping.)

1 Look for toys made of natural materials: cloth, paper, leather, natural fleece, wood (Good Wood, of course—see page 68) and metal.

2 Let children play with real things: put together a child-sized collection of pots and pans and dishes, instead of a purchased plastic kitchen (there is a lovely description of a child's kitchen in Louisa May Alcott's *Little Men*).

3 Secondhand or hand-me-down toys can be cleaned and mended. Let your child choose a new paint colour.

4 Invest in beautiful, adaptable toys. One example is the wooden train sets made by the Swedish firm Brio, available at many toy shops. For splendid, mostly maple toys—from basic blocks to climbing frames and a wooden ironing board and iron—write to Community Playthings for their mail order catalogue (address on page 347).

5 Toy libraries will give your children much variety and save you money (which can go towards buying more expensive 'permanent' toys). Swapping toys with friends is another idea.

6 Make playthings. Penelope Leach's *Baby & Child* (Penguin, 1979) has good ideas in a special section at the back of the book, many made from 'recycled' household items, and other books about children have similar information.

7 Have a special box or drawer for any sort of miniature that comes your way: tiny boxes, Marmite jars, desk supplies. These always come in handy.

8 Make a dolls' house, perhaps in an old sideboard table with its doors removed. Use scraps of gift wrapping paper for the walls, leftover bits of carpet for the floors. You can make—or help your child to make—much of the furniture. Toothpaste caps make lampshades, or drinking glasses for larger dolls, and all sorts of odds and ends can be put to good use.

9 A dress-up box is essential: children love long, sparkly, over-the-top clothes, so if you don't have that sort of thing to pass on pick up some at a jumble sale. They also adore funny shoes and hats—perhaps you can rustle these up from a great aunt or younger sister. Old leather shoes

can be washed in a basin of soapy water (dry away from heat).

10 In general, stick with pencils, chalk and crayons, instead of plastic pens. And watch out for marking pens that contain chemical solvents—these can be dangerous.

11 Some children adore filling in colouring books (I did) but they don't encourage a child's imagination like plain paper. Let children use the back of printed sheets of paper to draw on (you can save this from junk mail), or buy drawing pads made of recycled paper. Blackboards and writing slates are fun too (and good for messages).

12 All those postpaid return envelopes which come with bills can be used to play office (if you, sensibly, pay by bank giro—or perhaps even by computer), along with spare order forms and other bits of paper you would otherwise throw away.

13 Magazines and colour catalogues can be cut up and pasted in various ways. (Establish a specific place for used magazines, or you'll find your latest *Computer World* being hacked to bits.)

14 A buttonbox, handy for sewing and mending, can be a treasure trove. So can a collection of seashells, or whatever your particular passion is.

15 A Wendy house is wonderful. My father built us one the size of a small room, with a table and benches at one end and a kitchen at the other. This is an excellent way to use scrap wood, mouldings, carpet and wallpaper left from a bigger project.

16 Toys shouldn't be substitutes for hands-on assistance from parents. Often a child just needs a little adult aid to turn a cardboard box into a spaceship or a sturdy fruit crate into a cooker.

17 Let children join in your tasks whenever you can. They may not be able to make the same economic contribution to the family that children did a century ago, but it's good for them to feel that they can help. They can also acquire useful skills early in life (sewing on buttons may seem great fun to an 8 year old).

Community Playthings in East Sussex suggest the following criteria when buying toys and equipment (keep this list in mind when the inevitable crunch comes, at Christmas or birthdays):

1 Free of detail as possible.
2 Versatile in use.
3 Involve the child in play.
4 Large, easily manipulated.
5 Material warm and pleasant to touch.
6 Durable.
7 Work as intended.
8 Construction easily comprehended.
9 Sufficient quantity and roominess.
10 Encourage cooperative play.
11 Price based on durability and design.
● Community Playthings, Darvell, Robertsbridge, E. Sussex TN32 5DR, telephone Robertsbridge (0580) 880 626. Write for their catalogue and leaflet on choosing play equipment.

Television

If you spend every evening slumped in front of the box, you can hardly complain about its effect on your children or tell them they should be outside playing instead of watching cartoons on Saturday morning.

Although the effects of television violence haven't been proved, I recently read a suggestion that it creates a climate of social dis-ease, a feeling that the world outside is a dangerous place, and that as a result we become more likely to accept authoritarian government in the hope that this will protect us.

Joyce Nelson, author of *The Perfect Machine: TV in the Nuclear Age* (Toronto: Between the Lines Press, 1988), writes that 'The most powerful impact of TV's hidden curriculum is simply that of keeping people switched off from life outside the living room.' ('Tuned in and switched off', *New Internationalist*, February 1988).

She cites a number of observed characteristics of addicted TV viewers: short attention span, lack of 'reflectiveness' (the ability to think), poor logical ability and atrophy of the imagination. Children raised on television often do not know how to play—they simply imitate characters and situations they've seen on the telly—and there is persuasive evidence that television is a significant factor in failure at school.

Using the television to get the kids out of your hair may be okay on rare occasions, but it's well worth keeping tabs on how much they watch. Using TV as a childminder is *not* a good idea.

A child is not going to be so amenable to homemade toys if s/he has just seen fifteen advertisements for the Dark Star Wargames Set. In the US there have been protests about breakfast cereal commercials on children's TV—advertising on children's programmes does raise ethical questions.

Think about getting rid of the television: at least talking about this option might help you to focus on why you want to keep it around.

● *Four Arguments for the Elimination of Television*, Jerry Mander (New York: Morrow, 1980).

Other children

The ability to develop close relationships in later life is linked to childhood friendships. Some studies suggest that other children are even more important than the mother in a child's emotional development. When people lived in extended families (rather than the modern 'nuclear' family), children grew up not only with their brothers and sisters but with cousins, grandparents and aunts and uncles.

Children need to spend informal time together, not only school time or organized visits. This can be difficult, depending on where you live and whether there are other children of roughly the same age nearby. Solving this is a complicated issue—which is discussed in Alexander's *A Pattern Language*, pages 341–7—but I'm mentioning it because I suspect an over-dependence on toys has a lot to do with not having enough companionship, and you may want to think about this aspect of provision for your child or children.

EDUCATION

Many parents are dissatisfied with the education their children receive, for a wide variety of reasons. Access to good education is fundamental to any democratic society, and the information and attitudes that today's children acquire at school will affect the future for each of us, whether we have children ourselves or not.

We should be thinking about what we want from our children's education—about what the role of formal education should be. An approach to education which took account of what children want out of it would also be a healthy change from today's autocratic system.

Schools have traditionally served a social function in communities, for parents as well as children. Local schools are an important factor in neighbourhood or village life. This is one of the reasons parents have so strongly rejected the closing of small rural schools.

The notion that large schools can provide a better education simply by virtue of offering more exam subjects shows a sad misunderstanding of the complex role a school plays in pupils' and parents' lives.

A number of Maria Montessori's ideas about education, particularly about children's connection with the natural world, are relevant to *Home Ecology*. (See 'Nature in Education' in her *The Discovery of the Child*.)

● The Human Scale Education Movement, Ford House, Hartland, Bideford, Devon EX39 6EE, telephone (02374) 672 or 426.
● Montessori Society A.M.I. (UK), 26 Lyndhurst Gardens, London NW3, telephone 01–435 7874.

The values which our children need to face and resolve the challenges and problems of the next century are not going to be acquired in school lessons, but school lessons can provide the information and skills to help each child find his or her place in a changing, frequently worrying, world.

We can help to foster a sense of responsibility towards the planet we live on, and of obligation not only to the people we share it with now but to future generations. Our children need to learn to think of that 'seventh generation'.

POSTSCRIPT

Where do we go from here? How do we change the world around us, influence our friends, politicians, and the companies which make the products we use every day? *Home Ecology* is about changing what we do at home, but I hope that you will feel inspired to get involved in some of the larger issues.

Becoming better informed is an essential first step. This gets easier every day. Read the newspaper without skipping over unpleasant details about wood treatment chemicals or aluminium in drinking water. (A handy way to keep up on current information is with a subscription to the *Environment Digest*—see bibliography.)

The layperson is easily bewildered by conflicting information. Dervla Murphy's point about statistics (page 243) is worth keeping in mind: assess the *motives* of the person or organization who presents you with 'scientific facts'. Another difficulty is the way in which experts in any particular environmental field—whether nutrition or radiation or toxic chemicals—tend, understandably, to see their particular area as being of supreme importance. It may be easier for us non-experts to maintain a clear perspective, seeing the links between different subjects.

Collect some basic books—what you choose depends on your particular interests, but the following seem essential to me:

- Frances Moore Lappé's *Diet for a Small Planet*, especially the section 'Lessons for the Long Haul'.
- Jonathan Porritt's *Seeing Green*, with its excellent reading list at the back.
- Christopher Alexander's *A Pattern Language*. Stewart Brand, founder of the *Whole Earth Catalog*, says that this book 'should be in the hands of every citizen, city dweller, home builder, office worker'.

- The Worldwatch Institute's annual *State of the World* report (available from Books for a Change) is fascinating to dip into.
- For practical information, get hold of several good cook-books (suggestions on pages 44–5), John Button's *Green Pages* and *How to be Green*, and Richard Ballantine's *Richard's Bicycle Book.*

Writing letters—to your MP, local council and retailers—is a good habit to get into. Here are a few ideas: (1) Keep your letter short and specific, and give it a subject heading. (2) Type it if possible, or at least see that it is legible, and use a reasonable quality recycled paper. (3) Make it clear that you are a voter/ratepayer/customer, so the person to whom you are writing will want to keep you on their side. (4) Ronald Higgins, author of *The Seventh Enemy* (Hodder & Stoughton, 1978), suggests concluding your letter with a question so the addressee will be obliged to reply. (5) Keep a copy. (Friends of the Earth can send you a leaflet called 'How to Write an Effective Letter'.)

Even better is joining with other people in a cause you care about. Join Friends of the Earth and Greenpeace, as well as local environmental and conservation groups. At the very least, they need your financial support. Go to meetings—you may not find soulmates at every one, but you will almost certainly hit upon a group and a campaign which fits your personal interests and concerns.

Don't underestimate the power of your personal example. Seeing you using cotton nappies or save tea leaves for your compost heap will inevitably influence your friends. This isn't a matter of making them feel guilty, but of showing what is possible—ecological principles in action. Even more important is the example you set for your children and their friends. The other day my little son asked why there were so many people in cars, where were they all going? The Ministry of Transport should be asking the same question, and it's something all of us will have to think about over the next decade.

Summarizing the 'most important things to do' isn't easy, but here is a list to get you started:

- ☛ Buy less, and recycle whenever and whatever you can.
- ☛ Cut down on the amount you drive, get a bicycle, and switch to lead-free petrol.

☛ Don't buy tropical hardwoods or aerosol sprays, and use as little plastic as possible.

☛ Choose organically-grown products and humanely-reared meat (if you eat meat), and cut back on processed food.

☛ Switch to non-toxic household products.

CONTACTS

- **Friends of the Earth**, 26–28 Underwood Street, London N1 7JQ, telephone 01–490 1555. Membership enquiries to Friends of the Earth, Membership Department, Freepost, Mitcham, Surrey CR4 9AR. Campaign issues include recycling, pesticides, transport, rainforests and nuclear power. FoE's range of literature is formidable, and there are local groups throughout the country.
- **Greenpeace**, 30–31 Islington Green, London N1 8BR, telephone 01–354 5100 campaigns internationally for a nuclear-free world, fresh air, clean waters and the protection of wildlife and natural habitats.
- **Common Ground**, 45 Shelton Street, London WC2H 9HJ, telephone 01–379 3109. 'A small charity working to conserve nature, landscape and place with the help of people in all walks of the arts.'
- **Women's Environmental Network**, 287 City Road, London EC1V 1LA, telephone 01–490 2511. A new organization which is taking up issues of special importance to women.

BIBLIOGRAPHY

MAIL ORDER BOOK SUPPLIERS

- Books for a Change, 52 Charing Cross Road, London WC2H OBB, telephone 01–836 2315. Write or phone for catalogue – wide range of books and useful mail order service.
- Changes Bookshop, 242 Belsize Road, London NW6 4BT, telephone 01–328 5161. Mail order service.
- Schumacher Book Service, Ford House, Hartland, Bideford, Devon EX39 6EE, telephone (02374) 293.
- Green Books, Ford House, Hartland, Bideford, Devon EX39 6EE, telephone (02374) 293. Publishers.

AMERICAN BOOKS

Many US books are available through UK distributors, and I have tried to indicate these. Another source, indicated by 'WEA' following entry, is:

- Whole Earth Access (WEA), 2990 Seventh Street, Berkeley, CA 94710, USA. Payment by Access or VISA, or bank draft in US dollars.
- Airlift Book Co, 26 Eden Grove, London N7 8EF, telephone 01–607 5792, distribute for North Point, Celestial Arts and Ten Speed Press books.

BIBLIOGRAPHY

OP means, sadly, out of print. These can often be obtained through interlibrary loan.

Alexander, Christopher *et al.*, *A Pattern Language* (New York: Oxford University Press, 1977). Usually available at the Design Centre in London, or by mail from Building Communities Bookshop, PO Box 28, Dumfries, Scotland DG2 ONS, telephone (0387) 720755.

Artley, Alexandra (ed.), *Putting Back the Style* (Evans Brothers, 1982).

Ballantine, Richard, *Richard's Bicycle Book* (Pan, 1975).

Bates, W. H., *Better Eyesight Without Glasses* (Grafton, 1979).

Beech, Beverley Lawrence, *Who's Having your Baby?* (Camden Press, 1987).

Berry, Wendell, *The Landscape of Harmony* (Five Seasons Press, 1987). Includes a checklist of other books by Wendell Berry, with details of trade agents and suppliers.

Bertell, Rosalie, *No Immediate Danger* (Women's Press, 1985).

Brodeur, Paul, *The Zapping of America* (New York: W. W. Norton, 1977). OP.

Brown, Michael, *The Toxic Cloud* (New York: Harper & Row, 1987).

Bryan, Felicity, *The Town Gardener's Companion* (Penguin, 1983).

Bullock, Rob and Gillie Gould, *The Allotment Book* (Macdonald Optima, 1988).

Bunyard, Peter, *Health Guide for the Nuclear Age*, (Papermac, 1988).

Bunyard, Peter and Fern Morgan-Grenville (eds). *The Green Alternative Guide to Good Living* (Methuen, 1987).

Button, John, *Green Pages* (Optima, 1988), *The Green Guide to England* (Green Print, 1989) and *How to be Green, a Friends of the Earth handbook to looking after yourself and the planet* (Century, 1989).

Campbell, Rona and Alison Macfarlane, *Where to be born? The debate and the evidence* (National Perimatal Epidemiology Unit, Radcliffe Infirmary, Oxford, 1987).

Cannon, Geoffrey and Felicity Lawrence, *Additives: Your Complete Survival Guide* (Century, 1986).

Canter, David, Kay Canter and Daphne Swan, *The Cranks Recipe Book* (J. M. Dent, 1982).

Capra, Fritjof, *The Turning Point* (Wildwood House, 1982).

Chaitow, Leon, *Vaccination and Immunisation* (C. W. Daniel, 1987) and *The Radiation Protection Plan* (Thorsons, 1988).

Chapman, Carolyn, *Style on a Shoestring, a Guide to Conspicuous Thrift* (Hutchinson, 1984).

Curwell, S. R. and C. G. Marsh (eds.), *Hazardous Building Materials, A Guide to the Selection of Alternatives* (E. & F. N. Spon, 1986).

Dadd, Debra Lynn, *Nontoxic & Natural* (Los Angeles: J. P. Tarcher, 1984) and *The Nontoxic Home* (J. P. Tarcher, 1986). Available from Genesis Books, see page 237.

Davidson, John, *Radiation: What It Is, How It Affects Us And What We Can Do About It* (C. W. Daniel, 1986) and *Subtle Energy* (C. W. Daniel, 1988).

Davis, Adele, *Let's Have Healthy Children* (Unwin, 1981).

Davis, Patricia, *Aromatherapy, an A–Z* (C. W. Daniel, 1988).

Elkington, John and Julia Hailes, *The Green Consumer Guide* (Gollancz, 1988).

Elphinstone, Margaret and Julia Langley, *The Holistic Gardener* (Thorsons, 1988).

Ewald, Ellen, *Recipes for a Small Planet* (New York: Ballantine, 1973). From Wholefood, see page 44.

Gaskin, Ina May, *Babies, Breastfeeding and Bonding* (New York: Bergin & Garvey, 1987). From Changes Bookshop or the La Leche League.

Gear, Alan, *The New Organic Food Guide* (Dent, 1987).

Goldemberg, José *et al.*, *Energy for a Sustainable World*, World Resources Institute, Washington DC (Wiley, 1988).

Goodrich, Janet, *Natural Vision Improvement* (David & Charles, 1987).

Grant, Doris and Jean Joice, *Food Combining for Health* (Thorsons, 1984).

Green, Henrietta (ed.) *British Food Finds 1987* (Rich & Green, 1987) and *RAC Food Routes* (George Philip & Co, 1988).

Grigson, Jane, *Vegetable Book* (Michael Joseph, 1978) and *Fruit Book* (Michael Joseph, 1982).

Hardyment, Christine, *From Mangle to Microwave* (Polity Press, 1987).

Huxley, Aldous, *The Art of Seeing* (Panther, 1985).

Inch, Sally, *Birthrights* (Hutchinson, 1982).

Illich, Ivan, *Limits to Medicine* (Marion Boyars, 1976).

Innes, Jocasta, *The Pauper's Homemaking Book*

Jeavons, John, *Grow More Vegetables (than you ever thought possible on less land than you can imagine)* (Berkeley, CA; Ten Speed Press, 1982). Available from the Soil Association, address page 306.

Katzen, Mollie, *The Moosewood Cookbook* (Berkeley, CA: Ten Speed Press, 1977) and *The Enchanted Broccoli Forest* (Ten Speed Press, 1982). Airlift Books, and many bookshops.

Kenton, Branton, *Quantum Carrot* (Edbury Press, 1987).

Kenton, Leslie, *Ageless Ageing* (Century, 1984), *The Biogenic Diet* (Century, 1986), and *Ultrahealth* (Ebury Press, 1984).

Kenton, Leslie and Susannah, *Raw Energy* (Century, 1984).

Kinderlehrer, Jean, *Confessions of a Sneaky Organic Cook* (Emmaus, PA: Rodale, 1971).

Kitto, Dick, *Composting* (Thorsons, 1988).

Kitzinger, Sheila and J. Davis (eds.), *Place of Birth* (Oxford University Press, 1978).

La Leche League, *The Art of Breastfeeding*, revised edition 1988.

Larkcom, Joy, *Vegetables from Small Gardens* (Faber, 1976) and *Salads the Year Round* (Hamlyn, 1980).

Lazarus, Pat, *Keep Your Pet Healthy the Natural Way* (New York: Macmillan, 1983). Available from the Green Farm Nutrition Centre, Burwash Common, East Sussex TN19 7LX, telephone (0435) 882482.

Lewith, George T. and Julian N. Kenyon, *Clinical Ecology* (Thorsons, 1985).

Lobstein, Tim, The London Food Commission *Children's Food* (Unwin Hyman, 1988).

Loewenfeld, Claire, *Herb Gardening* (Faber, 1964).

Longacre, Doris, *Living More with Less* (Hodder & Stoughton, 1980). OP.

Luce, Gay, *Body Time* (Paladin, 1974). OP.

Makkar, Lali and Mary Ince, *How to Cut your Food Bills* (Kogan Page, 1982). OP.

Mander, Jerry, *Four Arguments for the Elimination of Television* (New York: Morrow, 1978). WEA.

Marshall, Janette, *Shopping for Health* (Penguin, 1987).

Mendelsohn, Robert, *How to Raise a Healthy Child in Spite of Your Doctor* (Chicago: Contemporary Books, 1984).

Monro, Jean and Peter Mansfield, *Chemical Children* (Century, 1987).

Montessori, Maria, *The Discovery of the Child* (New York: Ballantine, 1972).

Moore Lappé, Frances, *Diet for a Small Planet*, 10th anniversary edition (New York: Ballantine, 1982). From Wholefood, see page 44.

Moore Lappé, Frances and Joseph Collins, *Food First* (Abacus, 1982).

Mott, Lawrie and Karen Synder, *Pesticide Alert* (San

Francisco: Sierra Club Books, 1987). Available from Random House (UK) Limited, Isaac Newton Way, Alma Park Industrial Estate, Grantham, Lincs.

Murphy, Dervla, *In Ethiopia with a Mule* (John Murray, 1968), *Race to the Finish? The nuclear stakes* (John Murray, 1981), and *Muddling through in Madagascar* (John Murray, 1985).

National Trust Manual of Housekeeping, compiled by Hermione Sandwith and Sheila Stainton (Penguin, 1985).

North, Richard, *The Real Cost* (Chatto & Windus, 1986).

Odent, Michel, *Genèse de l'Homme Ecologique, L'instinct retrouvé* (Paris: Epi, 1979), *Birth Reborn* (Souvenir Press, 1984), *Entering the World* (Marion Boyars, 1984) and *Primal Health* (Century, 1986).

Ott, John, *Health and Light* (New York: Pocket Books) and *Light, Radiation and You* (New York: Devin-Adair, 1982, rev. 1985).

Patterson, Walter, *Nuclear Power* (Penguin, 1976) and *Going Critical* (Paladin, 1985).

Pearse, Innes H. and Lucy H. Crocker, *The Peckham Experiment* (Allen & Unwin, 1943 and Scottish Academic Press, 1985).

Pirsig, Robert, *Zen and the Art of Motorcycle Maintenance* (Bodley Head, 1974).

Porritt, Jonathan, ed., *Friends of the Earth Handbook* (Macdonald Optima, 1987).

Porritt, Jonathan, *Seeing Green* (Blackwell, 1984) and *The Coming of the Greens* (Collins, 1988).

Price, Shirley, *Practical Aromatherapy* (Thorsons, 1984).

Rifkin, Jeremy, *Time Wars: The Primary Conflict in Human History* (New York: Henry Holt & Co, 1987).

Rivers, Patrick and Shirley, *Diet for a Small Island* (Turnstone, 1981).

Rousseau, David, *Your Home, Your Health, and Well-Being* (Berkeley: Ten Speed Press, 1988). Airlift Book Company.

Samuels, Mike and Hal Zina Bennett, *Well Body, Well Earth* (San Francisco, Sierra Club Books, 1983).

Schaeffer, Edith, *Hidden Art* (Norfolk, 1971) and *What is a Family* (Highland, 1983).

Schumacher, E. F., *Small is Beautiful* (Abacus, 1974).

Shulman, Martha Rose, *The Vegetarian Feast* (Thorsons, 1982) and *Fast Vegetarian Feasts* (Thorsons, 1983).

Sekers, Simone, *Fine Food* (Hodder & Stoughton, 1987).

Seymour, John, *The Forgotten Arts* (Dorling Kindersley, 1984).

Seymour, John and Herbert Giradet, *Blueprint for a Green Planet* (Dorling Kindersley, 1987).

Smith, Drew and David Mabey (eds.), *The Good Food Directory* (Consumers' Association, 1987).

Smyth, Bob, *City Wildspace* (Hilary Shipman, 1987).

Stanway, Penny and Andrew, *Breast is Best* (Pan, 1978).

Stevens, John, *The National Trust Book of Wildflower Gardening* (Dorling Kindersley, 1987).

Templeton, Louise, *The Right Food for Your Kids* (Century, 1984).

Thevenin, Tina, *The Family Bed* (Thevenin, 1976). Available from the La Leche League.

Thomas, Anna, *The Vegetarian Epicure* (Penguin, 1973).

Tisserand, Robert, *The Art of Aromatherapy* (C. W. Daniel, 1977).

Vale, Brenda and Robert, *The Self-Sufficient Home* (Macmillan, 1980). OP.

Venolia, Carol, *Healing Environments* (Berkeley, CA: Celestial Arts, 1988). Airlift Book Company.

Vogler, John, *Recycling for Change* (Christian Aid, 1985).

Webb, Tony, *Radiation and Your Health* (Camden Press, 1988).

Webb, Tony and Tim Lang, *Food Irradiation: The Facts* (Thorsons, 1987).

Weiner, Michael, *Maximum Immunity* (Bath: Gateway Books, 1986).

Winston, Stephanie, *Getting Organized* (New York: Warner, 1978).

Worldwatch Institute, Brown, Lester R. *et al., State of the World 1988* (New York: W. W. Norton, 1988).

Yudkin, John, *Pure, White and Deadly*, 2nd edition (Penguin, 1988).

Magazines

The Ecologist, Subscriptions Department, Worthyvale Manor Farm, Camelford, Cornwall PL32 9TT, telephone (0840) 212711. Important stuff, but heavy going for the casual reader.

The Environment Digest, Subscriptions Office, Worthyvale

Manor Farm, Camelford, Cornwall PL32 9TT. Useful if you want to keep up on developments around the world without reading half a dozen newspapers.

The Food Magazine, The London Food Commission, 88 Old Street, London EC1V 9AR, telephone 01–253 9513.

The Living Earth, published by the Soil Association Ltd, 86–88 Colston Street, Bristol BS1 5BB, telephone (0272) 290661.

New Consumer – to be published by the Creative Consumer Project, first issue September 1989. On the newstand.

The New Internationalist, Subscription Offices, 120–126 Lavender Avenue, Mitcham, Surrey CR4 3HP, telephone 01–685 0372.

Resurgence, Subscriptions Department, Worthyvale Manor Farm, Camelford, Cornwall PL32 9TT, telephone (0840) 212711.

Utne Reader, Subscriptions Department, Box 1974, Marion, OH 43305, USA. Editorial offices: The Fawkes Building, 1624 Harmon Place, Minneapolis, MN 55403.

Whole Earth Review, 27 Gate Five Road, Sausalito, CA 94965, USA. Published quarterly by POINT, who also publish the Whole Earth Catalog.

INDEX